T0213194

Communicating and Mobile Systems: the π-Calculus

Communication is a fundamental and integral part of computing, whether between different computers on a network, or between components within a single computer. In this book Robin Milner introduces a new way of modelling communication that reflects its position. He treats computers and their programs as themselves built from communicating parts, rather than adding communication as an extra level of activity. Everything is introduced by means of examples, such as mobile phones, job schedulers, vending machines, data structures, and the objects of object-oriented programming. But the aim of the book is to develop a theory, the π-calculus, in which these things can be treated rigorously.

The π-calculus differs from other models of communicating behaviour mainly in its treatment of mobility. The movement of a piece of data inside a computer program is treated exactly the same as the transfer of a message – or indeed an entire computer program – across the internet. One can also describe networks which reconfigure themselves.

The calculus is very simple but powerful. Its most prominent notion is that of a name, and it has two important ingredients: the concept of behavioural (or observational) equivalence, and the use of a new theory of types to classify patterns of interactive behaviour. The internet, and its communication protocols, fall within the scope of the theory just as much as computer programs, data structures, algorithms and programming languages.

This book is the first textbook of the subject; it has been long-awaited by professionals and will be welcomed by them, and their students.

π

Communicating and Mobile Systems: the π-Calculus

ROBIN MILNER

Computer Laboratory, University of Cambridge

CAMBRIDGE
UNIVERSITY PRESS

University Printing House, Cambridge CB2 8BS, United Kingdom

One Liberty Plaza, 20th Floor, New York, NY 10006, USA

477 Williamstown Road, Port Melbourne, VIC 3207, Australia

314-321, 3rd Floor, Plot 3, Splendor Forum, Jasola District Centre, New Delhi - 110025, India

79 Anson Road, #06-04/06, Singapore 079906

Cambridge University Press is part of the University of Cambridge.

It furthers the University's mission by disseminating knowledge in the pursuit of
education, learning and research at the highest international levels of excellence.

www.cambridge.org
Information on this title: www.cambridge.org/9780521658690

First published 1999
Fifth printing 2004

A catalogue record for this publication is available from the British Library

Library of Congress Cataloging in Publication data
Milner, R. (Robin). 1934–
Communicating and mobile systems : the π-calculus / Robin Milner.
p.   cm.
ISBN 0 521 64320 1 (hc.). – ISBN 0 521 65869 1 (pbk.).
1. Mobile computing.   2. Telecommunication systems.
3. Pi-calculus.   I. Title.
QA76.59.M55   1999
004.6´2–dc21   98-39479 CIP

ISBN 978-0-521-64320-7 Hardback
ISBN 978-0-521-65869-0 Paperback

Contents

v

Glossary

The important notations, with the section number of their first appearance.

ENTITY SET	ENTITY	DESCRIPTION	
$\mathcal{N}$	$a,\ldots,x,\ldots$	names	3.1
$\overline{\mathcal{N}}$	$\overline{a},\ldots,\overline{x},\ldots$	co-names	3.1
$\mathcal{L}$	λ	labels	3.1
$\mathcal{Q}$	$p,q,\ldots$	states	3.1
	$\mathcal{R},\mathcal{S},\ldots$	simulation, bisimulation	3.2
$\mathcal{P}^{\text{seq}}$	$P,Q,\ldots$	sequential processes	3.4
Act	$\alpha,\beta,\ldots$	actions	4.2
	τ	silent action	4.2
$\mathcal{P}$	$P,Q,\ldots$	concurrent processes	4.3
	$\mathcal{C}$	process contexts	4.4
$\mathcal{P}^{\pi}$	$P,Q,\ldots$	π-calculus processes	9.1
	π	action prefixes	9.1
Σ	σ	sorts	11.2
Γ	C	sort constructors	11.3
	$F,G,\ldots$	abstractions	12.1
	$C,D,\ldots$	concretions	12.1
$\mathcal{A}^{\pi}$	$A,B,\ldots$	π-calculus agents	12.1

ACTION RELATIONS

$\xrightarrow{\alpha}$	labelled transition	3.1
$\xrightarrow{\alpha}$	commitment	12.2
$\rightarrow$	reaction	4.5
$\Rightarrow$	empty experiment	6.1
$\xRightarrow{e}$	experiment	6.1

BASIC CONSTRUCTIONS

$A(\vec{a}) \stackrel{\text{def}}{=} P_A$	process definition	3.4
$\Sigma \alpha_i . P_i$	summation	3.4
$A\langle a_1, \dots, a_n \rangle$	process instance	3.4
$\{\vec{b}/\vec{a}\}P$	substitution	3.4
$P \mid Q$	composition	4.3
new $a\ P$	restriction	4.3
$P \frown Q$	linking	4.4

EQUIVALENCES

$\equiv$	structural congruence	4.4
$\sim$	strong equivalence	3.3
$\approx$	weak equivalence	6.2

π-CALCULUS CONSTRUCTIONS

$x(y)$, $\overline{x}\langle y \rangle$	action prefix (monadic)	9.1
$\Sigma \pi_i . P_i$	summation	9.1
$!P$	replication	9.1
$x(\vec{y})$, $\overline{x}\langle \vec{y} \rangle$	action prefix (polyadic)	9.4
$F;G$	sequential composition	9.6
$(\vec{x}).P$	abstraction	12.1
new $\vec{x}\ \langle \vec{y} \rangle .P$	concretion	12.1
$F@C$	application	12.1
$\Sigma \alpha_i A_i$	summation of agents	12.1

Preface

Over the last thirty years or so, computer science has seriously taken up the challenge to understand the behaviour of communicating systems in the same way as it understands the behaviour of computer programs.

There is little pre-existing theory which can help. This is perhaps surprising, because the theory of computing has developed over a very long period as a part of mathematics and logic, and indeed it influenced the design of early stored-program computers. By comparison, a theory of communication as a smooth extension of programming is in its adolescence.

But theories usually arise to explain practice. Recently there has been a sea-change in computing practice; due to techological advances interactive systems are becoming the norm rather than the exception, and our whole view of computing has changed correspondingly. The new technology has created the need to expand our theory of sequential algorithmic processes to systems where interaction plays a significant and even dominant rôle.

One of the most challenging developments, both technically and conceptually, is the advent of mobile computing. People, computers and software now continually move among each other; moreover, some of the movement is physical and some (e.g. the movement of links) is virtual. As we experience this, we must somehow distil basic ideas which will help us to create reliable mobile systems which do what we want them to do.

Analysing the behaviour of mobile systems at the design stage is much harder than it ever was for sequential computer programs. This is partly because we lack ways even to express such behaviour accurately, in order to specify what must be designed. The π-calculus was developed in the late 1980s with just this goal in mind; this book introduces it with motivation and examples, but also with mathematical precision.

Who should read the book The book has grown out of a lecture course of sixteen lectures to final-year undergraduate students at Cambridge. It is

designed for such a course. In making the book from the lecture notes I have
resisted adding more material; I have only added explanations. The material
is challenging for undergraduates; the book can also be used as a basis for
graduate courses.

How to read the book The book divides clearly into two parts. Part I deals
with interactive systems which are not mobile, and represents a self-contained
review of previous work on CCS (a Calculus of Communicating Systems) [9,
10]. Part II introduces mobility, in the form of the dynamic creation of new
links between active processes. But one need not read all of Part I before Part
II. The diagram below shows the dependency of chapters.

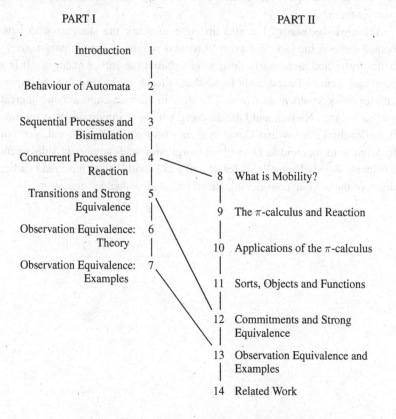

PART I

Introduction   1

Behaviour of Automata   2

Sequential Processes and   3
Bisimulation

Concurrent Processes and   4
Reaction

Transitions and Strong   5
Equivalence

Observation Equivalence: 6
Theory

Observation Equivalence: 7
Examples

PART II

8   What is Mobility?

9   The π-calculus and Reaction

10   Applications of the π-calculus

11   Sorts, Objects and Functions

12   Commitments and Strong
Equivalence

13   Observation Equivalence and
Examples

14   Related Work

There are many paths through some or all of the chapters:

- Part I, by itself, is a good introduction to the algebraic treatment of
  communicating systems; it emphasizes the kind of theoretical problem
  which arises with concurrency, but preserves a balance between theory
  and examples.

- Chapters 1–4 and 8–11 make a good introduction to mobile interactive systems, with emphasis on applications and less upon the behavioural theory. The examples of Chapter 7 can be added to this diet; they can be appreciated to a reasonable extent without the preparation of Chapters 5 and 6.
- Chapters 1–5 and 8–12 make a coherent whole, dealing with everything except the concept of observation equivalence. Chapters 6, 7 and 13 can then be tackled together.

Thus the mixture of theory and examples can be varied to taste. The theorems are important, but very often the practical applications can be appreciated without them.

Acknowledgements I would first like to thank the students who have helped me over the last three years to write down these ideas in progressively better form, and particularly those who suffered the earlier attempts. It is a continual source of excitement to me that to teach a new subject is so important for one's understanding of it. The ideas in the π-calculus are due in great part to Mogens Nielsen and Uffe Engberg who took important steps towards it, to Joachim Parrow and David Walker who first worked the calculus out in detail with me, and to Davide Sangiorgi who made important subsequent advances. Alexis Donnelly, Peter Sewell and David Walker have read earlier drafts of the book in considerable detail and made valuable suggestions.

Part I

Communicating Systems

1

Introduction

This book introduces a calculus for analysing properties of concurrent communicating processes, which may grow and shrink and move about.

Building communicating systems is not a well-established science, or even a stable craft; we do not have an agreed repertoire of constructions for building and expressing interactive systems, in the way that we (more-or-less) have for building sequential computer programs.

But nowadays most computing involves interaction – and therefore involves systems with components which are concurrently active. Computer science must therefore rise to the challenge of defining an underlying model, with a small number of basic concepts, in terms of which *interactional* behaviour can be rigorously described.

The same thing was done for *computational* behaviour a long time ago; logicians came up with Turing machines, register machines (on which imperative programming languages are built) and the lambda calculus (on which the notion of parametric procedure is founded). None of these models is concerned with interaction, as we would normally understand the term. Their basic activity consists of reading or writing on a storage medium (tape or registers), or invoking a procedure with actual parameters. Instead, we shall work with a model whose basic action is to communicate across an interface with a *handshake*, which means that the two participants synchronize this action.

Let us think about some simple examples of processes which do this handshaking. They can be physical or virtual, hardware or software. As a very physical system, consider a vending machine e.g. for selling drinks. It has links with its environment: the slot for money, the drink-selection buttons, the button for getting your change, the delivery point for a drink. The machine's pattern of interaction at these links is not entirely trivial – as we shall see in Chapter 2.

Physical systems tend to have permanent physical links; they have *fixed* structure. But most systems in the informatic world are not physical; their links may be virtual or symbolic. An obvious modern example is the linkage among agents on the internet or worldwide web. When you click on a symbolic link on your screen, you induce a handshake between a local process (your screen agent) and a remote process. These symbolic links can also be created or destroyed on the fly, by you and others. Virtual links can also consist of radio connection; consider the linkage between planes and the control tower in an air-traffic control system. Systems like these, with transient links, have *mobile* structure. In Chapter 8 we shall look at a very simple example involving mobile telephones.

We do not normally think of vending machines or mobile phones as doing computation, but they share with modern distributed computing systems the notion of interaction. This common notion underlies a theory of a huge range of modern informatic systems, whether computational or not. This is the theory we shall develop.

This book is not about design; for example, it will not teach you how best to design a concurrent operating system. Instead, we shall try to isolate concepts which allow designers to think clearly, not only when analysing interactive systems but even when expressing their designs in the first place. So we shall proceed with the help of examples – not large systems, but small ones illustrating key notions and problems.

A central question we shall try to answer is: when do two interactive systems have equivalent behaviour, in the sense that we can unplug one and plug in the other – in any environment – and not tell the difference? This is a theoretical question, but vitally important in practice. Until we know what constitutes similarity or difference of behaviour, we cannot claim to know what 'behaviour' *means* – and if that is the case then we have no precise way of explaining what our systems do!

Therefore our theory will focus on equivalence of behaviour. In fact we use this notion as a means of specifying how a designed system should behave; the designed system is held to be correct if its actual behaviour is equivalent to the specified behaviour. Chapters 7 and 13 contain several examples of how to prove such behavioural equivalence.

We shall begin at a familiar place, the classical theory of automata. We shall then extend these automata to allow them to run concurrently and to interact – which they will do by synchronizing their transitions from one state to another. This allows us to consider each system component, whether elementary or containing subcomponents, as an automaton.

For such systems of interacting automata we shall find it useful to represent their interconnection by diagrams, such as the following:

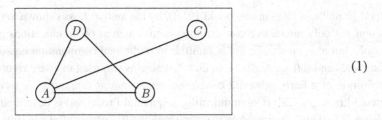

(1)

Here, an arc between two component automata A and B of a system means that they *may* interact – that is, A and B may sometimes synchronize their state transitions.

In many systems this linkage, or spatial structure, remains fixed as the system's behaviour unfolds. But in certain applications the spatial structure may *evolve*; for example the component D may *die* $(1{\rightarrow}2)$:

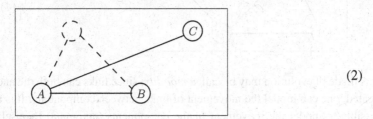

(2)

or may *divide* into two components $(1{\rightarrow}3)$:

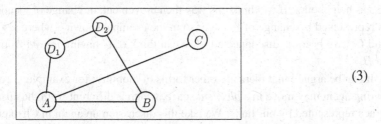

(3)

This mode of evolution covers a large variety of behaviour. For example, in understanding a high-level programming language one can treat each activation of a recursive procedure as a system component, whose lifetime lasts from a call of the procedure to a return from it; this extends smoothly to the case in which concurrent activations of the same procedure are allowed. Again, a communication handler may under certain conditions create a 'subagent' to deal with certain transactions; the subagent will carry out certain delegated interactions, and die when its task is done.

A calculus called CCS (Calculus of Communicating Systems) was developed along these lines in two books [9, 10] by the author. It was shown to represent not only interactive concurrent systems, such as communications protocols, but also much of what is familiar in traditional computation e.g. data structures and storage regimes. In fact the calculus was used to give a rigorous definition of a fairly powerful concurrent programming language. A similar model known as CSP (Communicating Sequential Processes) is described by Hoare [6]. These two models were independently conceived at roughly the same time, around 1980.

Returning to modes of evolution, there is a further mode in which new links are *created* between existing components, e.g. between B and C (1→4):

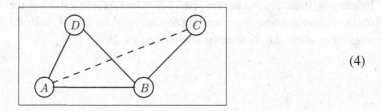

$$(4)$$

This mode of evolution may be called *mobility*; since links can both die and be created, one can model the movement of links between components. It is also possible to model the movement of the components (automata) themselves. For we may consider the location of a component of an interactive system to be determined by the links which it possesses, i.e. which other components it has as neighbours. If we think this way then movement, or change of location, is represented by change of linkage; so in the example shown – where also A and C have become disconnected – we can think of C having *moved* from A to B.

It can be argued that there are other forms of mobility; for example, a computing agent may move in a *physical* space, which is different from the *virtual* space represented by our links. We take this discussion up again in Chapter 8. Mobility – of whatever kind – is important in modern computing. It was not present in CCS or CSP, and we do not cover it here in Part I; but the theory we develop here extends smoothly to the π-*calculus*, introduced in Part II, which takes mobility of linkage as a primitive notion.

Any conceptual model, particularly in a young subject, has a problem with terminology. Ours is no exception; should we talk of automata, or processes, or systems, or components, or agents? All five have been used in this introduction. We shall mainly talk of *processes*, and of *process expressions* when we discuss mathematical notation for processes. At the beginning of the book we talk of *automata*, but only to relate our process theory to the pre-existing theory. When we discuss how processes combine to make larger processes we talk of *systems* of *component* processes. For most of the book we shall avoid using the word *agent*, except when we are dealing with examples where the word appears appropriate in a non-technical sense; but in Part II we shall adopt a precise technical meaning for the word.

2

Behaviour of Automata

We shall begin by considering the components of a system to be automata which interact with one another.

In the standard mathematical definition an automaton has a set of possible *states*, and moves from one state to another by performing certain *actions*. There is a well-developed theory, which we shall call the classical theory, of such automata. It deals with such matters as when two different automata may be regarded as having the same behaviour, and how automata can be classified in terms of this behaviour. Particularly important classes are the *finite state* automata (those with finitely many states) and the *deterministic automata* (those in which, in a given state, any action has only one possible outcome).

In the classical theory, rather little attention is paid to the way in which two automata may interact, in the sense that an action by one entails a complementary action by another. This kind of interaction requires us to look at automata in a new light; in particular, this interdependency of automata via their actions seems to demand a new approach to behavioural equivalence.

Nonetheless, classical automata theory is so important in many aspects of computing (e.g. in parsing theory) that we must take account of it in presenting any new theory, and must clearly indicate the points of agreement and difference. We therefore begin this chapter with a brief review of the classical theory and show where we shall depart from it. For a detailed account, see for example Hopcroft and Ullman [8] or Sudkamp [19].

2.1 Automata

We presume a given set *Act* of actions, sometimes called an alphabet. The classical definition of an automaton is as follows.

Definition 2.1 Automaton *An* automaton *A* over Act *has four ingredients:*

- *a set* $\mathcal{Q} = \{q_0, q_1, \dots\}$ *of* states;
- *a state* $q_0 \in \mathcal{Q}$ *called the* start state;
- *a subset* $\mathcal{F}$ *of* $\mathcal{Q}$ *called the* accepting states;
- *a subset* $\mathcal{T}$ *of* $\mathcal{Q} \times$ Act $\times \mathcal{Q}$ *called the* transitions.

A transition $(q, a, q') \in \mathcal{T}$ *is usually written* $q \xrightarrow{a} q'$. *The automaton A is said to be* finite-state *if* $\mathcal{Q}$ *is finite, and* deterministic *if for each pair* $(q, a) \in \mathcal{Q} \times$ Act *there is exactly one transition* $q \xrightarrow{a} q'$.

An automaton is usually represented by a *transition graph*, whose nodes are the states and whose arcs are the transitions. As an example consider the following finite automaton A_0 over the alphabet $Act = \{a, b, c\}$:

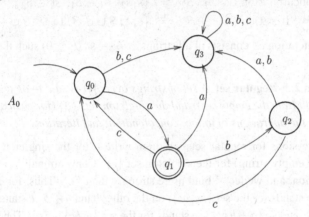

The state-set of A_0 is $\{q_0, q_1, q_2, q_3\}$; it has just one accepting state q_1 (indicated by a double circle) and it is clearly deterministic. In the diagram, two transitions $\xrightarrow{b}$ and $\xrightarrow{c}$ between the same states are combined as $\xrightarrow{b,c}$.

(In some definitions the determinacy condition 'exactly one transition' is relaxed to 'at most one transition'. But there is little difference, because if this weaker condition is satisfied then one can always meet the stronger condition by adding new transitions which all lead to some new non-accepting state. Such a state is called a *sink*; you can think of q_3 in A_0 above as a sink.)

In the classical theory the behaviour of an automaton A is usually taken to be the set of strings over Act which it accepts; this set is often called the language of A, defined as follows:

Definition 2.2 Language of an automaton *Let A be an automaton over Act, and* $s = a_1 \cdots a_n$ *a string over Act. Then A is said to* accept *s if there is a path in A, from* q_0 *to an accepting state, whose arcs are labelled successively*

$a_1, \ldots, a_n$. *The* language *of A, denoted by* $\hat{A}$, *is the set of strings accepted by A.*

For example A_0 accepts *abca* via the path whose successive states are $q_0 q_1 q_2 q_0 q_1$.

2.2 Regular sets

We shall be concerned with sets of strings over *Act*, and we shall need to build bigger such sets from smaller ones. Three important operations for building sets of strings are:

$$\text{Union}: \quad S_1 \cup S_2$$
$$\text{Concatenation}: \quad S_1 \cdot S_2 \stackrel{\text{def}}{=} \{s_1 s_2 \mid s_1 \in S_1,\ s_2 \in S_2\}$$
$$\text{Iteration}: \quad S^* \stackrel{\text{def}}{=} \{\epsilon\} \cup S \cup S \cdot S \cup S \cdot S \cdot S \cup \cdots$$

Thus the iteration S^* consists of all strings $s_1 s_2 \cdots s_n$ ($n \geq 0$) such that $s_i \in S$ for each i.

Definition 2.3 Regular set *A set of strings over Act is said to be* regular *if it can be built from the empty set $\emptyset$ and the singleton sets $\{a\}$ (for each $a \in Act$), using just the operations of union, concatenation and iteration.*

In expressions for regular sets we often write a for the singleton set $\{a\}$, and ϵ (the empty string) for the singleton set $\{\epsilon\}$. Conventionally '$+$' is used for set union, and we let '$\cdot$' bind more strongly than '$+$'. Thus, for example, $(a + b) \cdot c$ stands for the set $\{ac, bc\}$; on the other hand $a + b \cdot c$ stands for the set $\{a, bc\}$, and so $(a + b \cdot c)^* \cdot c$ stands for the set $\{a, bc\}^* \cdot \{c\}$. The latter set contains exactly all those strings of the form $s_1 s_2 \cdots s_n c$ ($n \geq 0$) where each s_i is either a or bc.

It is well-known and easy to verify that concatenation obeys the following equations:

$$(S_1 \cdot S_2) \cdot S_3 = S_1 \cdot (S_2 \cdot S_3) \qquad (S_1 + S_2) \cdot T = S_1 \cdot T + S_2 \cdot T$$
$$S \cdot \epsilon = S \qquad S \cdot \emptyset = \emptyset \qquad T \cdot (S_1 + S_2) = T \cdot S_1 + T \cdot S_2 \,.$$

Iteration also satisfies interesting equations; one which will be useful later is

$$S \cdot (T \cdot S)^* = (S \cdot T)^* \cdot S \,.$$

You can see this by noting that each side of the equation contains exactly all those strings of the form $s_1 t_1 s_2 t_2 \cdots s_n t_n s_{n+1}$ with each $s_i \in S$ and each $t_i \in T$.

The algebra of regular sets is interesting in its own right, but we shall not explore it here. The main point which we want to recall is that the language $\hat{A}$

of any finite-state automaton A is known to be regular. This depend on the following important fact:

Proposition 2.4 Arden's Rule *For any sets of strings S and T, the equation $X = S \cdot X + T$ has $X = S^* \cdot T$ as a solution. Moreover, this solution is unique if $\epsilon \notin S$.*

For example, the solution of $X = (a + b) \cdot X + c$ is $X = (a + b)^* \cdot c$. From now on we shall often drop the concatenation symbol '$\cdot$', writing SX for $S \cdot X$ etc.

2.3 The language of an automaton

Given an automaton A, we now recall how to find its language $\widehat{A}$.

Let A have states $\{q_0, \ldots, q_n\}$ with start state q_0. For $1 \le i \le n$, let X_i denote the set of strings accepted by A starting in state q_i; thus $\widehat{A} = X_0$. We can write an equation for each X_i, defining it in terms of the sets corresponding to its successor states. For example, for A_0 as in Section 2.1 above we have

$$
\begin{aligned}
(0) \quad & X_0 = aX_1 + bX_3 + cX_3 \\
(1) \quad & X_1 = aX_3 + bX_2 + cX_0 + \epsilon \\
(2) \quad & X_2 = aX_3 + bX_3 + cX_0 \\
(3) \quad & X_3 = aX_3 + bX_3 + cX_3 \, .
\end{aligned}
$$

(Note that X_1 contains ϵ because q_1 is an accepting state.) So we use Arden's Rule to solve the equations. First note that (3) can be written in the form $X_3 = (a + b + c)X_3 + \emptyset$, so Arden's Rule yields

$$
X_3 = (a + b + c)^* \emptyset = \emptyset \, .
$$

(We are using the fact that $S\emptyset = \emptyset$.) Using this, we can simplify the remaining equations:

$$
\begin{aligned}
(0) \quad & X_0 = aX_1 \\
(1) \quad & X_1 = bX_2 + cX_0 + \epsilon \\
(2) \quad & X_2 = cX_0 \, .
\end{aligned}
$$

Substituting (0) and (2) in (1) we get $X_1 = (bc + c)aX_1 + \epsilon$, so by Arden's Rule we deduce $X_1 = ((bc + c)a)^*$, and from (0) finally

$$
\widehat{A_0} = X_0 = a((bc + c)a)^* \, .
$$

Note that in reaching this solution we have used algebraic properties of union and concatenation; for example, after substituting (0) and (2) in (1) we used $bcaX_1 + caX_1 = (bc + c)aX_1$, justified by the first distributive law

$(S_1 + S_2)T = S_1T + S_2T$. In other examples, one also needs the second distributive law, $T(S_1 + S_2) = TS_1 + TS_2$. But we shall shortly look at another interpretation for our algebra in which the second law is *not* valid.

We have seen in this particular case that the language of a finite-state automaton is regular. In fact, this method of solution can be applied to any finite-state automaton, and this constitutes a proof that its language is always regular.

2.4 Determinism versus nondeterminism

Let us now ask whether the languages of deterministic automata differ somehow from those of nondeterministic ones. A simple example will suffice. Consider first A_1, defined by the following transition graph:

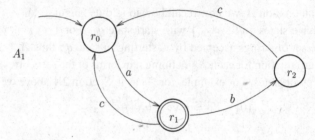

A_1 is deterministic, since there is at most one transition for each pair (q, a). In contrast consider A_2; it is very like A_1 but non-deterministic, because there are two a-transitions out of r_0:

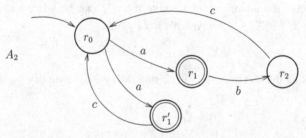

By writing down the appropriate equations (as we did for A_0), and solving them, we can show that A_1 and A_2 possess the same language, and indeed it is the same as $\widehat{A_0}$. We leave this as an exercise.

Exercise 2.5 In Section 2.2 the equation $S{\cdot}(T{\cdot}S)^* = (S{\cdot}T)^*{\cdot}S$ was mentioned. What alternative expression can be derived for $\widehat{A_0}$, using this equation? By solving equations using Arden's rule, find the languages $\widehat{A_1}$ and $\widehat{A_2}$; then, using the algebraic equations mentioned in Section 2.2, show that they are identical with $\widehat{A_0}$. ∎

We now ask whether it is inevitable – or even desirable – that the automata A_1 and A_2 be regarded as equivalent, just because they accept the same language. Language-equivalence has some advantages; for example, every automaton can be converted to a deterministic one which accepts the same language. (You may recall that the conversion to a deterministic automaton is done by the so-called *subset construction*; see any text-book on automata theory.)

But realistic systems can be nondeterministic in an *intrinsic* way which should not just be explained away like this! We shall now demonstrate this with a simple example from everyday life.

2.5 Black boxes, or reactive systems

Let us now think of an automaton over $Act = \{a, b, c\}$ as a black box

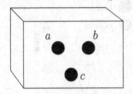

with three buttons marked a, b and c. We interact with it by trying to press the buttons in some sequence. Sometimes the button goes down i.e. we succeed – and sometimes it doesn't; this is the only way we can tell the difference between black boxes with the same alphabet. In particular, we can't tell the difference between an accepting and a non-accepting *state*; we can't tell anything about states except indirectly through the behaviour of the buttons. (We shall often use the words 'button' and 'port', interchangeably, for the means of access to a process.)

Thus we diverge in a subtle but important way from the classical notion of automaton. What matters about a string s – a sequence of actions – is not whether it drives the automaton into an accepting state (since we cannot detect this by interaction) but whether the automaton is able to perform the sequence s interactively. We reflect this by confining our attention to automata in which *every* state is an accepting one, A consequence is that if an automaton accepts s, then it also accepts any initial part of s. We now make this precise:

Definition 2.6 Prefix closure *If a string s can be expressed in the form $s_1 s_2$, then s_1 is said to be a* prefix *of s. A language S is said to be* prefix-closed *if, whenever $ss' \in S$ then also $s \in S$. The* prefix-closure *of a language S is the larger language $Pref(S)$ which contains all the prefixes of every string in S. It is the smallest prefix-closed language which includes S.*

For example, if $S = \{a, bcd\}$ then its prefix-closure is $Pref(S) = \{\epsilon, a, b, bc, bcd\}$.

Exercise 2.7 By considering accepting paths (as in Section 2.1), verify informally for any automaton A that if all its states are accepting then $\widehat{A}$ is prefix-closed.   ■

Example 2.8 Vending machine Here is a tea/coffee vending machine, a black box with a three-symbol alphabet $\{2p, \overline{tea}, \overline{coffee}\}$. (For now ignore the overbars.)

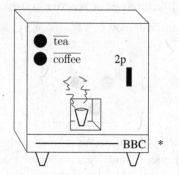

* Black Box Corporation

Its internal state-transition diagram could be as follows:

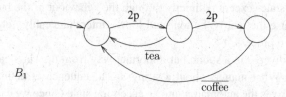

This means that after putting in 2p, you can get tea by pressing the $\overline{tea}$ button, or you can put in another 2p and then get coffee by pressing $\overline{coffee}$, and so on.   ■

Exercise 2.9 By solving equations or otherwise, show that the set of strings which take B_1 back to its start state is given by $(2p \cdot (\overline{tea} + 2p \cdot \overline{coffee}))^*$. Then, assuming that every state is accepting, deduce that $\widehat{B_1} = Pref((2p \cdot (\overline{tea} + 2p \cdot \overline{coffee}))^*)$.   ■

Exercise 2.10 Consider a variant of the machine B_1, as follows:

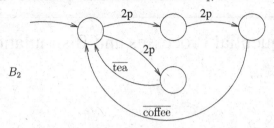

Verify that $\widehat{B_2} = \widehat{B_1}$.   ■

Despite the fact that B_1 and B_2 are language-equivalent, they are annoyingly different for a thirsty user! This is because B_2 is more nondeterministic; after we have put in the first 2p, it may be in a state in which we can only get tea (it will not accept a further 2p), or it may be in a state in which we can only put in more money to get coffee (it will not allow the $\overline{\text{tea}}$ button to be pressed). If you bought a vending machine and found it to behave like this, you would ask for your money back.

So what is wrong with the theory which has allowed you to deduce that $\widehat{B_2} = \widehat{B_1}$, in Exercise 2.10? The answer is that you had to use an instance of the second distributive law, i.e. you used

$$2p \cdot (\overline{\text{tea}} + 2p \cdot \overline{\text{coffee}}) \;=\; 2p \cdot \overline{\text{tea}} + 2p \cdot 2p \cdot \overline{\text{coffee}} \,,$$

in order to equate a deterministic machine with a less reliable non-deterministic one.

2.6 Summary

We have briefly reviewed classical automata theory, especially its notion of language-equivalence. We found that this notion of equivalence is not suitable for all purposes. In particular, it does not appear to be correct when an automaton's actions consist of *reactions* between it and another automaton; an example was given in the form of a vending machine interacting with a purchaser.

It has appeared that if we are interested in interactive behaviour, then a non-deterministic automaton cannot correctly be equated behaviourally with a deterministic one. So a radical departure from the classical theory is required; we take up this challenge in the chapters which follow.

3

Sequential Processes and Bisimulation

In this chapter we define nondeterministic sequential processes, and introduce a form of equivalence which respects their nondeterminism. It is based on a concept of mutual simulation, which we shall call *bisimulation*. Although the chapter does not treat concurrency, the same equivalence will apply later to concurrent processes.

3.1 Labelled transition systems

We shall begin by refining the notion of *action*. First we presuppose an infinite set $\mathcal{N}$ of *names*; we shall usually denote them by letters like $a, b, \ldots$, but in examples we shall use helpful names like 'tea', '2p' etc. Then we introduce the set $\overline{\mathcal{N}} = \{\overline{a} \mid a \in \mathcal{N}\}$, which we call *co-names*; thus $\overline{\text{coffee}}$ is a co-name. We assume that $\mathcal{N}$ and $\overline{\mathcal{N}}$ are disjoint, and we denote their union $\mathcal{N} \cup \overline{\mathcal{N}}$, by $\mathcal{L}$, the set of *labels* (the kind of label which identifies the buttons on our black boxes). For the time being we take Act, the set of actions, to be just $\mathcal{L}$; we shall use $\alpha, \beta, \ldots$ to range over Act. We think of a and $\overline{a}$ as complementary actions, being the two parts of an interaction between two processes. (For example, the vending machine of Example 2.8 may perform the action '$\overline{\text{tea}}$' to complement the customer's action 'tea'.)

Definition 3.1 Labelled transition system   *A labelled transition system (LTS) over Act is a pair $(\mathcal{Q}, \mathcal{T})$ consisting of*

  – *a set $\mathcal{Q}$ of* states;
  – *a ternary relation $\mathcal{T} \subseteq (\mathcal{Q} \times Act \times \mathcal{Q})$, known as a* transition relation.

If $(q, \alpha, q') \in \mathcal{T}$ we write $q \xrightarrow{\alpha} q'$, and we call q the source *and q' the* target *of the transition. If $q \xrightarrow{\alpha_1} q_1 \xrightarrow{\alpha_2} \cdots \xrightarrow{\alpha_n} q_n$ then we call q_n a* derivative *of q under $\alpha_1 \alpha_2 \cdots \alpha_n$.*

An LTS can be thought of as an automaton without a start state or accepting states. We have already explained why accepting states are omitted; by omitting the start state too, we gain the freedom to consider *any* state as the start. In fact each different selection of a start state defines a different automaton, but based upon the same LTS.

3.2 Strong simulation

When should two states in an LTS (or the automata defined by two such states) be considered equivalent?

Example 3.2 Consider again our two vending machines B_1 and B_2 (in Example 2.8 and the sequel). The essential difference between them is the difference between p_0 and q_0, whose transitions are as follows:

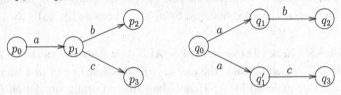

– and we argued that these should *not* be equivalent. ∎

To pinpoint the way they differ, we now introduce a notion of simulation according to which (the automaton defined by) p_0 can simulate q_0, but not vice versa. Informally, to say 'p simulates q' will mean that p's behaviour pattern is at least as rich as that of q.

Definition 3.3 Strong simulation *Let* (Q, T) *be an LTS, and let S be a binary relation over Q. Then S is called a* strong simulation *over* (Q, T) *if, whenever pSq,*

if $p \xrightarrow{\alpha} p'$ then there exists $q' \in Q$ such that $q \xrightarrow{\alpha} q'$ and $p'Sq'$.

We say that q strongly simulates p if there exists a strong simulation S such that pSq.

The condition for S to be a strong simulation can be expressed in diagrams:

$$
\begin{array}{ccc}
 & p \; S \; q & \\
\textit{if} & \Big\downarrow\alpha & \textit{then, for some } q', \\
 & p' &
\end{array}
\qquad
\begin{array}{c}
q \\
\Big\downarrow\alpha \\
p' \; S \; q'
\end{array}
$$

Thus 'q strongly simulates p', or 'p is strongly simulated by q', means that whatever transition path p takes, q can match it by a path which retains all of p's options.

Notice that we define a simulation to be a relation over the states in a single LTS, rather than between the states of one LTS and those of another. Often an LTS consists intuitively of two or more distinct automata, as in Example 3.2. But we also need our notion of simulation to allow one state to simulate another in the *same* LTS.

Example 3.4 Illustrating simulation Continuing Example 3.2, define $\mathcal{S}$ by

$$\mathcal{S} = \{(q_0, p_0), (q_1, p_1), (q_1', p_1), (q_2, p_2), (q_3, p_3)\} \, ;$$

then $\mathcal{S}$ is a strong simulation; hence p_0 strongly simulates q_0. To verify this, for every pair $(q, p) \in \mathcal{S}$ we have to consider each transition $q \xrightarrow{\alpha} q'$ of the first member q, and show that it is properly matched by some transition $p \xrightarrow{\alpha} p'$ of the second member p. Consider the pair (q_1', p_1) for example; q_1' has just one transition $q_1' \xrightarrow{c} q_3$, and it is matched by $p_1 \xrightarrow{c} p_3$ because $(q_3, p_3) \in \mathcal{S}$.   ■

Exercise 3.5 Check all other pairs of $\mathcal{S}$. Also show that there can be no strong simulation $\mathcal{R}$ which contains the pair (p_1, q_1), because one of p_1's transition could never be matched by q_1. Hence show that no strong simulation $\mathcal{R}$ can contain the pair (p_0, q_0), and thus q_0 does not strongly simulate p_0.   ■

Thus we have found a criterion for distinguishing between the two automata of Example 3.2, and hence between our two vending machines. We shall now refine simulation into an equivalence relation – one in which the two vending machines are *not* equivalent (even though they are language-equivalent).

3.3 Strong bisimulation

Recall that the *converse* $\mathcal{R}^{-1}$ of any binary relation $\mathcal{R}$ is the set of pairs (y, x) such that $(x, y) \in \mathcal{R}$.

Definition 3.6 Strong bisimulation, strong equivalence *A binary relation $\mathcal{S}$ over $\mathcal{Q}$ is said to be a* strong bisimulation *over the LTS $(\mathcal{Q}, \mathcal{T})$ if both $\mathcal{S}$ and its converse are simulations. We say that p and q are* strongly bisimilar *or* strongly equivalent, *written $p \sim q$, if there exists a strong bisimulation $\mathcal{S}$ such that $p\mathcal{S}q$.*

Example 3.7 Illustrating bisimulation Consider the following LTS (intuitively, it is two separate automata):

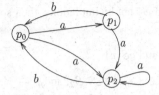 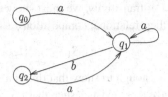

Then $p_0 \sim q_0$. To prove this, we define

$$\mathcal{S} = \{(p_0, q_0), (p_0, q_2), (p_1, q_1), (p_2, q_1)\} ;$$

then we show that $\mathcal{S}$ is a bisimulation, and this is enough because $p_0 \mathcal{S} q_0$. ∎

It often helps to show a bisimulation graphically, by linking the related states on a transition graph. For Example 3.7 it looks like this:

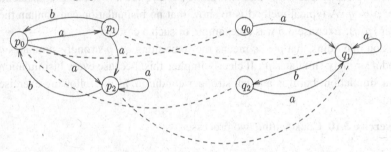

Exercise 3.8 In Example 3.7, prove first that $\mathcal{S}$ is a strong simulation (consider every pair). Then write down $\mathcal{S}^{-1}$, and show that it is also a strong simulation. ∎

Bisimilarity has many applications, even outside the theory of processes. Here are some of its properties.

Proposition 3.9

   (1) $\sim$ *is an equivalence relation, i.e. the following hold:*
       $p \sim p$ *(reflexivity)*
       $p \sim q$ *implies* $q \sim p$ *(symmetry)*
       $p \sim q$ *and* $q \sim r$ *imply* $p \sim r$ *(transitivity);*
   (2) $\sim$ *is itself a strong bisimulation.*

Proof (1) For reflexivity, it is enough to show that the identity relation over $\mathcal{Q}$, that is the relation $Id_{\mathcal{Q}} = \{(p, p) \mid p \in \mathcal{Q}\}$, is a bisimulation. This is easy.

For symmetry, we have to show that if $\mathcal{S}$ is a bisimulation then so is its converse $\mathcal{S}^{-1}$. But this is obvious from Definition 3.6.

For transitivity, we must show that if S_1 and S_2 are bisimulations, then so is their relational composition

$$S_1S_2 = \{(p,r) \mid \exists q.\ pS_1q \text{ and } qS_2r\}\ .$$

It is enough to show that this is a simulation. Let $(p,r) \in S_1S_2$, and $p \xrightarrow{\alpha} p'$. Since there exists q such that pS_1q and qS_2r, there exist also q' such that $q \xrightarrow{\alpha} q'$ and $p'S_1q'$, and hence r' such that $r \xrightarrow{\alpha} r'$ and $q'S_2r'$. So $(p',r') \in S_1S_2$, and we have established the simulation condition for S_1S_2.

(2) Let $p \sim q$. Then by definition pSq for some bisimulation S. Therefore if $p \xrightarrow{\alpha} p'$, there exists q' for which $q \xrightarrow{\alpha} q'$ and $p'Sq'$ – hence also $p' \sim q'$. Thus $\sim$ satisfies the simulation condition, and by symmetry so does its converse.

□

We often wish to show that two processes p, q are *not* strongly equivalent, i.e. $p \not\sim q$. A typical method is to show that no bisimulation can contain the pair (p, q). Exercise 3.5 was an example of such a case.

You may think that $p \sim q$ means the same thing as 'p strongly simulates q and q strongly simulates p'. It clearly implies this, because every bisimulation is a simulation; but it is a much stronger condition, as the following exercise shows.

Exercise 3.10 Consider the two processes

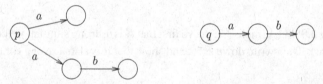

Prove that p strongly simulates q, and vice-versa. You need two simulations, one in each direction. On the other hand show that $p \not\sim q$, i.e. there cannot be a simulation S containing the pair (p, q) such that S^{-1} is also a simulation.

■

In the last exercise, intuitively p is less reliable than q; in performing the action a, p can reach a *deadlock* – a state in which no action is possible. We surely care about the possibility of deadlock, so we do not wish to regard p and q as equivalent.

3.4 Sequential process expressions

In the work that follows, especially when we introduce concurrency, it will help to represent each state of a system by a *process expression*, which carries information about both the behaviour and the structure of the system. In the simple case of sequential processes, this information will indicate explicitly the possible transitions from a state.

Since we wish to define processes rather like procedures in a standard programming language, we presuppose an infinite set *Id* of *process identifiers*. We denote these by capital letters like $A, B, \ldots$, but in examples we shall use helpful names like 'Vending-machine', 'Buffer' and so on. We consider processes to be parametric on names; for example we write $A\langle a, b, c\rangle$ to mean the process A with name parameters a, b, c.

We need a little notation. We shall often write $\vec{a}$ for a sequence $a_1, \ldots, a_n$ of names. If $\vec{a}$ and $\vec{b}$ are name-sequences of length n (the $\vec{a}$ being distinct) and P is a process expression, then $\{\vec{b}/\vec{a}\}P$ means the result of replacing a_i by b_i in P ($1 \le i \le n$). The set of names which occur in the process expression P is denoted by $\text{fn}(P)$. ('fn' stands for *free names*; later we shall extend our process expressions to contain *bound* i.e. not free – names, and then $\text{fn}(P)$ will denote just the free names in P.)

We are now ready to define our language of sequential processes.

Definition 3.11 Sequential process expression *The set $\mathcal{P}^{\text{seq}}$ of* sequential process expressions *is defined by the following syntax:*

$$P ::= A\langle a_1, \ldots, a_n\rangle \mid \sum_{i \in I} \alpha_i.P_i$$

where I is any finite indexing set. We use $P, Q, P_i, \ldots$ to stand for process expressions.

If $I = \{1, 2, 3\}$ for example, we write the summation $\sum_{i \in I} \alpha_i.P_i$ as $\alpha_1.P_1 + \alpha_2.P_2 + \alpha_3.P_3$, the order of the terms being insignificant. If $I = \emptyset$ then $\sum_{i \in I} \alpha_i.P_i$ is the empty sum, written 0.

We assume that every process identifier A has a *defining equation* of the form

$$A(\vec{a}) \stackrel{\text{def}}{=} P_A$$

where P_A is a summation, and the names $\vec{a} = a_1, \ldots, a_n$ (all distinct) include all the free names $\text{fn}(P_A)$ of P_A. We intend that if $\vec{b}$ is any sequence of n names, not necessarily distinct, then the process expression $A\langle \vec{b}\rangle$ should mean the same as $\{\vec{b}/\vec{a}\}P_A$. We capture this intention by the following definition:

Definition 3.12 Structural congruence *Two sequential process expressions P and Q are* structurally congruent, *written $P \equiv Q$, if we can tranform one into the other by replacing occurrences of $A\langle\vec{b}\rangle$ by $\{\vec{b}/\vec{a}\}P_A$, or vice versa, for arbitrary A defined by $A(\vec{a}) \stackrel{\text{def}}{=} P_A$.*

For example, consider the process definitions

$$A(a, b) \stackrel{\text{def}}{=} a.A\langle a, b \rangle + b.B\langle a, a \rangle$$
$$B(c, d) \stackrel{\text{def}}{=} c.d.0 \ ;$$

then we have structural congruences $B\langle a, a \rangle \equiv a.a.0$ and $A\langle a, b \rangle \equiv a.(a.A\langle a, b \rangle + b.B\langle a, a \rangle) + b.a.a.0$. In passing, note the convention of *introducing* name parameters with round brackets, and representing their *use* with angle brackets.

It is clear that if $P \equiv Q$ then $\text{fn}(P) = \text{fn}(Q)$, because we required all the names in P_A to appear as parameters in the defining equation for A. Sometimes, when we don't wish to vary the parameters, we shall omit them. Thus instead of the above definitions for A and B we might write $A \stackrel{\text{def}}{=} a.A + b.B\langle a, a \rangle$ and $B(c, d) \stackrel{\text{def}}{=} c.d.0$. If we do this, we have to remember that a and b are in the set $\text{fn}(A)$, even if not mentioned explicitly.

We now define a labelled transition system containing all sequential processes, as follows:

Definition 3.13 The LTS of sequential processes *The labelled transition system of sequential processes over Act is defined to have states* $\mathcal{P}^{\text{seq}}$*, and transitions as follows: if* $P \equiv \sum_{i \in I} \alpha_i.P_i$ *then, for each* $j \in I$*,* $P \stackrel{\alpha_j}{\rightarrow} P_j$*.*

In the next few sections we give examples of some sequential processes which will appear in later chapters. Although we have just defined a giant labelled transition system containing *all* sequential processes, we can think of each example as a small LTS containing just the states accessible from those which are explicitly identified.

3.5 Boolean buffer

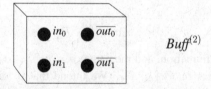

$Buff^{(2)}$

We shall design a buffer process with capacity two, $Buff^{(2)}$ (initially empty). It is parametric on the names in_i, out_i ($i \in \{0, 1\}$), but we omit these name parameters as described above. It receives boolean values (the receipt of 0 is the action in_0) and transmits them in the same order (e.g. the transmission of 1 is the action $\overline{out_1}$). While storing the sequence s, where $s \in \{0, 1, 00, 01, 10, 11\}$, it is in the state $Buff_s^{(2)}$. Thus we have seven process identifiers $Buff^{(2)}$, $Buff_0^{(2)}$,

$Buff_1^{(2)}$, $Buff_{00}^{(2)}$, ..., whose defining equations can be presented schematically as follows:

$$
\begin{aligned}
Buff^{(2)} &\overset{\text{def}}{=} \textstyle\sum_{i\in\{0,1\}} in_i.Buff_i^{(2)} \\
Buff_i^{(2)} &\overset{\text{def}}{=} \overline{out_i}.Buff^{(2)} + \textstyle\sum_{j\in\{0,1\}} in_j.Buff_{ji}^{(2)} \\
Buff_{ij}^{(2)} &\overset{\text{def}}{=} \overline{out_j}.Buff_i^{(2)} \ .
\end{aligned}
$$

We shall see later how buffers can be combined to make buffers of larger capacity, and also how $Buff^{(2)}$ can be decomposed into simpler processes. Note how the indexed family $\{in_i \mid i \in \{0,1\}\}$ of actions is used to represent input of values from a finite value space (similarly for output). We can think of '*in*' as a port through which 0 or 1 is received.

Exercise 3.14 (a) Write an analogous definition of a buffer $Buff^{(3)}$ of capacity three. (b) Modify the defining equations of $Buff^{(2)}$ to allow the stored values to be transmitted in either order. ∎

3.6 Scheduler

A set of agents P_i, $1 \le i \le n$, is to be scheduled to perform a certain task repeatedly. More precisely, each P_i wishes to perform the task repeatedly, and a scheduler is required to ensure that they initiate the task in cyclic order, beginning with P_1. Each agent signals its completion of the task to the scheduler. The different task-performances may overlap each other in time, but the scheduler must ensure that each P_i finishes one performance before it starts another.

We suppose that P_i requests to start the task by pressing the button a_i on the scheduler, and signals completion of the task by pressing b_i.

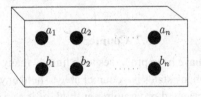

Scheduler

Informally the scheduler's specification is:

(1) it must require $a_1, \ldots, a_n$ to occur cyclically, beginning with a_1;
(2) for each i, it must require a_i and b_i to occur alternately, beginning with a_i.
(3) it must permit any of its buttons to be pressed at any time provided (1) and (2) are not violated.

In a later chapter we shall see how the scheduler may be implemented as a little network of communicating automata. Here, we merely write its specification as a sequential process.

To do this we define a state $Sched_{i,X}$ of the scheduler, for each $i \in \{1, \ldots, n\}$ and $X \subseteq \{1, \ldots, n\}$). The parameter i indicates that it is P_i's turn to initiate the task next; the parameter X represents the set of agents currently performing the task. Thus in state $Sched_{i,X}$:

– only P_i can initiate (provided that $i \notin X$);
– any P_j ($j \in X$) can complete.

The specification is therefore represented by the following defining equations, in which we write $X \cup i$ and $X - i$ instead of $X \cup \{i\}$ and $X - \{i\}$:

$$Scheduler \stackrel{\text{def}}{=} Sched_{1,\emptyset}$$
$$Sched_{i,X} \stackrel{\text{def}}{=} \begin{cases} \sum_{j \in X} b_j.Sched_{i,X-j} & (i \in X) \\ \sum_{j \in X} b_j.Sched_{i,X-j} + a_i.Sched_{i+1,X \cup i} & (i \notin X) \end{cases}$$

where $i + 1$ is interpreted modulo n. Again, this is a schematic presentation of the defining equations for the process identifiers $Sched_{1,\emptyset}$, $Sched_{1,\{1\}}$, $Sched_{1,\{1,2\}}$, ...

Exercise 3.15 (a) Show that the scheduler is never deadlocked – it always permits at least one action. (b) Draw its transition graph when $n = 2$. (c) What's the difference if we define

$$Sched_{i,X} \stackrel{\text{def}}{=} \sum_{j \in X} b_j.Sched_{i,X-j} + a_i.Sched_{i+1,X \cup i}$$

whether or not $i \in X$?   ∎

3.7 Counter

Hitherto our examples have been processes with finitely many states. A simple process with infinitely many states is a counter able to hold any natural number. In the spirit of object-oriented programming, think of it as a number capable of interaction.

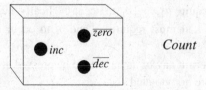

You can always increment it by pressing *inc*; when it's zero you can detect the fact by successfully pressing $\overline{zero}$; otherwise you can detect that it's nonzero and simultaneously decrement it by successfully pressing $\overline{dec}$. Its states are $Count_n$ ($n \geq 0$) with behaviour defined by the equations

$$Count_0 \stackrel{\text{def}}{=} inc.Count_1 + \overline{zero}.Count_0$$
$$Count_{n+1} \stackrel{\text{def}}{=} inc.Count_{n+2} + \overline{dec}.Count_n$$

and we set $Count \stackrel{\text{def}}{=} Count_0$.

Exercise 3.16 The idea of a counter generalises smoothly to a *stack*. Define a process to represent a stack of boolean values, with states $Stack_s$ ($s \in \{0,1\}^*$) and actions $push_i$, $\overline{pop_i}$ ($i \in \{0,1\}$) and $\overline{empty}$.

Can you modify your definition to give not a stack (last-in-first-out) but a *queue* (last-in-last-out)? ∎

As with the scheduler, one can implement these infinite-state processes as networks of very simple components; but in this case the components must be able to *die* and *divide* as in diagrams (2) and (3) of Chapter 1. This mode of evolution is therefore capable of representing dynamically changing data structures.

3.8 Summary

In this chapter we have introduced sequential processes, in the form of labelled transition systems, and we have motivated and defined an important equivalence relation – bisimilarity – which respects the nondeterminism inherent in such processes.

We have also given a few practical examples of such processes; we shall be able to build each of these processes from interacting components, once we have introduced further process constructions in the next section.

4

Concurrent Processes and Reaction

Hitherto we have dealt with only sequential processes. Now we shall consider how processes may run concurrently and interact. This means extending our simple process language. It also means making a distinction between those actions of a (concurrent) system which are *externally* observable and those which are *internal* – being interactions between components of the system. Thus the true sense of 'black box' becomes apparent; things can happen inside which we can't see.

4.1 Labels and flowgraphs

In Section 3.1 we defined the labels $\mathcal{L} \overset{\text{def}}{=} \mathcal{N} \cup \overline{\mathcal{N}}$. They were used as labels in a labelled transition system, but the term fits them for another reason – they are the labels on the buttons of our black boxes. From now on we shall use $\lambda, \mu, \ldots$ to stand for labels. We call $\overline{a}$ the *complement* of a, and we extend complementation to all labels by defining $\overline{\overline{a}} \overset{\text{def}}{=} a$. (*Act* will be a slightly larger set than $\mathcal{L}$, as we shall soon see.)

From now on we shall often draw a black box A, with buttons $a, \overline{b}$ say, as a node with labelled *ports*:

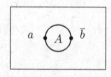

Every complementary pair $(a, \overline{a})$ of labels will represent a means of interaction between black boxes; we think of the action a of one black box as pressing the button labelled $\overline{a}$ on the other. So if B has buttons labelled $b, \overline{c}$ then the system containing both A and B will be drawn

26

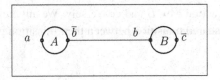

This is a simple example of a *flowgraph*, not to be confused with a transition graph; a flowgraph depicts the structure of a system, i.e. the linkage among its components, not its dynamic properties. To help make the distinction, in Part I of this book we shall consistently draw every flowgraph inside a rectangle. (The diagrams in Chapter 1 were flowgraphs.) As another example we show the flowgraph for the scheduler of Section 3.6 with its client processes $P_1, \ldots, P_n$:

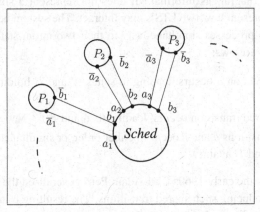

Note that each P_i may have many other labelled ports. Also, in general, a port may bear any number of arcs.

4.2 Observations and reactions

A complementary label-pair $(b, \overline{b})$ is not to be thought of as a buffer or channel having some capacity; it is a means for synchronized action, or handshake. Let us turn back to transition graphs to see what this means. Think of the black boxes A and B in Section 4.1 as separate sequential processes, whose defining equations are

$$A \stackrel{\text{def}}{=} a.A' \qquad B \stackrel{\text{def}}{=} b.B'$$
$$A' \stackrel{\text{def}}{=} \overline{b}.A \qquad B' \stackrel{\text{def}}{=} \overline{c}.B$$

Now consider the composite system consisting of A and B running concurrently, with no interdependence except that any action $\overline{b}$ by A must be synchronised with an action b by B and conversely. We might represent this synchronization by a shared transition between their transition graphs:

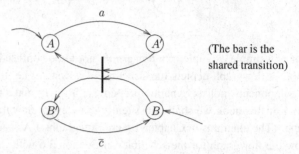

(The bar is the shared transition)

Note that this diagram is informal. It does not represent a single LTS, but attempts to represent how two LTS's may interact. The system begins with the two sequential processes simultaneously in their two initial states, A and B, and behaves as follows:

- the transition a occurs, leading to states A' and B holding simultaneously;
- the shared transition occurs, leading to A and B';
- the transitions a and $\bar{c}$ occur in either order, or simultaneously, leading to A' and B again;

– and so on. In the early 1960s Carl-Adam Petri generalised the theory of automata by introducing such shared transitions. The resulting transition graphs have become famous as *Petri nets*, and have many applications. Petri's was the first substantial theory of concurrent processes and – like the theory of sequential automata – makes great use of graphical representation. Transition graphs and Petri nets are intuitive in many ways, and assist in applications; however, in the theory we develop we shall use transition graphs only from time to time, informally. One reason for this is that we are strongly interested in the way processes are built from others by constructions such as composition and restriction (see below), and such constructions are not greatly enlightened by graphical models. Also we need algebraic methods to represent the parametric dependence of a process upon its link-names.

We shall think of the labels $b, \bar{b}$ as representing *observable* actions, or *observations*. We observe b by interacting with it, i.e. by performing its complement $\bar{b}$, and conversely. Thus we are equating the concepts of interaction and observation. But the shared transition in the diagram above is itself *unobservable*; we can think of it as an internal action, or *reaction* as we shall call it, which is the interaction (i.e. mutual observation) between two components of the system. This internal action will be denoted by τ; being unobservable, it has no complement.

Thus our full class of actions, both observable and internal (i.e. both observations and reactions), consists of $Act \stackrel{\text{def}}{=} \mathcal{L} \cup \{\tau\}$. We continue to denote members of Act by $\alpha, \beta, \ldots$ and we shall denote members of $\mathcal{L}$ by $\lambda, \mu, \ldots$.

4.3 Concurrent process expressions

Hitherto *summation* $\sum_{i \in I} \alpha_i.P_i$ has been our only process construction. We now add two more: *composition* $P|Q$ to run P and Q concurrently, and *restriction* new $a\,P$ to restrict the scope of a name to a process.[1]

Definition 4.1 Concurrent process expression *The set* $\mathcal{P}$ *of* (concurrent) process expressions *is defined by the following syntax:*

$$P \quad ::= \quad A\langle a_1, \ldots, a_n \rangle \quad | \quad \sum_{i \in I} \alpha_i.P_i \quad | \quad P_1 \mid P_2 \quad | \quad \text{new}\,a\,P$$

where I is any finite indexing set.

We shall often use M, N to stand for summations. Note that the order of terms in a summation is insignificant. Prefixed operations (α. and new a) bind more tightly than summation and composition, so for example new $a\,P|Q$ means $(\text{new}\,a\,P)|Q$, not new $a\,(P|Q)$. Also, if a sum with more than one term occurs inside a restriction or composition, we write it in brackets thus: $(a.P + b.Q)|c.R$. Occasionally, to avoid ambiguity, we write a restriction new $a\,P$ as $(\text{new}\,a)P$.

One or two abbreviations are convenient. We shall often omit '.0'; for example we write $a.b$ instead of $a.b.0$. Also, we shall write new $a, b\,P$ or new $ab\,P$ for new a new $b\,P$.

In a restriction new $a\,P$ we say that a is a *bound* name. We denote by $\text{fn}(P)$ the set of all names occurring *free*, i.e. not bound, in P. Changing a bound name into a fresh name is called *alpha-conversion*, and we shall treat two terms as structurally congruent if one is derived from the other by alpha-conversion. Thus for example $(\text{new}\,b)a.b \equiv (\text{new}\,b')a.b'$. We may have to alpha-convert a term in order to perform a substitution properly; for example if $P = (\text{new}\,b)a.b$ then $\{^b/a\}P = (\text{new}\,b')b.b'$.

---

[1] In CCS [10] the constructions differed a little. The restriction new $a\,P$ was written $P \backslash a$. There was also a *renaming construction* $P[b_1/a_1, \ldots, b_n/a_n]$, which is not present here; its job is largely done by syntactic substitution of names for names, which we are writing as $\{\vec{b}/\vec{a}\}P$. In spite of these minor discrepancies, the CCS book is still useful auxiliary reading for the present approach.

We assume that every process identifier A is equipped with a *defining equation* $A(\tilde{a}) \overset{\text{def}}{=} P_A$, where $\tilde{a}$ is a list of $\text{fn}(P_A)$, and P_A may be any summation.

Before formally defining reaction, let us look at examples which show reactions occurring within a process P, leading to a new state P'. We write such a reaction as $P \to P'$.

Example 4.2 Illustrating reaction Let $P = A'|B$, as defined at the head of Section 4.2. Thus $P \equiv \overline{b}.A|b.B'$, so a reaction between b and $\overline{b}$ can occur. Thus we have the reaction

$$P \to A \mid B' .$$ ∎

Example 4.3 Illustrating alternative reactions Let $P = \text{new}\, a\,((a.Q_1 + b.Q_2)|\overline{a}.0) \mid (\overline{b}.R_1 + \overline{a}.R_2)$. Then a reaction can occur either between $a.Q_1$ and $\overline{a}.0$, or between $b.Q_2$ and $\overline{b}.R_1$. In each case, alternative choices in a sum are discarded; thus, using from Definition 4.4 (below) that $Q_1|0 \equiv Q_1$,

$$P \to \text{new}\, a\, Q_1 \mid (\overline{b}.R_1 + \overline{a}.R_2)$$
$$\text{and} \quad P \to \text{new}\, a\,(Q_2 \mid \overline{a}) \mid R_1 .$$

The example illustrates how nondeterminism arises via reaction; once either of these reactions occurs, the other can no longer occur since the possibility of a complementary action has been discarded.

Note that $\overline{a}.R_2$ is not in the scope of the restriction new a, so the a's in $a.Q_1$ and $\overline{a}.R_2$ are different, and these two cannot react; so $P \not\to \text{new}\, a\,(Q_1 \mid \overline{a}) \mid R_2$.   ∎

One may think of new $a\, P$ as a kind of local declaration of a in P. So in the last example the locally declared a has nothing to do with the a in $\overline{a}.R_2$. It is natural to allow a bound name to be changed to a new name, which is not used in the expression under consideration; if we change the local name a to an new name a', then we shall allow ourselves to enlarge the scope of the local name and write P as

$$P \equiv \text{new}\, a'\,((a'.Q'_1 + b.Q'_2) \mid \overline{a'} \mid (\overline{b}.R_1 + \overline{a}.R_2)) \qquad (*)$$

without change of meaning. (Q_1 and Q_2 may contain a, so they have changed to $Q'_1 = \{a'/a\}Q_1$ and $Q'_2 = \{a'/a\}Q_2$.) This makes it easier to see the possible reactions. We shall now make this idea more precise, by extending our notion of structural congruence.

4.4 Structural congruence

Now that we have widened our process language, we wish to extend our definition of structural congruence (Definition 3.12). However, we must first define precisely what is meant by the term 'congruence' of processes, since we shall meet several congruence relations in the rest of this book.

Definition 4.4 Process context *A process context $\mathcal{C}$ is, informally speaking, a process expression containing a hole, represented by $[\ ]$. Formally, process contexts are given by the syntax*

$$\mathcal{C} ::= \ [\ ] \ \mid \ \alpha.\mathcal{C} + M \ \mid \ \text{new}\,a\,\mathcal{C} \ \mid \ \mathcal{C} \mid P \ \mid \ P \mid \mathcal{C}\,.$$

$\mathcal{C}[Q]$ denotes the result of filling the hole in the context $\mathcal{C}$ by the process Q. The elementary contexts are $\alpha.[\ ] + M$, $\text{new}\,a\,[\ ]$, $[\ ] \mid P$ and $P \mid [\ ]$.

Note in particular that $\mathcal{C} = [\ ]$ is the identity context; in this case $\mathcal{C}[Q] = Q$.

Definition 4.5 Process congruence *Let $\cong$ be an equivalence relation over $\mathcal{P}$, i.e. it is reflexive ($P \cong P$), symmetric (if $P \cong Q$ then $Q \cong P$) and transitive (if $P \cong Q$ and $Q \cong R$ then $P \cong R$). Then $\cong$ is said to be a* process congruence *if it is preserved by all elementary contexts; that is, if $P \cong Q$ then*

$$\begin{aligned}
\alpha.P + M \ &\cong\ \alpha.Q + M \\
\text{new}\,a\,P \ &\cong\ \text{new}\,a\,Q \\
P \mid R \ &\cong\ Q \mid R \\
R \mid P \ &\cong\ R \mid Q\,.
\end{aligned}$$

The following is an easy consequence:

Proposition 4.6 *An arbitrary equivalence relation $\cong$ is a process congruence if and only if, for all process contexts $\mathcal{C}$, $P \cong Q$ implies $\mathcal{C}[P] \cong \mathcal{C}[Q]$.*

From now on, when there is no confusion, we shall often drop the word 'process' qualifying the terms 'context' and 'congruence'.

Sometimes a particular congruence $\cong$ is defined by writing down a set $\mathcal{E}$ of equations which $\cong$ is decreed to satisfy, and also decreeing that $Q_1 \cong Q_n$ whenever there is a sequence $Q_1, Q_2, \dots, Q_n$ ($n \geq 1$) such that, for each i, Q_i is $\mathcal{C}[P]$ and Q_{i+1} is $\mathcal{C}[P']$ where $\mathcal{C}$ is a context and $P \cong P'$ or $P' \cong P$ is an equation in $\mathcal{E}$. In other words, $Q \cong R$ holds if Q can be transformed into R by repeatedly applying any equation from $\mathcal{E}$, in either direction, to any term or subterm. If $\cong$ is defined in this way, we say that it is *determined* by the equations $\mathcal{E}$.

Definition 4.7 Structural congruence Structural congruence, *written $\equiv$, is the process congruence over $\mathcal{P}$ determined by the following equations:*

(1) *Change of bound names (alpha-conversion)*

(2) *Reordering of terms in a summation*

(3) $P|0 \equiv P, \quad P|Q \equiv Q|P, \quad P|(Q|R) \equiv (P|Q)|R$

(4) $\text{new}\, a\,(P|Q) \equiv P|\text{new}\, a\, Q \quad \text{if}\, a \notin \text{fn}(P)$

  $\text{new}\, a\, 0 \equiv 0, \quad \text{new}\, ab\, P \equiv \text{new}\, ba\, P$

(5) $A\langle \vec{b} \rangle \equiv \{\vec{b}/\vec{a}\} P_A \quad \text{if}\, A(\vec{a}) \stackrel{\text{def}}{=} P_A$

The first law in (4) means that parts of a process not containing a can be included in the scope of new a or not, with no difference. For example the equation $(*)$ above has been derived by replacing the bound a by a new a' (alpha-conversion) and then using some of the laws in (3) and (4).

It is easy to see that if $P \equiv Q$ then $\text{fn}(P) = \text{fn}(Q)$, i.e. the notion of 'free name' is not sensitive to structural congruence.

Related to structural congruence is the notion of standard form, defined as follows:

Definition 4.8 Standard form *A process expression* new $\vec{a}\,(M_1|\cdots|M_n)$, *where each M_i is a non-empty sum, is said to be in* standard form. *(If $n = 0$ we take $M_1|\cdots|M_n$ to mean 0. If $\vec{a}$ is empty then there is no restriction.)*

The following is an important result, but easy to prove:

Theorem 4.9 *Every process is structurally congruent to a standard form.*

Proof For any restriction new a not inside a summation, we can bring it to the outermost by using alpha-conversion (if necessary) followed by the rule $P|\text{new}\, a\, Q \equiv \text{new}\, a\,(P|Q)$ in conjunction with some of the laws in 4.7(3). □

Exercise 4.10 Prove that new $a\, P \equiv P$ if a is not free in P. Hence prove that in any standard form we can ensure that the outermost restriction new $\vec{a}$ only involves names free in some M_i. Show also how we can arrange that, up to structural congruence, each components M_i $(1 \leq i \leq n)$ in a standard form is a non-empty sum. ■

Example 4.11 Linking Consider a process P with two ports labelled ℓ, r.

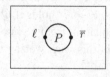

We often want to make a chain of such processes, linking the right port of one with the left of the next:

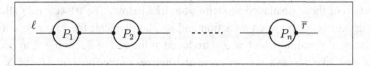

For the purpose we can define a binary *linking* operator

$$P \frown Q \stackrel{\text{def}}{=} \text{new } m \left(\{ {}^m/_r \} P \mid \{ {}^m/_\ell \} Q \right)$$

where m is not free in P or Q. It doesn't matter which name m is chosen, as long as it is not free in P or Q, because any choice yields the same result up to alpha-conversion.

Linking can also be defined in the more general case where there are many left ports and an equal number of right ports:

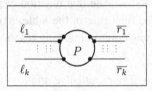

Denote the sequence $\ell_1, \dots, \ell_k$ by $\vec{\ell}$; define $\vec{r}$ similarly. Then the linking operator can be generalised thus:

$$P \frown Q \stackrel{\text{def}}{=} \text{new } \vec{m} \left(\{ {}^{\vec{m}}/_{\vec{r}} \} P \mid \{ {}^{\vec{m}}/_{\vec{\ell}} \} Q \right)$$

where the members of $\vec{m}$ are distinct and not free in P or Q. Of course the definition of linking depends upon the port sequences $\vec{\ell}$ and $\vec{r}$; we can rely on the context to determine these. A natural use of linking is when we are concerned with a finite data domain $V = \{ v_1, \dots, v_k \}$; then we can think of the port sequence $\vec{\ell}$ as a *single* port at which a value $v \in V$ is transmitted. ∎

Of course chaining makes little sense unless we can prove that the linking operator is associative, but this is not hard.

Exercise 4.12 Prove that the linking operator $\frown$ is associative up to structural congruence, i.e.

$$P \frown (Q \frown R) \equiv (P \frown Q) \frown R.$$ ∎

4.5 Reaction rules

We now proceed to define how the different concurrent components of a process can react one with another. With the help of structural congruence, we determine the reactions possible within any process by two simple rules – the first two of those displayed in Definition 4.13 below. The REACT rule allows reaction to occur between an action and its complement; the TAU rule allows the internal τ action, which was introduced at the end of Section 4.2, to occur. Note that, in each case, zero or more alternatives represented by M and N are discarded.

But these rules cannot be applied just anywhere in a process. For example, in $Q = \overline{a}.(b.B|\overline{b}.C)$ the interaction between $b.B$ and $\overline{b}.C$ cannot occur until the action $\overline{a}$ has been observed. This can happen in the context $a.A|Q$; so we can have

$$ a.A \mid Q \;\rightarrow\; A \mid (b.B \mid \overline{b}.C) \;\rightarrow\; A \mid (B \mid C)\,. $$

The two rules PAR and RES indicate that reaction can occur inside a composition or a restriction. The final rule in the table, STRUCT, allows structural congruence to be used at any point in inferring reactions.

Definition 4.13 Reaction *The reaction relation $\rightarrow$ over $\mathcal{P}$ contains exactly those transitions which can be inferred from the rules in the table below:*

REACTION RULES

TAU : $\tau.P + M \rightarrow P$

REACT : $(a.P + M) \mid (\overline{a}.Q + N) \rightarrow P \mid Q$

PAR : $\dfrac{P \rightarrow P'}{P \mid Q \rightarrow P' \mid Q}$ RES : $\dfrac{P \rightarrow P'}{\mathsf{new}\, a\, P \rightarrow \mathsf{new}\, a\, P'}$

STRUCT : $\dfrac{P \rightarrow P'}{Q \rightarrow Q'}$ *if* $P \equiv Q$ *and* $P' \equiv Q'$

As an example of applying these rules, let us see how to infer the reactions for the process in Example 4.3,

$$ P = \mathsf{new}\, a\left((a.Q_1 + b.Q_2)|\overline{a}.0\right) \mid (\overline{b}.R_1 + \overline{a}.R_2)\,. $$

First, $(a.Q_1 + b.Q_2)|\overline{a}$ matches the left side of the REACT rule, so we have $(a.Q_1 + b.Q_2)|\overline{a} \rightarrow Q_1|0$. Then using STRUCT, RES and PAR we can infer a reaction in P. The inference can be diagrammed thus:

$$\frac{}{(a.Q_1 + b.Q_2) \mid \overline{a} \to Q_1 \mid 0} \text{ REACT}$$

$$\frac{}{(a.Q_1 + b.Q_2) \mid \overline{a} \to Q_1} \text{ STRUCT}$$

$$\frac{}{\text{new } a\,((a.Q_1 + b.Q_2) \mid \overline{a}) \to \text{new } a\,.Q_1} \text{ RES}$$

$$\frac{}{\text{new } a\,((a.Q_1 + b.Q_2) \mid \overline{a}) \mid (\overline{b}.R_1 + \overline{a}.R_2) \to \text{new } a\,.Q_1 \mid (\overline{b}.R_1 + \overline{a}.R_2)\,.} \text{ PAR}$$

Exercise 4.14 Using the laws of structural congruence, show that P has the standard form

$$P \equiv \text{new } a'\,(((a'.Q_1' + b.Q_2') \mid (\overline{b}.R_1 + \overline{a}.R_2)) \mid \overline{a'})\,;$$

where a' is fresh and $Q_i' = \{a'/a\}Q_i$. Hence show by an inference diagram, whose last step is by the STRUCT rule, that

$$P \to \text{new } a'\,((Q_2' \mid R_1) \mid \overline{a'})\,.$$

Transform this result by structural congruence to reduce the scope of new a'. ∎

Bear in mind that internal reactions are only half the story of the behaviour of a process, the other half being its observable actions. Of course, sometimes a system P needs an observation (i.e. external interaction) to proceed any further; in this case, i.e. when $P \nrightarrow$, we shall call P *stable*. However, in large systems with many localised (i.e. restricted) labels, most of the behaviour will be internal. Here is an example with a decent amount of internal behaviour i.e. many unstable states.

Example 4.15 Lottery We would like to build a lottery machine L, which will choose randomly a 'ball' from the set $\{b_1, \dots, b_n\}$, and when it has ejected the ball (an observable action!) it will repeat the performance. (For simplicity we assume that it can repeatedly choose the same ball, and that it continues indefinitely.) Using τ to represent internal choice, we could specify the lottery's behaviour as the process

$$Lotspec \stackrel{\text{def}}{=} \tau.b_1.Lotspec + \dots + \tau.b_n.Lotspec\,.$$

But this requires a different definition for each size n of the ball-set. Can we build lotteries for arbitrary n from a fixed stock of components? Here is an attempt, for $n = 3$:

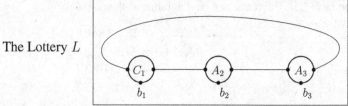

The Lottery L

The components are as follows. First, a generic cell $A(a, b, c)$ is defined by

$$A \stackrel{\text{def}}{=} \overline{a}.C, \quad C \stackrel{\text{def}}{=} \tau.B + c.A, \quad B \stackrel{\text{def}}{=} b.C.$$

(Of course A, B and C are all parametric upon the names a, b, c, but in such simple cases we take the liberty of dropping the parameters). The action $\overline{a}$ of a cell occurs when its left-hand button (port) is pressed; the cell performs c to press the left-hand button (port) of its right neighbour. Next, we define instances

$$A_i \stackrel{\text{def}}{=} A\langle a_i, b_i, a_{i+1} \rangle$$
$$B_i \stackrel{\text{def}}{=} B\langle a_i, b_i, a_{i+1} \rangle$$
$$C_i \stackrel{\text{def}}{=} C\langle a_i, b_i, a_{i+1} \rangle$$

($1 \leq i \leq 3$, with arithmetic modulo 3), and three states of the lottery are defined by

$$L_1 = \text{new } a_1 a_2 a_3 \, (C_1 \mid A_2 \mid A_3)$$
$$L_2 = \text{new } a_1 a_2 a_3 \, (A_1 \mid C_2 \mid A_3)$$
$$L_3 = \text{new } a_1 a_2 a_3 \, (A_1 \mid A_2 \mid C_3).$$

Now it is not hard to see that, starting in any of these states, the lottery can cycle indefinitely through L_1, L_2 and L_3 but may at any time reach a state in which a particular ball b_i must be dropped (an observable action). ∎

Exercise 4.16 Using the reaction rules, show that

$$L_1 \rightarrow L_2$$
$$\text{and} \quad L_1 \rightarrow \text{new } \vec{a} \, (B_1 \mid A_2 \mid A_3),$$

with similar reactions for L_2 and L_3, and that the resulting state in the second case is stable. Draw the transition graph for the whole lottery (six states), giving only the reactions. ∎

It's clear from this example that the reactions '$\rightarrow$' only tell the story of the lottery's *internal* behaviour. For its *external* behaviour we need transition relations like $\xrightarrow{b}$. Then we shall be able to make clear that, in the state new $\vec{a} \, (B_1 \mid A_2 \mid A_3)$, the external action b_1 must be performed before anything else happens.

We can underline this comment by considering bisimulation equivalence $\sim$, to which we shall shortly return. The point of bisimulation is to make processes equivalent if the have the same 'pattern of behaviour', and one reason for this is to ensure that if $P \sim Q$ then P and Q are interchangeable *in all contexts* without disturbing the behaviour pattern of the whole. (This is what is meant by saying that $\sim$ is a *congruence* relation.) If we limited ourselves to just reactions $P \to P'$ in defining bisimulation, then it would not be a congruence relation.

We can see this for the lottery. Write $L\langle b_1, b_2, b_3 \rangle$ for the lottery using balls b_1, b_2, b_3. Changing the names of the balls clearly makes no difference to the pattern of reactions, so if bisimulation were defined only in terms of reactions we would have $L\langle b_1, b_2, b_3 \rangle \sim L\langle b_1', b_2', b_3' \rangle$. But now place them in contact with an external process $\overline{b_1}$ $(= \overline{b_1}.0)$ say; then if $b_1 \neq b_1'$ we find that $L\langle b_1, b_2, b_3 \rangle | \overline{b_1} \not\sim L\langle b_1', b_2', b_3' \rangle | \overline{b_1}$, since their reaction patterns differ; in other words, $\sim$ would fail the congruence condition. With this in mind, we shall now define the labelled transition system for both internal and external actions of concurrent processes.

Exercise 4.17 Identify a reaction which is possible for $L\langle b_1, b_2, b_3 \rangle | \overline{b_1}$ but not possible for $L\langle b_1', b_2', b_3' \rangle | \overline{b_1}$.　　　■

4.6 Summary

In this chapter we have introduced concurrent processes, which are built using four constructions: summation (or choice), parallel composition, restriction and process definition. We have seen how a pair $(b, \overline{b})$ of complementary names represent a means of interaction between two processes. With the help of the important concept of structural congruence, we have defined the reactions $P \to P'$ which represent the process interactions occurring *internally* within the process P.

We are now ready to consider the other aspect of behaviour, the capability of a process P to interact *externally* with other processes.

5

Transitions and Strong Equivalence

We begin this chapter by setting up the labelled transition system for concurrent processes, and we analyse its relationship both with structural congruence and with the reaction relation of the preceding chapter. We then apply the general definition of strong bisimulation, Definition 3.6, to the LTS of concurrent processes. Finally we examine some properties of this equivalence relation, and prove it to be a congruence. This ensures that it is a practically useful notion of behavioural equivalence.

5.1 Labelled transitions

The process transitions $P \xrightarrow{\alpha} P'$, which we now define, will in effect extend the reactions $P \to P'$ which we defined earlier. In fact the case $\alpha = \tau$ corresponds to a reaction, while the case $\alpha = a$ or $\alpha = \bar{a}$ corresponds to a capability of P to participate in a reaction provided that another process, running concurrently, can perform the complementary transition.

The following LTS does not employ the notion of structural congruence. However alpha-conversion is always allowed.

Definition 5.1 The LTS of concurrent processes *The labelled transition system $(\mathcal{P}, \mathcal{T})$ of concurrent processes over the action-set $Act = \mathcal{L} \cup \{\tau\}$ has the process expressions $\mathcal{P}$ as its states, and its transitions $\mathcal{T}$ are exactly those which can be inferred from the rules in the table below, together with alpha-conversion:*

TRANSITION RULES

$$\text{SUM}_t : \quad M + \alpha.P + N \xrightarrow{\alpha} P \qquad\qquad \text{REACT}_t : \quad \frac{P \xrightarrow{\lambda} P' \qquad Q \xrightarrow{\bar{\lambda}} Q'}{P \mid Q \xrightarrow{\tau} P' \mid Q'}$$

$$\text{L-PAR}_t : \quad \frac{P \xrightarrow{\alpha} P'}{P \mid Q \xrightarrow{\alpha} P' \mid Q} \qquad\qquad \text{R-PAR}_t : \quad \frac{Q \xrightarrow{\alpha} Q'}{P \mid Q \xrightarrow{\alpha} P \mid Q'}$$

$$\text{RES}_t : \quad \frac{P \xrightarrow{\alpha} P'}{\text{new } a\, P \xrightarrow{\alpha} \text{new } a\, P'} \quad \text{if } \alpha \notin \{a, \bar{a}\}$$

$$\text{IDENT}_t : \quad \frac{\{\vec{b}/\vec{a}\} P_A \xrightarrow{\alpha} P'}{A\langle \vec{b} \rangle \xrightarrow{\alpha} P'} \quad \text{if } A(\vec{a}) \overset{\text{def}}{=} P_A$$

In the rules REACT_t, L-PAR_t, R-PAR_t and RES_t a transition of a composite process is inferred from transitions of its components. Recall that λ can be of the form a or $\bar{a}$, but not τ. SUM_t is the basic rule to which all transitions are ultimately traced.

As an example of applying the rules, take A and B as defined in Section 4.2. We have $A' \overset{\text{def}}{=} \bar{b}.A$, so using SUM_t and IDENT_t we can infer $A' \xrightarrow{\bar{b}} A$; then using L-PAR_t we get

$$A' \mid B \xrightarrow{\bar{b}} A \mid B. \tag{1}$$

Similarly, using SUM_t and IDENT_t we can infer $B \xrightarrow{b} B'$; so using R-PAR_t with $B \xrightarrow{b} B'$ as hypothesis yields the transition

$$A' \mid B \xrightarrow{b} A' \mid B'. \tag{2}$$

A third transition of $A'|B$, inferred using REACT_t with $A' \xrightarrow{\bar{b}} A$ and $B \xrightarrow{b} B'$ as hypotheses, is

$$A' \mid B \xrightarrow{\tau} A \mid B'. \tag{3}$$

Our system of rules also makes it easy to enumerate *all* possible transitions of a given process. For example, we argue as follows that (1),(2) and (3) are the only transitions of $A'|B$. Since $A'|B$ is a composition, the last step in inferring any transition must be by one of L-PAR_t, R-PAR_t or REACT_t. If by L-PAR_t, then it must be inferred from a transition of A', which in turn can only be inferred by IDENT_t from a transition of $\bar{b}.A$, and this transition (inferred by SUM_t) can only be $\bar{b}.A \xrightarrow{\bar{b}} A$. Similar arguments show that (2) and (3) are the only transitions of $A'|B$ which may be inferred by R-PAR$_t$ and by REACT$_t$ respectively.

From (1), (2) and (3) we see that $A'|B$ is capable of both (external) observation and (internal) reaction. Now consider any transition of new $b\,(A'|B)$. It must be inferred by RES$_t$ (since no other rule can infer a transition of a restricted term), from a transition of the form $A'|B \xrightarrow{\alpha} \cdots$ where α is neither b nor $\bar{b}$. But by our previous reasoning (3) is the only such transition. Therefore the only transition of $A'|B$ is

$$\mathsf{new}\,b\,(A' \mid B) \xrightarrow{\tau} \mathsf{new}\,b\,(A \mid B')\,.$$

The inference of this transition can be drawn as a tree, thus:

$$
\cfrac{
  \cfrac{
    \cfrac{\rule{2cm}{0.4pt}}{\bar{b}.A \xrightarrow{\bar{b}} A}\ \text{SUM}_t
    \qquad
    \cfrac{\rule{2cm}{0.4pt}}{A' \xrightarrow{\bar{b}} A}\ \text{IDENT}_t
  }{}
  \quad
  \cfrac{
    \cfrac{\rule{2cm}{0.4pt}}{b.B' \xrightarrow{b} B'}\ \text{SUM}_t
    \qquad
    \cfrac{}{B \xrightarrow{b} B'}\ \text{IDENT}_t
  }{}
}{A' \mid B \xrightarrow{\tau} A \mid B'}
$$

$$
\cfrac{A' \mid B \xrightarrow{\tau} A \mid B'}{\mathsf{new}\,b\,(A' \mid B) \xrightarrow{\tau} \mathsf{new}\,b\,(A \mid B')}\ \text{RES}_t
$$

The inference of any transition $P \xrightarrow{\alpha} P'$ can be represented as a tree in this way. When we prove a property of transitions, we often do it by induction upon the depth of their inference trees; we sometimes call this proof method *induction on (the depth of) inference*.

We are now ready to show how our LTS relates to structural congruence. It is simple and satisfying to state; it asserts that two structurally congruent processes have essentially the same transitions. The observant reader will see that this is just the same as asserting that the structural congruence relation is a simulation – something we shall pick up again in the following section.

Proposition 5.2 Structural congruence respects transition *If $P \xrightarrow{\alpha} P'$ and $P \equiv Q$, then there exists Q' such that $Q \xrightarrow{\alpha} Q'$ and $P' \equiv Q'$.*

Proof We outline the proof, which proceeds by induction on the depth of the inference of $P \xrightarrow{\alpha} P'$.

It is clearly enough to prove the result in the special case that the congruence $P \equiv Q$ is due to a single application of a structural congruence rule from Definition 4.7; the general case follows just by iterating the special case.

The full proof must treat all possible cases for the final step of the inference of $P \xrightarrow{\alpha} P'$. Here we consider just one case; suppose that it is inferred by L-PAR$_t$, where P is $P_1|P_2$ and P' is $P_1'|P_2$, with $P_1 \xrightarrow{\alpha} P_1'$ inferred by a shorter inference. Now there are many ways in which $P_1|P_2 \equiv Q$ may be due to a single use of a structural congruence rule; we shall confine ourselves to considering just two cases.

(1) Suppose that the commutativity rule is used, so that Q is $P_2|P_1$. In this case we use R-PAR$_t$ to deduce $Q \xrightarrow{\alpha} P_2|P_1'$. Now take Q' to be $P_2|P_1'$; we have $P' \equiv Q'$ as required.

(2) Suppose that a single rule of structural congruence is used within P_1, so that $P_1 \equiv Q_1$ and Q is $Q_1|P_2$. Then, since $P_1 \xrightarrow{\alpha} P_1'$ is inferred by a shorter inference, by appeal to induction we have $Q_1 \xrightarrow{\alpha} Q_1'$ and $P_1' \equiv Q_1'$. Now take Q' to be $Q_1'|P_2$; by using L-PAR$_t$ we deduce that $Q \xrightarrow{\alpha} Q'$ and $P' \equiv Q'$ as required.

So the result follows by a fairly lengthy case analysis, both for the structural congruence rule used and for the last step of the transition inference. □

Now, what is the relationship between the reaction relation $\rightarrow$ and the labelled transition relations $\xrightarrow{\alpha}$? It would be confusing if $\rightarrow$ and $\xrightarrow{\tau}$ were different, since both represent reaction!

Actually, the transition rules mimic the reaction rules (and do more besides). For example, every instance of the REACT rule can be mimicked by the transition rules SUM$_t$ and REACT$_t$.

Exercise 5.3 To prove this, suppose that $P \rightarrow P'$ is an instance of the REACT rule. What form must P and P' take? Use this to show that the transition $P \xrightarrow{\tau} P'$ can be inferred by using SUM$_t$ twice and then REACT$_t$. ∎

More generally, we can prove the following:

Lemma 5.4 *If $P \rightarrow P'$ then $P \xrightarrow{\tau}\equiv P'$.*

Note: $P \xrightarrow{\tau}\equiv P'$ is an instance of relational composition; it means that, for some P'', $P \xrightarrow{\tau} P''$ and $P'' \equiv P'$.

Proof We use induction on the inference of $P \rightarrow P'$ using the reaction rules. Consider the possible cases for the last step of the inference.

Case inferred by TAU. Then P is $\tau.P' + M$, and the transition $P \xrightarrow{\tau} P'$ follows by SUM$_t$.

Case inferred by REACT. Then P takes the form $(a.Q + M)|(\overline{a}.R + N)$ and

P' is $Q|R$. The required transition is then inferred using SUM$_t$ and REACT$_t$ as follows:

$$\frac{\rule{3cm}{0.4pt}}{a.Q + M \xrightarrow{a} Q} \text{ SUM}_t \qquad \frac{\rule{3cm}{0.4pt}}{\overline{a}.R + N \xrightarrow{\overline{a}} R} \text{ SUM}_t$$

$$\frac{}{(a.Q + M) \mid (\overline{a}.R + N) \xrightarrow{\tau} Q \mid R} \text{ REACT}_t$$

Case inferred by PAR. Then P and P' take the form $Q|R$ and $Q'|R$ respectively, with $Q \to Q'$ by a shorter inference; so by induction $Q \xrightarrow{\tau}\equiv Q'$, and hence easily $P \xrightarrow{\tau}\equiv P'$ with the help of L-PAR$_t$.

Case inferred by RES. A similar argument.

Case inferred by STRUCT. Then we have $Q \equiv P$ and $Q' \equiv P'$, with $Q \to Q'$ by a shorter inference – whence $Q \xrightarrow{\tau}\equiv Q'$ by induction, and so $P \xrightarrow{\tau}\equiv P'$ follows from Proposition 5.2. □

Before we can prove the converse, we need another result which is of interest in its own right. To illustrate it, consider a transition of form $P \xrightarrow{\lambda} P'$; recalling that $\lambda \neq \tau$, we intuitively see that the transition has to arise from some summation $\lambda.Q + M$ inside P, with λ unrestricted. We now make this intuition precise.

Lemma 5.5 *Let $P \xrightarrow{\lambda} P'$. Then P and P' can be expressed, up to structural congruence, in the form*

$$P \;\equiv\; \text{new } \vec{z}\,((\lambda.Q + M) \mid R)$$
$$P' \;\equiv\; \text{new } \vec{z}\,(Q \mid R)$$

where λ is not restricted by new $\vec{z}$.

Proof By induction on the inference of $P \xrightarrow{\lambda} P'$. As usual, we need to do a case analysis on the last step of this inference. The details are straightforward; only note that, since $\lambda \neq \tau$, the last step cannot be by the rule REACT$_t$. □

We are now ready for the other half of the proof that $\to$ and $\xrightarrow{\tau}$ coincide, up to structural congruence.

Theorem 5.6 Reaction agrees with τ-transition $P \xrightarrow{\tau}\equiv P'$ *if and only if* $P \to P'$.

Proof The implication from right to left follows directly from Lemma 5.4. For the other direction it will be enough to prove that $P \xrightarrow{\tau} P'$ implies $P \to \equiv P'$, which we do by induction on the inference of the transition $P \xrightarrow{\tau} P'$. Consider the possible cases for the last step of the inference.

Case inferred by SUM$_t$. Then P is $M + \tau.P' + N$, and $P \to P'$ follows directly by TAU and STRUCT.

Case inferred by REACT$_t$. Then P is $P_1 | P_2$, where $P_1 \xrightarrow{\lambda} P_1'$, $P_2 \xrightarrow{\bar\lambda} P_2'$ and P' is $P_1' | P_2'$. So by Lemma 5.5 there exist $\lambda, \vec{z_i}, Q_i, R_i, M_i$ such that for $i = 1, 2$

$$P_i \equiv \text{new } \vec{z_i} \left((\lambda.Q_i + M_i) \mid R_i \right) \text{ and } P_i' \equiv \text{new } \vec{z_i} \left(Q_i \mid R_i \right) \quad \text{with } a \notin \vec{z_i} .$$

With the help of the STRUCT rule, it is now easy to show that $P_1 | P_2 \to P_1' | P_2'$, as required.

Case inferred by L-PAR$_t$, R-PAR$_t$, RES$_t$ or IDENT$_t$. Then the result follows by a simple use of induction. $\qquad\square$

Thus we have demonstrated a tight relationship between the reaction relation ($\to$) and the silent transition relation ($\xrightarrow{\tau}$), via structural congruence.

We now deduce some properties of transitions which we need later. The first says that the branching of a process's behaviour is finite; the second says that a process can only 'use' the names which it already contains; the third says that transitions are preserved by substitutions.

Proposition 5.7

(1) *Given P, there are only finitely many transitions $P \xrightarrow{\alpha} P'$.*

(2) *If $P \xrightarrow{\alpha} P'$ then $\text{fn}(P', \alpha) \subseteq \text{fn}(P)$.*

(3) *If $P \xrightarrow{\alpha} P'$ and σ is any substitution then $\sigma P \xrightarrow{\sigma\alpha} \sigma P'$.*

Proof (1) If P is $\sum_{i \in I} \alpha_i.P_i$ then its only transitions (inferred by SUM$_t$) are $P \xrightarrow{\alpha_i} P_i$ for $i \in I$ and these are finite in number. If P is $A\langle \vec{b} \rangle$ then its transitions (inferred by IDENT$_t$) are exactly those of $\{\vec{b}/\vec{a}\} P_A$, which is a summation, so a similar argument applies. For other forms of P, the result is proved simply by structural induction upon P.

Parts (2) and (3) are proved by induction on the inference of $P \xrightarrow{\alpha} P'$. $\qquad\square$

Now that we have set up a labelled transition system for concurrent processes, we naturally proceed to use it to examine the behaviour of systems by drawing their transition graphs.

Example 5.8 Two-way message buffer Define $A(a, a', b, b')$ by

$$A \stackrel{\text{def}}{=} a.\bar{b}.A + b'.\bar{a'}.A .$$

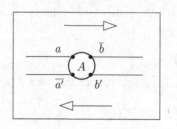 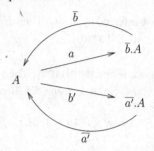

We can think of $A \xrightarrow{a} \overline{b}.A \xrightarrow{\overline{b}} A$ as the transmission of a message from left to right. Clearly A can transmit arbitrarily many messages in both directions.

Now define $B \overset{\text{def}}{=} A\langle b, b', c, c' \rangle$, compose it with A and restrict:

$$P = \text{new } bb' \, (A \mid B) .$$

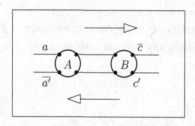 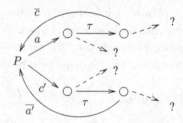

We can deduce for P the transition graph shown partially above. It indicates that, with the help of an internal τ reaction, P can behave more-or-less as A does. But unfortunately it can also behave less reliably!　■

Exercise 5.9 Work out the expressions for the intervening states in the above transition graph. One of them is $\text{new } bb' \, (\overline{b}.A \mid B)$. Now complete the graph, indicated vaguely by the dashed lines. Show that P can reach a deadlocked state in which no further transition is possible.　■

Example 5.10 Lottery Let us revisit the lottery of Example 4.15. Previously we only looked at its internal reactions, and found that it can reach stable states such as $L_1' = \text{new } \vec{a} \, (B_1 | A_2 | A_3)$ (when it is ready to drop the ball b_1). It is easy to see that L_1' only has one transition $L_1' \xrightarrow{b_1} L_1$.

Exercise 5.11 Verify this, from the transition rules.　■

Therefore the full transition graph is as follows:

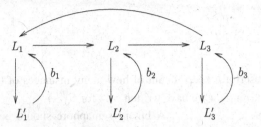

(Note that we naturally drop the τ label from reactions.) It is an accident that this transition graph looks very like the flowgraph in Example 4.15. ■

Exercise 5.12 What happens to the transition graph if $B(a, b, c)$ is defined instead by $B \overset{\text{def}}{=} b.c.A$? ■

5.2 Strong bisimilarity and applications

We are now in a position to apply bisimilarity (Definition 3.6) to the labelled transition system of concurrent processes. First, we point out the relationship between structural congruence and bisimilarity.

Theorem 5.13

(1) *Structural congruence is a strong bisimulation over concurrent processes.*

(2) *If $P \equiv Q$ then $P \sim Q$.*

Proof The first part is just a restatement of Proposition 5.2, and the second part then follows directly. □

We now look at some examples, and derive an important technique which cuts down the work of exhibiting bisimulations.

Example 5.14 Semaphores

An n-ary *semaphore* $S^{(n)}(p, v)$ is a process used to ensure that no more than n instances of some activity run concurrently. It is simpler than the scheduler specified in Section 3.6, since it imposes no cyclic discipline upon its clients. Traditionally the activity is started by the action p and terminated by the action v.

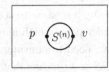

The defining equations for a unary and binary semaphore are respectively

$$S^{(1)} \overset{\text{def}}{=} p.S_1^{(1)} \qquad\qquad\qquad S^{(2)} \overset{\text{def}}{=} p.S_1^{(2)}$$
$$S_1^{(1)} \overset{\text{def}}{=} v.S^{(1)} \qquad\qquad\qquad S_1^{(2)} \overset{\text{def}}{=} p.S_2^{(2)} + v.S^{(2)}$$
$$\qquad\qquad\qquad\qquad\qquad S_2^{(2)} \overset{\text{def}}{=} v.S_1^{(2)}$$

where the subscript k keeps count of how many instances of the activity are running concurrently. (We have written $S^{(n)}$ for $S_0^{(n)}$.)

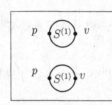

A binary semaphore should behave like two unary ones side-by-side, i.e. $S^{(1)}|S^{(1)}$. (Note that in a flowgraph two ports can have the same label, as shown.) The intuition is that each unary semaphore represents a single unit of resource, and that an n-ary one is nothing but n units of resource. We formalise this statement for $n = 2$ as follows:

Proposition 5.15 $S^{(1)} \mid S^{(1)} \sim S^{(2)}$.

Proof It is enough to show that

$$\mathcal{R} =$$
$$\{\, (S^{(1)}|S^{(1)}, S^{(2)}),\ (S_1^{(1)}|S^{(1)}, S_1^{(2)}),\ (S^{(1)}|S_1^{(1)}, S_1^{(2)}),\ (S_1^{(1)}|S_1^{(1)}, S_2^{(2)}) \,\}$$

is a strong bisimulation. □

Exercise 5.16 Do this. You must show that for all $i, j \in \{0, 1\}$ each transition of $S_i^{(1)}|S_j^{(1)}$ is matched in $\mathcal{R}$ by a transition of $S_{i+j}^{(2)}$, and conversely. ∎

Note that two copies of $S^{(1)}$ can never interact with one another – and hence no τ transitions occur in $S^{(1)}|S^{(1)}$. This is not typical; in most systems of interest the components interact. But the example illustrates the expressive power of parallel composition.

The semaphore example raises an important point about bisimulations. Note that the bisimulation $\mathcal{R}$ of Proposition 5.15 lists two pairs

$$(S_1^{(1)}|S^{(1)}, S_1^{(2)}),\ (S^{(1)}|S_1^{(1)}, S_1^{(2)})$$

which are the same up to structural congruence ($\equiv$). It would be nice, when checking a relation to see if it is a simulation or bisimulation, if we need not consider pairs which agree up to $\equiv$. We now justify this intuition. In doing so, we need to consider relational compositions such as $\equiv \mathcal{S} \equiv$; recall that $P \equiv \mathcal{S} \equiv Q$ means that for some P_1 and Q_1 we have $P \equiv P_1$, $P_1 \mathcal{S} Q_1$ and $Q_1 \equiv Q$.

Definition 5.17 Strong simulation up to $\equiv$ *A binary relation* S *over* $\mathcal{P}$ *is a strong simulation up to* $\equiv$ *if, whenever* PSQ,

if $P \xrightarrow{\alpha} P'$ *then there exists* Q' *such that* $Q \xrightarrow{\alpha} Q'$ *and* $P' \equiv S \equiv Q'$.

S *is a* strong bisimulation up to $\equiv$ *if its converse also has this property.*

Thus for S to be a strong simulation up to $\equiv$ we must be able to complete the following diagram, given the top row and the left transition:

$$
\begin{array}{ccc}
P & S & Q \\
\Big\downarrow{\alpha} & & \Big\downarrow{\alpha} \\
P' \equiv & S \equiv & Q'
\end{array}
$$

Proposition 5.18 *If* S *is a strong bisimulation up to* $\equiv$ *and* PSQ, *then* $P \sim Q$.

Proof Clearly PSQ implies $P \equiv S \equiv Q$. So it will be enough to show that $\equiv S \equiv$ is a strong bisimulation, for then $P \equiv S \equiv Q$ implies $P \sim Q$ and we are done.

Let $P \equiv S \equiv Q$ and $P \xrightarrow{\alpha} P'$. We wish to find Q' which completes the following diagram:

$$
\begin{array}{ccc}
P \equiv & S \equiv & Q \\
\Big\downarrow{\alpha} & & \Big\downarrow{\alpha} \\
P' \equiv & S \equiv & Q'
\end{array}
$$

To do this, first note that for some P_1 and Q_1 we have $P \equiv P_1$, $P_1 S Q_1$ and $Q_1 \equiv Q$. Thus with the help Theorem 5.13 and knowing that S is a strong bisimulation up to $\equiv$, we can fill in the following three diagrams in sequence from left to right:

$$
\begin{array}{cc}
P \equiv P_1 \\
\Big\downarrow{\alpha} \;\; \Big\downarrow{\alpha} \\
P' \equiv P_1'
\end{array}
\qquad
\begin{array}{cc}
P_1 \; S \; Q_1 \\
\swarrow{\alpha} \quad \searrow{\alpha} \\
P_1' \equiv S \equiv Q_1'
\end{array}
\qquad
\begin{array}{cc}
Q_1 \equiv Q \\
\Big\downarrow{\alpha} \;\; \Big\downarrow{\alpha} \\
Q_1' \equiv Q'
\end{array}
$$

Composing these, using the transitivity of $\equiv$, we obtain the required diagram. $\square$

Now, return to Proposition 5.15; it is easy to show that the smaller relation

$$
\mathcal{R}' = \{ (S^{(1)}|S^{(1)}, S^{(2)}), (S_1^{(1)}|S^{(1)}, S_1^{(2)}), (S_1^{(1)}|S_1^{(1)}, S_2^{(2)}) \}
$$

is a bisimulation up to $\equiv$, and by Proposition 5.18 we can conclude that $S^{(1)}|S^{(1)} \sim S^{(2)}$. We only save one pair in this case, but in more complex cases the saving can be considerable. So in practice we only look for bisimulations up to $\equiv$.

Exercise 5.19 Define $D(a, c)$ by

$$D \stackrel{\text{def}}{=} a.\tau.D', \ D' \stackrel{\text{def}}{=} a.D'' + \overline{c}.D, \ D'' \stackrel{\text{def}}{=} \overline{c}.\tau.D' .$$

Draw its transition graph and prove that $D \sim \text{new } b\,(A|B)$, where A and B are as defined in Section 4.2. You will need a bisimulation with four pairs. ∎

In Chapter 6 we shall find that τ transitions such as those in the preceding exercise can often be 'ignored'. More precisely, there is a weaker form of equivalence, $\approx$, for which $D \approx \text{new } b\,(A|B)$ will hold even if we omit the τ's in defining D. In this case a composite system with internal behaviour is equivalent, in this weaker sense, to a system having no internal behaviour.

For the present, we need to derive a few more properties of strong equivalence, $\sim$.

5.3 Algebraic properties of strong equivalence

We need to know how strong equivalence interacts with our three process constructions – sum, composition and restriction. We begin by showing that every process is equivalent to a sum.

Exercise 5.20 For example, prove that $a \mid b \sim a.b + b.a$. ∎

What this means is that when you interact with a process as a black box you cannot tell its structure; a parallel composition is behaviourally indistinguishable from a sum. This shows that strong equivalence is a much more generous relation than structural congruence. More generally:

Proposition 5.21 *For all processes* $P \in \mathcal{P}$, $P \sim \Sigma\{\beta.Q \mid P \stackrel{\beta}{\to} Q\}$.

Proof Let $S = \{\beta.Q \mid P \stackrel{\beta}{\to} Q\}$, so that the right-hand side is ΣS. We show that the transitions of P and ΣS are actually identical. In one direction, suppose $P \stackrel{\alpha}{\to} P'$; then by definition $\alpha.P' \in S$, and hence $\Sigma S \stackrel{\alpha}{\to} P'$ by SUM$_t$. In the other direction suppose $\Sigma S \stackrel{\alpha}{\to} P'$; then it must have been inferred by SUM$_t$, and hence $P \stackrel{\alpha}{\to} P'$ by definition of S. □

The next result asserts that each transition of a multiple composition is either due to one component, or to a reaction between two components:

Proposition 5.22 *For all* $n \geq 0$ *and processes* $P_1, \ldots, P_n$:

$$
\begin{aligned}
P_1 \mid &\cdots \mid P_n \sim \\
&\left\{\Sigma\{\alpha.(P_1|\cdots|P_i'|\cdots|P_n) \mid 1 \leq i \leq n, \ P_i \stackrel{\alpha}{\to} P_i'\}\right. \\
&\left.+ \Sigma\{\tau.(P_1|\cdots|P_i'|\cdots|P_j'|\cdots|P_n) \mid 1 \leq i < j \leq n, \ P_i \stackrel{\lambda}{\to} P_i', \ P_j \stackrel{\overline{\lambda}}{\to} P_j'\}\right.
\end{aligned}
$$

Proof By a simple induction on n. Note that any order of association of the P_i, e.g. $(P_1 \mid (\cdots (P_{n-1} \mid P_n) \cdots))$ can be used, since they all strongly congruent ($\equiv$) and hence strongly equivalent ($\sim$) by Theorem 5.13. $\qquad\square$

We now come to a result which helps to compute the transitions of standard forms. This is widely useful, since Theorem 4.9 tells us that every process can be expressed in standard form.

Proposition 5.23 The Expansion Law *For all $n \geq 0$, processes $P_1, \ldots, P_n$ and names $\vec{a}$:*

$$
\text{new } \vec{a} \, (P_1 \mid \cdots \mid P_n) \sim
$$
$$
\left\{
\begin{aligned}
&\Sigma\{\, \alpha.\text{new } \vec{a} \, (P_1 \mid \cdots \mid P_i' \mid \cdots \mid P_n) \\
&\qquad\qquad \mid 1 \leq i \leq n, \; P_i \xrightarrow{\alpha} P_i' \text{ and } \alpha, \overline{\alpha} \notin \vec{a}\,\} \\
&+ \Sigma\{\, \tau.\text{new } \vec{a} \, (P_1 \mid \cdots \mid P_i' \mid \cdots \mid P_j' \mid \cdots \mid P_n) \\
&\qquad\qquad \mid 1 \leq i < j \leq n, \; P_i \xrightarrow{\lambda} P_i' \text{ and } P_j \xrightarrow{\overline{\lambda}} P_j'\,\}
\end{aligned}
\right.
$$

Proof The left-hand side takes the form $\text{new } a_1 \cdots \text{new } a_k \, (P_1 \mid \cdots \mid P_n)$, and the result is proved by induction on k, starting from Prop 5.22 as the basis. $\qquad\square$

Exercise 5.24 With A and B defined as in Section 4.2, prove by the Expansion Law that

$$
\begin{aligned}
&\text{new } b \, (A \mid B) \sim a.\text{new } b \, (A' \mid B) \\
&\text{new } b \, (A' \mid B) \sim \tau.\text{new } b \, (A \mid B') \\
&\text{new } b \, (A \mid B') \sim a.\text{new } b \, (A' \mid B') + \overline{c}.\text{new } b \, (A \mid B) \\
&\text{new } b \, (A' \mid B') \sim \overline{c}.\text{new } b \, (A' \mid B) \, .
\end{aligned}
$$

$\blacksquare$

Exercise 5.25 Similarly expand all the reachable states of $P = \text{new } bb' \, (A \mid B)$ in Example 5.8. $\qquad\qquad\blacksquare$

Here are some further equivalences, either useful or amusing:

Exercise 5.26 Prove the following:

(1) $\alpha.P + \alpha.P + M \sim \alpha.P + M$

(2) $(\text{new } a)a.P \sim 0, \; (\text{new } a)\overline{a}.P \sim 0$

(3) $\text{new } c \, (a.c.P \mid b.\overline{c}.Q) \sim \text{new } c \, (a.c.Q \mid b.\overline{c}.P) \, .$

$\blacksquare$

Example 5.27 Sequential composition In contrast with the parallel composition $P \mid Q$, which allows concurrent activity of P and Q, we may wish to define *sequential* composition $P; Q$ to mean that 'when P finishes, Q starts'.

We have not taken this as a primitive operator because it can be modelled easily if we adopt the convention (for the class of processes which we wish to compose sequentially) that each process performs a special action $\overline{done}$ as its last action before termination. In fact, we define

$$P; Q \stackrel{\text{def}}{=} \text{new } start\,(\{^{start}/done\}P \mid start.Q)$$

where we assume $start$ not free in P or Q. Clearly, if $\overline{done}$ is the last action of P and of Q then it will also be the last action of $P; Q$. But without any assumption about when, if ever, processes perform the action $\overline{done}$ we can show that sequential composition is well-behaved.   ■

Exercise 5.28 Prove that sequential composition is associative, up to strong equivalence; that is,

$$P; (Q; R) \sim (P; Q); R\,.$$ ■

It is interesting to compare sequential composition with linking (Example 4.11). The linking operator $\frown$ was associative up to structural congruence, but the same is not true of sequential composition. The reason is that sequential composition only 'works' because of the semantics of reaction, as represented by the reaction rules; linking, on the other hand, is merely a question of wiring ports together in a disciplined manner.

5.4 Congruence

We have established many properties of $\sim$; in particular, we showed it to be an equivalence relation in Proposition 3.9(1). But we have not yet shown that it has an essential property of equality – namely that we can 'substitute equals for equals'. in other words, we have not shown it to be a relation process congruence relation, as defined in Definition 4.5.

It is important to prove that strong equivalence is a congruence, because it means that if $P \sim Q$ then, in any system we can build with our constructions, we can replace P by Q without altering the behaviour of the system. The property does indeed hold.

Proposition 5.29 Strong process congruence *Strong equivalence is a process congruence; that is, if $P \sim Q$ then*

(1) $\alpha.P + M \sim \alpha.Q + M$
(2) $\text{new } a\, P \sim \text{new } a\, Q$
(3) $P \mid R \sim Q \mid R$
(4) $R \mid P \sim R \mid Q\,.$

Proof We shall just consider (3); the others are similar. We prove that

$$\mathcal{S} = \{\,(P|R, Q|R) \mid P \sim Q\}$$

is a strong bisimulation. Let $P|R \xrightarrow{\alpha} U$. We must find V such that $Q|R \xrightarrow{\alpha} V$ and $(U, V) \in \mathcal{S}$. Now the transition of $P|R$ can be inferred by any of the rules L-PAR$_t$, R-PAR$_t$ or REACT$_t$; in each case we find that U has the form $P'|R'$, and that for some Q', $Q|R \xrightarrow{\alpha} Q'|R'$ with $P' \sim Q'$. Take V to be $Q'|R'$. $\qquad\square$

Note, by the way, that (4) need not be proved separately, since it follows from (3) by Theorem 5.13(2); for we have $R|P \equiv P|R \sim Q|R \equiv R|Q$, hence $R|P \sim R|Q$.

5.5 Summary

In this chapter the notion of bisimulation from Chapter 3 has been extended to concurrent processes, and we have found it to yield a useful equivalence relation which is also a congruence i.e. it is preserved by substitution in any process context. This so-called strong congruence relation differs greatly from structural congruence; despite its name it is much weaker, being insensitive to the concurrency within a system. Indeed, every concurrent system is strongly congruent to a sequential one.

On the other hand, strong congruence is still sensitive to the amount of re-action which occurs internally within a process. In the following chapter we shall set up a weaker congruence relation which is completely insensitive to internal reactions, except in so far as they influence the possibilities for external behaviour.

6

Observation Equivalence: Theory

A main goal of our theory is that systems with different internal structure, and hence different internal behaviour, may nevertheless be considered equivalent. So we look for a notion of equivalence expressed as far as possible in terms of external behaviour, i.e. the transitions $\xrightarrow{\lambda}$, $\lambda \in \mathcal{L}$.

Hitherto we have interleaved theoretical development with examples. For observation equivalence we change style; this chapter contains all the theory we need, with a few simple illustrations, while Chapter 7 will contain substantial examples and exercises.

6.1 Observations

We think of any action $\xrightarrow{\lambda}$, with $\lambda \in \mathcal{L}$, as an observation (see Section 4.2); $\xrightarrow{a}$ is an observation of $\xrightarrow{\bar{a}}$ and conversely, so an interaction 'at a' is just a mutual observation. In the system $\text{new } a\,(P|Q)$ such a mutual observation may be a reaction, itself unobservable, between the components P and Q.

Now think of an *experiment* e as a sequence $e = \lambda_1 \cdots \lambda_n$ of observable actions. In conducting an experiment, i.e. in making successive observations on a process, we cannot prevent its internal reactions occurring at any time. The following definitions will therefore be helpful:

Definition 6.1 Experiment relations *The relations* $\Rightarrow$ *and* $\xrightarrow{s}$, *for any* $s \in Act^*$, *are defined as follows:*

(1) $P \Rightarrow Q$ *means that there is a sequence of zero or more reactions* $P \rightarrow \cdots \rightarrow Q$. *Formally,* $\Rightarrow \overset{\text{def}}{=} \rightarrow^*$, *the transitive reflexive closure of* $\rightarrow$.

(2) *Let* $s = \alpha_1 \cdots \alpha_n$. *Then* $P \xrightarrow{s} Q$ *means* $P \Rightarrow \xrightarrow{\alpha_1} P_1 \cdots \Rightarrow \xrightarrow{\alpha_n} P_n \Rightarrow Q$. *Formally,* $\xrightarrow{s} \overset{\text{def}}{=} \Rightarrow \xrightarrow{\alpha_1} \Rightarrow \cdots \Rightarrow \xrightarrow{\alpha_n} \Rightarrow$.

In particular, $\xrightarrow{\lambda}$ is the observation $\xrightarrow{\lambda}$ accompanied (before and after) by any

52

number of reactions; $\overset{\tau}{\Rightarrow}$ means at least one reaction, whereas $\Rightarrow$ means zero or more reactions; $\overset{e}{\Rightarrow}$ is the performance of an experiment $e = \lambda_1 \cdots \lambda_n$ accompanied by any number of reactions. If $n = 0$ then $e = \epsilon$, the empty experiment; we have $\overset{\epsilon}{\Rightarrow} = \Rightarrow$, indicating that internal reactions may occur even if we observe nothing.

6.2 Weak bisimulation

We define weak simulation exactly as we did strong, but with reference to experiments $\overset{e}{\Rightarrow}$ instead of arbitrary actions $\overset{\alpha}{\rightarrow}$.

Definition 6.2 Weak simulation *Let S be a binary relation over $\mathcal{P}$. Then S is said to be a* weak simulation *if, whenever PSQ,*

if $P \overset{e}{\Rightarrow} P'$ then there exists $Q' \in \mathcal{P}$ such that $Q \overset{e}{\Rightarrow} Q'$ and $P'SQ'$.

We say that Q weakly simulates P if there exists a weak simulation S such that PSQ.

Although this follows Definition 3.3 (strong simulation) closely, there is a large difference in practice. To check whether any S is a weak simulation, we appear to have to check for all pairs $(P, Q) \in S$ whether Q can match P for all experiments $\overset{e}{\Rightarrow}$, and this would be an intolerable burden. For not only may e contain arbitrarily many observations λ, but also the transition $\overset{e}{\Rightarrow}$ allows an arbitrary number of interspersed reactions.

Luckily, we find that we only have to make a check for each single action $P \overset{\alpha}{\rightarrow} P'$ (we know there are only a finite number of these). The following result makes this precise:

Proposition 6.3 *S is a weak simulation if and only if, whenever PSQ,*

if $P \rightarrow P'$ then there exists $Q' \in \mathcal{P}$ such that $Q \Rightarrow Q'$ and $P'SQ'$;
if $P \overset{\lambda}{\rightarrow} P'$ then there exists $Q' \in \mathcal{P}$ such that $Q \overset{\lambda}{\Rightarrow} Q'$ and $P'SQ'$.

The proof is quite easy and we omit it. Note particularly that a reaction $\overset{\tau}{\rightarrow}$ of P can be matched by many reactions, and even *no reaction*, on the part of Q; there is freedom for disparity in the reaction-patterns of P and Q, in contrast with strong simulation.

The following is obvious, and shows that the term 'weak' is appropriate:

Proposition 6.4 *Every strong simulation is also a weak one.*

The proof of this relies on Proposition 6.3. In fact it is almost always better to use Proposition 6.3 than the original Definition 6.2 when checking a weak (bi)simulation.

Definition 6.5 Weak bisimulation and equivalence *A binary relation S over $\mathcal{P}$ is said to be a* weak bisimulation *if both S and its converse are weak simulations. We say that P and Q are* weakly bisimilar, weakly equivalent, *or* observation equivalent, *written $P \approx Q$, if there exists a weak bisimulation S such that PSQ.*

We now easily see that:

Proposition 6.6 *$P \sim Q$ implies $P \approx Q$.*

Proof Immediate from Proposition 6.4.   □

The elementary theory of weak equivalence is the same as for strong. By analogy with Proposition 3.9 we have

Proposition 6.7

    (1) *$\approx$ is an equivalence relation;*

    (2) *$\approx$ is itself a weak bisimulation.*

We now turn to the notion of 'simulation up to'. In the previous chapter we defined strong simulation up to $\equiv$ and showed why it is useful. A completely analogous result holds for weak simulation up to $\equiv$. But we prefer to state something more general, and therefore more useful; we work not up to $\equiv$, but up to $\sim$. What it amounts to is that, in establishing *weak* equivalence, we can treat *strongly* equivalent processes as effectively identical. The definition and proposition are as follows:

Definition 6.8 Weak simulation up to $\sim$ *A binary relation S is a* weak simulation up to $\sim$ *if, whenever PSQ,*

    if $P \to P'$ then there exists Q' such that $Q \Rightarrow Q'$ and $P' \sim S \sim Q'$;

    if $P \xrightarrow{\lambda} P'$ then there exists Q' such that $Q \xRightarrow{\hat{\lambda}} Q'$ and $P' \sim S \sim Q'$.

S is a weak bisimulation up to $\sim$ *if its converse also has this property.*

So for S to be a weak simulation up to $\sim$ we must be able to complete the following diagrams, given the top row and the left transition:

$$
\begin{array}{ccc}
P & S & Q \\
{\scriptstyle\lambda}\big\downarrow & & \big\Downarrow{\scriptstyle\lambda} \\
P' \sim & S & \sim Q'
\end{array}
\qquad\qquad
\begin{array}{ccc}
P & S & Q \\
\big\downarrow & & \big\Downarrow \\
P' \sim & S & \sim Q'
\end{array}
$$

Proposition 6.9 *If S is a weak bisimulation up to $\sim$ and PSQ, then $P \approx Q$.*

Proof It will be enough to show that $\sim S \sim$ is a weak bisimulation, for then $P \sim S \sim Q$ implies $P \approx Q$ and we are done.

So we must find Q' which completes each of the following diagrams, given the top row and the left transition:

$$
\begin{array}{ccc}
P & \sim S \sim & Q \\
\downarrow{\scriptstyle\lambda} & & \Downarrow{\scriptstyle\lambda} \\
P' & \sim S \sim & Q'
\end{array}
\qquad\qquad
\begin{array}{ccc}
P & \sim S \sim & Q \\
\downarrow & & \Downarrow \\
P' & \sim S \sim & Q'
\end{array}
$$

It will be enough just to treat the first diagram. Note that for some P_1 and Q_1 we have $P \sim P_1$, $P_1 S Q_1$ and $Q_1 \sim Q$. Thus, since $\sim$ is a strong simulation and we are assuming that S is a weak bisimulation up to $\sim$, given the left-most transition we can fill in the following three diagrams in sequence from left to right:

$$
\begin{array}{ccc}
P & \sim & P_1 \\
\downarrow{\scriptstyle\lambda} & & \downarrow{\scriptstyle\lambda} \\
P' & \sim & P'_1
\end{array}
\qquad
\begin{array}{ccc}
P_1 & S & Q_1 \\
\downarrow{\scriptstyle\lambda} & & \Downarrow{\scriptstyle\lambda} \\
P'_1 \sim & S & \sim Q'_1
\end{array}
\qquad
\begin{array}{ccc}
Q_1 & \sim & Q \\
\downarrow{\scriptstyle\lambda} & & \downarrow{\scriptstyle\lambda} \\
Q'_1 & \sim & Q'
\end{array}
$$

Composing these, using the transitivity of $\sim$, we obtain the required result. (Note especially that multiple transitions are involved in the second and third diagrams.) $\qquad\square$

Having pursued the analogy between strong and weak equivalence, let us look at the differences. First, we see how weak equivalence is less sensitive to τ transitions.

Example 6.10 Illustrating weak bisimulation In Section 4.2 we defined two processes $A(a, b)$ and $B(b, c)$ by

$$
\begin{aligned}
A &\stackrel{\text{def}}{=} a.A' & B &\stackrel{\text{def}}{=} b.B' \\
A' &\stackrel{\text{def}}{=} \overline{b}.A & B' &\stackrel{\text{def}}{=} \overline{c}.B
\end{aligned}
$$

and in Exercise 5.19 we combined them as $\text{new } b\,(A|B)$, which we showed strongly equivalent to a sequential process. We can now show that it is weakly equivalent to a sequential process which has no τ transitions, i.e.

$$
E \stackrel{\text{def}}{=} a.E', \ E' \stackrel{\text{def}}{=} a.E'' + \overline{c}.E, \ E'' \stackrel{\text{def}}{=} \overline{c}.E' .
$$

In fact the following is a weak bisimulation:

$$
\{\, (\text{new } b\,(A|B), E), \ (\text{new } b\,(A'|B), E'),
$$
$$
(\text{new } b\,(A|B'), E'), \ (\text{new } b\,(A'|B'), E'') \,\} . \qquad\blacksquare
$$

Exercise 6.11 Verify this weak bisimulation, using Proposition 6.3.   ■

One may be tempted to think that, in a similar way, every process can be reduced to a weakly equivalent one with no τ transitions. But that is not true. The
following example shows the kind of subtle differences of behaviour which
arise from the presence of internal actions.

Example 6.12 Some inequivalences Consider the three processes P, Q
and R:

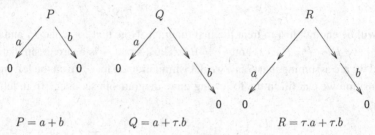

$$P = a + b \qquad Q = a + \tau.b \qquad R = \tau.a + \tau.b$$

In fact, no pair of these are weakly equivalent. Consider P and Q. Intuitively
they differ because Q can internally discard the possibility of doing a, whereas
P can make no such commitment – it preserves both the possibility of doing a
and the possibility of doing b until one of these has occurred. More formally,
we can show that no bisimulation S can contain the pair (P, Q). For suppose it
can; then since $Q \rightarrow b.0$, there must be some P' with $P \Rightarrow P'$ and $(P', b.0) \in$
S. But the only P' such that $P \Rightarrow P'$ is P itself, so $(P, b.0) \in S$. But this is
impossible if S is a weak bisimulation, since $P \xrightarrow{a} 0$ whereas $b.0 \not\Rightarrow$.   ■

Exercise 6.13 Prove similarly that no weak bisimulation can contain either
(P, R) or (Q, R).   ■

On the other hand, certain behaviour patterns *are* weakly equivalent. They
are best seen first in a simple example.

Example 6.14 Some equivalences In each of the following three cases, the
dashed transition(s) can be removed, up to weak equivalence:

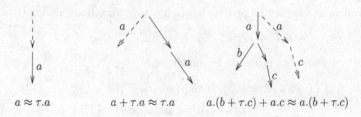

$$a \approx \tau.a \qquad a + \tau.a \approx \tau.a \qquad a.(b + \tau.c) + a.c \approx a.(b + \tau.c)$$

■

These properties are occasionally useful in a more general form, so we state them here. In a certain sense, they represent all the possible ways in which weak equivalence allows one to vary the pattern of τ transitions.

Theorem 6.15 *If P is any process and M, N any summations, then*

(1) $P \approx \tau.P$

(2) $M + N + \tau.N \approx M + \tau.N$

(3) $M + \alpha.P + \alpha.(\tau.P + N) \approx M + \alpha.(\tau.P + N)$.

Proof For each case, we can exhibit a simple weak bisimulation. For (2), take

$$\mathcal{S} = \{(M+N+\tau.N,\ M+\tau.N)\} \cup \mathrm{Id}_{\mathcal{P}}$$

where $\mathrm{Id}_{\mathcal{P}}$ is the identity relation on processes. $\square$

Equations (2) and (3) in the theorem look rather different. However, the following equation can be proved equivalent to equation (2):

$$M + \alpha.P + \tau.(\alpha.P + N) \approx M + \tau.(\alpha.P + N)\ . \qquad (*)$$

It pleasantly resembles equation (3), with τ and α swapped in two places. Both $(*)$ and (3) express the idea that a summand $\alpha.P$ is superfluous if there is another way of performing the reaction $\overset{\alpha}{\rightarrow} P$, but accompanied by a τ.

Exercise 6.16 Derive equation (2) from equation $(*)$ and vice versa.
Hint: Recall that any summation N takes the form $\sum \alpha_i P_i$. In one direction you will find the first equation in Exercise 5.26 useful. ∎

As with strong congruence, we also have a congruence property for $\approx$, allowing us to 'substitute equals for equals'. The proof is along the same lines.

Proposition 6.17 Weak process congruence *Weak equivalence is a process congruence; that is, if $P \approx Q$ then*

(1) $\alpha.P + M \approx \alpha.Q + M$ *(where M is any sum)*

(2) $\mathrm{new}\, a\, P \approx \mathrm{new}\, a\, Q$

(3) $P \mid R \approx Q \mid R$

(4) $R \mid P \approx R \mid Q$.

It is important to be clear what this asserts. Consider (1); it asserts that if $P \approx Q$ then we can substitute one for the other *under* a prefixed action α in a summation, and the result will be weakly equivalent. It does *not* assert that if $N_1 \approx N_2$ then $M + N_1 \approx M + N_2$; in other words, we cannot replace *a partial* summation by an equivalent one and expect to maintain weak equivalence. Indeed we know that $b \approx \tau.b$; but in Example 6.12 we found that $a + b \not\approx a + \tau.b$.

6.3 Unique solution of equations

We now come to our last general property, and one that is rather useful. It is to do with *solving equations*, of the form

$$X_1 \approx \alpha_{11}.E_{11} + \cdots + \alpha_{1n_1}.E_{1n_1}$$
$$X_2 \approx \alpha_{21}.E_{21} + \cdots + \alpha_{2n_2}.E_{2n_2}$$
$$\cdots \cdots ,$$

where the expressions E_{ij} contain process variables $X_1, X_2, \ldots$. An example is

$$X \approx a.X + b.Y$$
$$Y \approx c.X .$$

How many solutions do such equations have? First, it's clear that any such set of equations has at least one solution; for example, we can *define*

$$A \overset{\text{def}}{=} a.A + b.B$$
$$B \overset{\text{def}}{=} c.A$$

and then A and B certainly satisfy the equations – they even satisfy them for structural congruence, i.e. $A \equiv a.A + b.B$, $B \equiv c.A$. But are there any essentially different pairs of processes P, Q which satisfy $P \approx a.P + b.Q$ and $Q \approx c.P$? In this case, the answer will be: No, the solution of the equations is *unique up to* $\approx$; that is, for any P and Q satisfying the equations, $P \approx A$ and $Q \approx B$.

But the solution isn't always unique up to $\approx$. Consider the simple single equation

$$X \approx \tau.X ;$$

Theorem 6.15(1) tells us that *every* process P satisfies it! There are also intermediate cases of equations satisfied by many processes, as the following exercise shows.

Exercise 6.18 Consider the equation $X \approx a.P + \tau.X$, where P is any fixed process. Show that for any process Q, this equation has the solution $a.P + \tau.Q$. ∎

In fact, it is τ which allows this multiplicity of solutions. If it doesn't occur at top level in the equations, and the expressions E_{ij} satisfy certain other conditions, then we are sure of uniqueness. We shall be content with the case in which each E_{ij} is just a process variable. To be precise:

Theorem 6.19 Unique solution of equations *Let $\vec{X} = X_1, X_2, \ldots$ be a (possibly infinite) sequence of process variables. In the following formal equations*

$$X_1 \approx \alpha_{11}.X_{k(11)} + \cdots + \alpha_{1n_1}.X_{k(1n_1)}$$
$$X_2 \approx \alpha_{21}.X_{k(21)} + \cdots + \alpha_{2n_2}.X_{k(2n_2)}$$
$$\ldots \qquad \ldots \ldots$$

assume that each $\alpha_{ij} \neq \tau$. Then, up to $\approx$, there is a unique sequence $P_1, P_2, \ldots$ of processes which satisfies the equations.

Proof For convenience, write $M_i[\vec{X}]$ for the right-hand side of the equation for X_i. Let $\vec{P}, \vec{Q}$ be two different solutions, i.e. $P_i \approx M_i[\vec{P}]$ and $Q_i \approx M_i[\vec{Q}]$ for all i.

We shall show that $P_i \approx Q_i$ for each i. To this end, it is enough to show that

$$\mathcal{S} = \{(P, Q) \mid P \approx P_i \text{ and } Q \approx Q_i \text{ for some } i\}$$

is a weak bisimulation. So take an arbitrary pair $(P, Q) \in \mathcal{S}$.

First, suppose $P \Rightarrow P'$. Then $P \approx P_i \approx M_i[\vec{P}] \Rightarrow P'' \approx P'$, for some P''. But since $\alpha_{ij} \neq \tau$ for all i, j, it follows that $P \approx P'$. By choosing $Q' = Q$, we clearly have a Q' such that $Q \Rightarrow Q'$ and $(P', Q') \in \mathcal{S}$.

Now suppose $P \overset{\lambda}{\Rightarrow} P'$. Then $P \approx P_i \approx M_i[\vec{P}] \overset{\lambda}{\Rightarrow} P_k \Rightarrow P'' \approx P'$, where $\lambda = \alpha_{ij}$ and $P_k = P_{k(ij)}$ for some j. By a similar argument to above, $P_k \approx P'$. Also, we have $M_i[\vec{Q}] \overset{\lambda}{\Rightarrow} Q_k$; but $Q_i \approx M_i[\vec{Q}]$, so $Q \overset{\lambda}{\Rightarrow} Q' \approx Q_k$ for some Q', which is what we require. □

6.4 Summary

We have introduced a weak form of bisimulation which allows two processes to be considered equivalent even if they have greatly dissimilar patterns of internal reaction. We have developed the theory of this weak equivalence ($\approx$), and found that it follows that of strong equivalence ($\sim$) to a certain extent, but that it satisfies some extra properties such as $P \approx \tau.P$. Finally we have shown that a set of process equations has a unique solutions up to $\approx$, under certain conditions; this is a pleasant analogy to Proposition 2.4 concerning the language-equivalence of automata.

In the following chapter we exploit these results in some practical applications.

7

Observation Equivalence: Examples

In this chapter we look at several examples of systems and their specifications. In each case the specification is represented by a process which has little or no compositional structure, while the system itself is made up of several concurrent components which interact. In each case we are able to prove a theorem of the form

$$System \approx Specification .$$

This is done either by exhibiting and verifying a weak bisimulation, or by invoking Theorem 6.19, the unique solution of equations. In each case, since the *System* has many internal reactions while the *Specification* has virtually none, weak congruence is the best we can hope for.

7.1 Lottery

In Example 4.15 we specified a lottery system, for picking one of n balls at random, by

$$Lotspec \stackrel{\text{def}}{=} \tau.b_1.Lotspec + \cdots + \tau.b_n.Lotspec .$$

Then in Example 5.10 we designed a lottery, made from n identical components, to meet this specification. We need not recall the detailed implementation; we need only recall its transition graph:

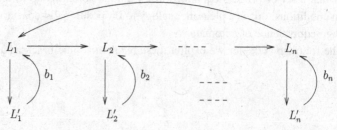

Now we can prove it is correct, i.e.

Theorem 7.1 $L_1 \approx Lotspec$.

Proof More generally, we shall show that $L_i \approx Lotspec$, for each i. In fact we show that the following is a weak bisimulation:

$$\mathcal{S} \stackrel{\text{def}}{=} \{\, (L_i, Lotspec) \mid 1 \le i \le n \,\} \cup \{\, (L'_i, b_i.Lotspec) \mid 1 \le i \le n \,\} \,.$$

Take a typical pair of the second kind, $(L'_1, b_1.Lotspec)$. We need to show that to each transition $\stackrel{\lambda}{\rightarrow}$ or $\rightarrow$ of one member there corresponds a 'matching' transition $\stackrel{\lambda}{\Rightarrow}$ or $\Rightarrow$ (respectively) of the other. But each member of the pair has only one transition; these are $L'_1 \stackrel{b_1}{\rightarrow} L_1$ and $b_1.Lotspec \stackrel{b_1}{\rightarrow} Lotspec$, and they match because $(L_1, Lotspec) \in \mathcal{S}$.

Now take a typical pair of the first kind, say $(L_1, Lotspec)$. Consider the transitions of L_1:

$L_1 \rightarrow L_2$ is matched by $Lotspec \Rightarrow Lotspec$;

$L_1 \rightarrow L'_1$ is matched by $Lotspec \rightarrow b_1.Lotspec$.

Note that the $\Rightarrow$ transition is empty. On the other hand, for transitions of $Lotspec$:

For each i, $Lotspec \rightarrow b_i.Lotspec$ is matched by $L_1 \Rightarrow L'_i$.

Note that this $\Rightarrow$ transition may involve many $\rightarrow$ transitions. □

It is striking that in this weak equivalence, one member (L_1) is capable of infinite 'idling', i.e. an infinite sequence of internal transitions, while the other (*Lotspec*) is not. Thus the equivalence rests on a *fairness* assumption that no transition, e.g. $L_1 \rightarrow L'_1$, can be enabled infinitely often without occurring. We shall not try to justify this assumption.

7.2 Job Shop

Two agents A are working together on an assembly line. They receive jobs off a conveyor belt represented by the port i, and dispatch them after assembly along another conveyor belt represented by $\overline{o}$. There are three grades of job: easy (E), neutral (N) and difficult (D). We represent this difference by dividing i into an indexed family of ports i_X, $X \in \{E, N, D\}$.

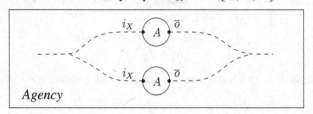

However the agents are experienced and no longer need to distinguish the grades of job. They treat them all alike, as reflected in the following definition of an agent:

$$A \stackrel{\text{def}}{=} i_E.A' + i_N.A' + i_D.A'$$
$$A' \stackrel{\text{def}}{=} \overline{o}.A .$$

The system consisting of the two agents is simply

$$Agency \stackrel{\text{def}}{=} A \mid A .$$

Since parallel composition is not clocked, this definition allows each agent to take an arbitrary amount of time per job, perhaps due to laziness or boredom.

The agents are promoted to become managers. They are replaced by two less capable people whom we shall call jobbers, J. A jobber can do a difficult (D) job only with the aid of a hammer, and can do a neutral (N) job only with the aid of either a hammer or a mallet – but can do an easy (E) job with bare hands. Unfortunately (since the promoted agents aren't yet good managers) there is only one hammer H and one mallet M which the two jobbers must share, picking one of them up and putting it down as required. The picking-up actions are gh, gm; the putting-down actions are ph, pm. The jobbers use the co-actions $\overline{gh}, \ldots$.

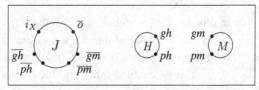

The hammer and mallet are just semaphores, $H \stackrel{\text{def}}{=} S\langle gh, ph \rangle$ and $M \stackrel{\text{def}}{=} S\langle gm, pm \rangle$; the parametric semaphore $S(p, v)$ was defined in Example 5.14. Thus they satisfy

$$H \equiv gh.H' \qquad\qquad M \equiv gm.M'$$
$$H' \equiv ph.H \qquad\qquad M' \equiv pm.M$$

The definition of a jobber is a little more complex:

$$J \stackrel{\text{def}}{=} \Sigma_{X \in \{E,N,D\}}\, i_X.J_X$$
$$J_E \stackrel{\text{def}}{=} \overline{o}.J$$
$$J_N \stackrel{\text{def}}{=} \overline{gh}.\overline{ph}.J_E + \overline{gm}.\overline{pm}.J_E$$
$$J_D \stackrel{\text{def}}{=} \overline{gh}.\overline{ph}.J_E$$

The whole system, two jobbers with a hammer and a mallet, is

$$Jobshop \stackrel{\text{def}}{=} \text{new}\,\vec{t}\,(J \mid J \mid H \mid M)$$

where $\vec{t}$ stands for gh, ph, gm, pm. Here is its flowgraph:

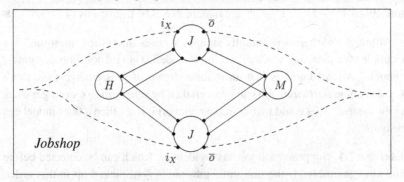

Now, to show that the jobshop is properly designed, we prove that

Theorem 7.2 *Agency* $\approx$ *Jobshop* .

Proof We exhibit a relation S which contains the pair (*Agency, Jobshop*) and is a weak bisimulation up to $\sim$. S contains the following pairs, where X, Y take any value in $\{E, N, D\}$:

$$(1) \quad A \mid A, \quad \text{new}\,\vec{t}(J \mid J \mid H \mid M)$$

$$(2) \quad A \mid A', \quad \text{new}\,\vec{t}(J \mid J_X \mid H \mid M)$$
$$A \mid A', \quad \text{new}\,\vec{t}(J \mid \overline{ph}.J_E \mid H' \mid M)$$
$$A \mid A', \quad \text{new}\,\vec{t}(J \mid \overline{pm}.J_E \mid H \mid M')$$

$$(3) \quad A' \mid A', \quad \text{new}\,\vec{t}(J_X \mid J_Y \mid H \mid M)$$
$$A' \mid A', \quad \text{new}\,\vec{t}(J_X \mid \overline{ph}.J_E \mid H' \mid M)$$
$$A' \mid A', \quad \text{new}\,\vec{t}(J_X \mid \overline{pm}.J_E \mid H \mid M')$$
$$A' \mid A', \quad \text{new}\,\vec{t}(\overline{ph}.J_E \mid \overline{pm}.J_E \mid H' \mid M') \ .$$

It is routine work to prove that this is indeed a bisimulation up to $\sim$; see the following exercise. $\qquad\square$

Note how working up to $\sim$ reduces the number of pairs we have to consider, because $A|A' \equiv A'|A$, $J|J_X \equiv J_X|J$ etc. (In this application we have not gained any extra advantage by working up to $\sim$ rather than $\equiv$.)

Exercise 7.3 Check some of the pairs in S, to see that the bisimulation conditions hold. For example, consider the first pair (P, Q) in (2) with $X = N$, i.e.

$$P = A \mid A', \ Q = \text{new}\,\vec{t}(J \mid J_N \mid H \mid M) \ .$$

List all the transitions $Q \xrightarrow{\lambda} Q'$ or $Q \to Q'$ and show that they are matched by a transition $P \stackrel{\lambda}{\Rightarrow} P'$ or $P \Rightarrow P'$ with $(P', Q') \in \mathcal{S}$. Similarly, show that all transitions $P \stackrel{\lambda}{\rightarrow} P'$ or $P \rightarrow P'$ are matched in $\mathcal{S}$ by transitions of Q. ∎

Although *Jobshop* is apparently simple, it raises interesting questions. For example, we may ask whether we have modelled a real jobshop accurately enough. All we know is that an infinite stream of jobs emerges; we don't know if some *particular* job can be overtaken by other jobs, or even get stuck in the system. This could matter in the real world; if so, then a finer model can be built.

Exercise 7.4 Suppose each job has an identity, which can be detected before and after assembly. If the first three jobs are $j_1 j_2 j_3$, picked up in that order, show that in both *Agency* and *Jobshop* they can be completed in the order $j_2 j_1 j_3$, whatever their degree of difficulty. (Reason informally, not necessarily in terms of process expressions.)

Now adjust the definition of a jobber J so that he or she, once in possession of the hammer, only releases it when having to assemble an easy (E) job – presumably so as to use both hands. If both jobbers are redefined in this way, show that the completion order $j_2 j_1 j_3$ is now impossible in the case that all three jobs are difficult (D).

This exposes a subtle, but possibly crucial, distinction between the two systems. Convince yourself that no shorter job sequence can expose the distinction. ∎

7.3 Scheduler

In Section 3.6 we specified the behaviour of a scheduler to control the repeated performance of a certain task by each of n agents, $P_1, \ldots, P_n$. Agent P_i requests each *initiation* of the task by performing the action a_i, and signals each *termination* of the task by performing the action b_i. The scheduler has to ensure that the actions a_i occur cyclically, starting with a_1, and that for each i the pair of actions (a_i, b_i) must alternate starting with a_i. Our specification was given in terms of process states $Sched_{i,X}$. The parameter i indicates that it is P_i's turn to initiate the task next; the parameter X represents the set of agents currently performing the task. The specification was

$$
\begin{aligned}
Scheduler &\stackrel{\text{def}}{=} Sched_{1,\emptyset} \\
Sched_{i,X} &\stackrel{\text{def}}{=} \begin{cases} \sum_{j \in X} b_j.Sched_{i,X-j} & (i \in X) \\ \sum_{j \in X} b_j.Sched_{i,X-j} + a_i.Sched_{i+1,X \cup i} & (i \notin X) \end{cases}
\end{aligned}
$$

where $i + 1$ is interpreted modulo n.

We would like to build the scheduler as a ring of n identical cells $A(a, b, c, d)$. The ith cell will have two ports for controlling the agent P_i, and two other ports to link it to its neighbour cells.

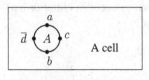

A cell

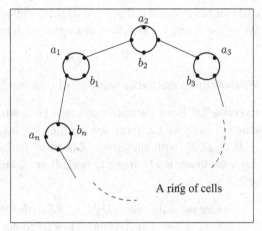

A ring of cells

A first attempt is to define $A(a, b, c, d)$ by the equation

$$A \overset{\text{def}}{=} a.c.b.\overline{d}.A \qquad (\textbf{?}) -$$

or, giving names to the four states of the cell:

$$A \overset{\text{def}}{=} a.C, \; C \overset{\text{def}}{=} c.B, \; B \overset{\text{def}}{=} b.D, \; D \overset{\text{def}}{=} \overline{d}.A \qquad (\textbf{?})$$

In order to link n such cells we define

$$A_i \overset{\text{def}}{=} A(a_i; b_i, c_i, c_{i-1}) \,,$$

and similarly for the intervening states C_i, B_i, D_i; then the initial state of this implementation of the scheduler is defined as

$$S \overset{\text{def}}{=} \text{new } c_1, \ldots, c_n \, (A_1 \mid D_2 \mid \cdots \mid D_n) \,.$$

Of course, we wish to show that $S \approx Scheduler$. Oddly enough, this is nearly true but not quite.

Exercise 7.5 Why does this weak equivalence not hold? Argue informally why it is not true. There is a state of S which is equivalent to no possible state of the specification *Scheduler*.

(*Hint*: This state only occurs after about $2n$ transitions from the start.) ∎

This is a good example of the kind of bug that can exist in a system design for years without detection, and even when detected can be very difficult to reproduce!

Luckily, the correct definition of a cell is not much more complex. It is

$$A \stackrel{\text{def}}{=} a.C, \ C \stackrel{\text{def}}{=} c.E, \ E \stackrel{\text{def}}{=} b.D + \bar{d}.B, \ B \stackrel{\text{def}}{=} b.A, \ D \stackrel{\text{def}}{=} \bar{d}.A \ .$$

(All that has changed is that b and $\bar{d}$ are now allowed to occur in either order.) We define $A_i, B_i, \dots$ as before, and again we define

$$S \stackrel{\text{def}}{=} \text{new } \vec{c}(A_1 \mid D_2 \mid \cdots \mid D_n) \ .$$

We show this correct via a sequence of exercises.

Exercise 7.6 Draw the transition graph of S, when $n = 2$. In general, every state is clearly of the form new $\vec{c}(Q_1 \mid Q_2 \mid \cdots \mid Q_n)$, where each Q is one of A, B, C, D, E (with subscript). Convince yourself that the only accessible states are those in which *one* Q is A, B or C, and all the others are either D or E.   ∎

Consider the state new $\vec{c}(D_1 \mid E_2 \mid A_3 \mid E_4)$. It can perform the action a_3, but no other a_i, so it should correspond to a scheduler state in which it is P_3's turn to initiate. Also, the actions b_2 and b_4 can occur but not b_1 and b_3; this means that P_2 and P_4 are currently performing the task, but not P_1 and P_3. So it must correspond to the state $Sched(3, \{2, 4\})$.

Exercise 7.7 What state of *Scheduler* does new $\vec{c}(E_1 \mid D_2 \mid C_3 \mid E_4)$ correspond to?   ∎

Exercise 7.8 Using the Expansion Law, Proposition 5.23, show that each of the following is strongly equivalent to a summation $\sum_r \alpha_r.S_r$, where each α_r is a_i, b_i or τ and each S_r an accessible state:

$$\text{new } \vec{c}(D_1 \mid D_2 \mid A_3 \mid E_4)$$
$$\text{new } \vec{c}(D_1 \mid E_2 \mid B_3 \mid D_4)$$
$$\text{new } \vec{c}(E_1 \mid D_2 \mid C_3 \mid E_4) \ .$$

∎

Now let us revert to the general case of n components. The accessible states of the system can be defined as follows:

$$A_{i,X,Y} \stackrel{\text{def}}{=} \text{new } \vec{c}(A_i \mid \Pi_{j \in X} D_j \mid \Pi_{k \in Y} E_k)$$
$$B_{i,X,Y} \stackrel{\text{def}}{=} \text{new } \vec{c}(B_i \mid \Pi_{j \in X} D_j \mid \Pi_{k \in Y} E_k)$$
$$C_{i,X,Y} \stackrel{\text{def}}{=} \text{new } \vec{c}(C_i \mid \Pi_{j \in X} D_j \mid \Pi_{k \in Y} E_k) \ .$$

where the sets $\{i\}$, X and Y are any partition of $\{1, \dots, n\}$ i.e. they are disjoint and their union is $\{1, \dots, n\}$. Note that $S = A_{1, \{2, \dots, n\}, \emptyset}$.

Exercise 7.9 Using the Expansion Law again, show the following strong equivalences:

$$A_{i,X,Y} \sim a_i \cdot C_{i,X,Y} + \Sigma_{k \in Y}\, b_k \cdot A_{i,X \cup k, Y-k}$$
$$B_{i,X,Y} \sim b_i \cdot A_{i,X,Y} + \Sigma_{k \in Y}\, b_k \cdot B_{i,X \cup k, Y-k}$$
$$C_{i,X,Y} \sim \Sigma_{k \in Y}\, b_k \cdot C_{i,X \cup k, Y-k} + $$
$$\begin{cases} \tau \cdot A_{i+1, X-(i+1), Y \cup i} & (i+1 \in X) \\ \tau \cdot B_{i+1, X, Y \cup i-(i+1)} & (i+1 \in Y). \end{cases}$$

∎

Exercise 7.10 Let the relation $\mathcal{R}$ containing the following pairs, where $\{i\}$, X and Y form any partition of the set $\{1, \dots, n\}$:

$$A_{i,X,Y}\,, \quad Sched_{i,Y}$$
$$B_{i,X,Y}\,, \quad Sched_{i,Y \cup i}$$
$$C_{i,X,Y}\,, \quad Sched_{i+1,Y \cup i}\,.$$

Then show that $\mathcal{R}$ is a weak bisimulation up to $\sim$. ∎

We are now ready for the main result.

Theorem 7.11 $S \approx Scheduler$.

Proof We need only observe that $\mathcal{R}$ contains the pair $(S, Scheduler)$, corresponding to the case $i = 1$, $X = \{2, \dots, n\}$, $Y = \emptyset$. □

7.4 Buffer

In this section we look at a data structure of fixed capacity, a buffer.

First, recall the boolean buffer of capacity two, defined in Section 3.5. Let us now generalise it to carry values in any finite domain $V = \{v_1, \dots, v_k\}$, and to have capacity n. So $Buff_{\vec{v}}^{(n)}$ stands for the buffer of capacity n holding the value sequence $\vec{v}$ of length no greater than n. (When $\vec{v}$ is empty we just write $Buff^{(n)}$.) For fixed $n \geq 1$, the processes $Buff_{\vec{v}}^{(n)}$ for varying $\vec{v}$ are defined by mutual recursion, as follows:

$$Buff^{(n)} \stackrel{\text{def}}{=} \Sigma_u\, in_u.Buff_u^{(n)}$$
$$Buff_{\vec{v},w}^{(n)} \stackrel{\text{def}}{=} \begin{cases} \Sigma_u\, in_u.Buff_{u,\vec{v},w}^{(n)} + \overline{out_w}.Buff_{\vec{v}}^{(n)} & (|\vec{v}| < n-1) \\ \overline{out_w}.Buff_{\vec{v}}^{(n)} & (|\vec{v}| = n-1) \end{cases}$$

Now write *Cell* for $Buff^{(1)}$, the buffer of capacity one; also $Cell_v$ for $Buff_v^{(1)}$. Using the linking operator of Example 4.11, we would like to show that

Theorem 7.12 $Buff^{(n)} \approx \overbrace{Cell \frown \cdots \frown Cell}^{n\ times}$.

Here we are linking with respect to the vector $in = in_{v_1}, \ldots, in_{v_k}$ of left ports and $out = out_{v_1}, \ldots, out_{v_k}$ of right ports. (We think of in, out as single ports at which a value in V can be transmitted.)

Note that in this chain of cells a lot of concurrent activity can go on, shuffling values from each cell to its right neighbour. A simple lemma, which concerns only two adjacent cells, helps us to cope with this activity:

Lemma 7.13 $Cell_v \frown Cell \approx Cell \frown Cell_v$.

Proof By the expansion law, and the equation $P \approx \tau.P$.   □

Note that the process on the right-hand side of the lemma is *stable*; that is, it can perform no τ actions initially. This suggests that we consider especially those cell chains whose values have percolated right as far as possible. So we define, for $0 \le k \le n$,

$$Chain^{(n)}_{v_1,\ldots,v_k} \stackrel{\mathrm{def}}{=} \overbrace{Cell \frown \cdots \frown Cell}^{n-k\ times} \frown Cell_{v_1} \frown \cdots \frown Cell_{v_k} .$$

Lemma 7.14 $Cell_u \frown Chain^{(n)}_{\vec{v}} \approx Chain^{(n+1)}_{u,\vec{v}}$.

Proof By the previous lemma.   □

Now, by the Unique Solution Theorem (Theorem 6.19) it will be enough to prove Theorem 7.12 if we can show that the processes $Chain^{(n)}_{\vec{v}}$ satisfy the defining equations of $Buff^{(n)}_{\vec{v}}$, up to $\approx$. That is, we wish to prove the following:

Lemma 7.15

$$Chain^{(n)} \approx \sum_u in_u.Chain^{(n)}_u$$

$$Chain^{(n)}_{\vec{v},w} \approx \begin{cases} \sum_u in_u.Chain^{(n)}_{u,\vec{v},w} + \overline{out_w}.Chain^{(n)}_{\vec{v}} & (|\vec{v}| < n-1) \\ \overline{out_w}.Chain^{(n)}_{\vec{v}} & (|\vec{v}| = n-1) \end{cases}$$

Proof By induction on n. The case $n = 1$ follows directly from the definition of $Buff^{(1)}$, since $Cell \equiv Buff^{(1)}$. Now assume the result for n, and consider the case $n + 1$. Let us prove the second equation:

$$Chain^{(n+1)}_{\vec{v},w} \approx \begin{cases} \sum_u in_u.Chain^{(n+1)}_{u,\vec{v},w} + \overline{out_w}.Chain^{(n+1)}_{\vec{v}} & (|\vec{v}| < n) \\ \overline{out_w}.Chain^{(n+1)}_{\vec{v}} & (|\vec{v}| = n). \end{cases}$$

We argue by cases on the length of $\vec{v}$.

Case $|\vec{v}| < n - 1$:

$Chain_{\vec{v},w}^{(n+1)}$

$\quad \equiv \quad Cell^\frown Chain_{\vec{v},w}^{(n)} \cdot$ $\qquad\qquad\qquad\qquad\qquad$ by definition

$\quad \approx \quad Cell^\frown (\sum_{u'} in_{u'}.Chain_{u',\vec{v},w}^{(n)} + \overline{out_w}.Chain_{\vec{v}}^{(n)})$ $\quad$ by induction

$\quad \sim \quad \sum_u in_u.(Cell_u {^\frown} Chain_{\vec{v},w}^{(n)})$

$\qquad\qquad + \overline{out_w}.(Cell^\frown Chain_{\vec{v}}^{(n)})$ $\qquad\qquad$ by expansion

$\quad \approx \quad \sum_u in_u.Chain_{u,\vec{v},w}^{(n+1)} + \overline{out_w}.Chain_{\vec{v}}^{(n+1)}$ $\qquad$ Lemma 7.14.

Case $|\vec{v}| = n - 1$:

$Chain_{\vec{v},w}^{(n+1)}$

$\quad \equiv \quad Cell^\frown Chain_{\vec{v},w}^{(n)}$ $\qquad\qquad\qquad\qquad\qquad\quad$ by definition

$\quad \approx \quad Cell^\frown \overline{out_w}.Chain_{\vec{v}}^{(n)}$ $\qquad\qquad\qquad\qquad$ by induction

$\quad \sim \quad \sum_u in_u.(Cell_u {^\frown} Chain_{\vec{v},w}^{(n)})$

$\qquad\qquad + \overline{out_w}.(Cell^\frown Chain_{\vec{v}}^{(n)})$ $\qquad\qquad$ by expansion

$\quad \approx \quad \sum_u in_u.Chain_{u,\vec{v},w}^{(n+1)} + \overline{out_w}.Chain_{\vec{v}}^{(n+1)}$ $\qquad$ Lemma 7.14.

Case $|\vec{v}| = n$, and $\vec{v} = u, \vec{v'}$:

$Chain_{\vec{v},w}^{(n+1)}$

$\quad \equiv \quad Cell_u {^\frown} Chain_{\vec{v'},w}^{(n)}$ $\qquad\qquad\qquad\qquad\qquad$ by definition

$\quad \approx \quad Cell_u {^\frown} \overline{out_w}.Chain_{\vec{v'}}^{(n)}$ $\qquad\qquad\qquad\qquad$ by induction

$\quad \sim \quad \overline{out_w}.(Cell_u {^\frown} Chain_{\vec{v'}}^{(n)})$ $\qquad\qquad\qquad$ by expansion

$\quad \equiv \quad \overline{out_w}.Chain_{\vec{v}}^{(n+1)} \cdot$ $\qquad\qquad\qquad\qquad\qquad$ by definition.

The first equation, $Chain^{(n+1)} \approx \sum_u in_u.Chain_u^{(n+1)}$, also follows easily by induction, using the definition $Chain^{(n+1)} \stackrel{\text{def}}{=} Cell^\frown Chain^{(n)}$. This concludes the proof of the lemma, and also of Theorem 7.12. $\qquad\qquad\qquad\qquad$ $\square$

7.5 Stack and Counter

All the processes we have considered so far have a fixed structure; the jobshop had a fixed number of jobbers and tools, the scheduler was a fixed ring of n cells, and buffer was a chain of fixed length. But many data structures – stacks, queues, lists, ordered trees, balanced tree, ..., change shape in various ways as they receive and relinquish items. They can all be modelled, like the buffer, by representing their elements or nodes as little processes of different kinds.

In Exercise 3.16 you should have written the specification for a stack of boolean values. Here is the specification for a stack on a finite value domain V:

$$Stack \stackrel{\text{def}}{=} \sum_u push_u.Stack_u + \overline{empty}.Stack$$
$$Stack_{v,\vec{w}} \stackrel{\text{def}}{=} \sum_u push_u.Stack_{u,v,\vec{w}} + \overline{pop_v}.Stack_{\vec{w}}$$

where u, v and the vector $\vec{w}$ are values in V. Since $\vec{w}$ is unbounded in length, any process structure which implements this specification must be able to grow without bound.

If we take V to have only one element then a stack becomes a unary counter, and indeed this specification degenerates into the counter of Section 3.7:

$$Count_0 \stackrel{\text{def}}{=} inc.Count_1 + \overline{zero}.Count_0$$
$$Count_{n+1} \stackrel{\text{def}}{=} inc.Count_{n+2} + \overline{dec}.Count_n$$

where $Count \stackrel{\text{def}}{=} Count_0$, the initially empty counter.

We shall now implement $Count_n$ as a chain of $n + 1$ cells, of two kinds C and B:

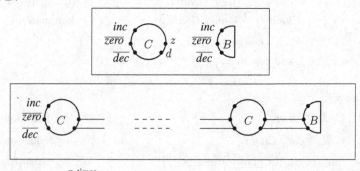

The chain is $\overbrace{C^\frown \cdots ^\frown C}^{n \text{ times}} {}^\frown B$, where linking (Example 4.11) is with respect to the left ports $inc, \overline{zero}, \overline{dec}$ and the right ports $\bar{\imath}, z, d$:

$$P^\frown Q \stackrel{\text{def}}{=} new\ i'z'd'\ (\{i'z'd'/\bar{\imath}zd\}P \mid \{i'z'd'/inc\ zero\ dec\}Q)$$

where i', z', d' are fresh. (The fact that the cell C doesn't use the right port $\bar{\imath}$ just means that no copy of C in the chain except the leftmost will be able to interact through its left port inc.)

First, we need a lemma which doesn't depend on the exact definition of B.

Lemma 7.16 *Assume that* $\text{fn}(B) \subseteq \{inc, zero, dec\}$ *and that B has no τ transitions; then* $B^\frown B \sim B$.

Proof Follows easily using structural congruence, and the fact that new $i'z'd'\,B \sim 0$ by Prop 5.7 and the Expansion Law. □

We now define B and C in terms of a third 'state', D:

$$B \stackrel{\text{def}}{=} inc.(C{\frown}B) + \overline{zero}.B$$
$$C \stackrel{\text{def}}{=} inc.(C{\frown}C) + \overline{dec}.D$$
$$D \stackrel{\text{def}}{=} d.C + z.B$$

Note that after the *inc* action both B and C generate a new C cell.

Exercise 7.17 By allowing C to have an $\bar{\imath}$ port, can you see how to modify this design so that only B, but not C, generates a new cell after *inc*? You should be able to see this intuitively, without formal proof. ∎

Here are a few sample transitions between chains. Note the τ transitions in each row; the chains in the lower row all stand for 0, those in the middle all stand for 1, the upper row for 2, and so on.

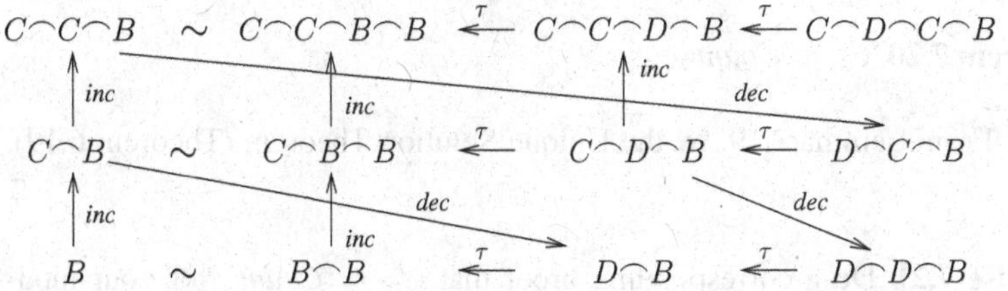

Note also that all the chains in the left column are stable; this is the state into which each number will settle, given time, but as the diagram shows incrementing and decrementing may occur before settling. We now have a key lemma which says that 'settling' doesn't change the observation equivalence class of a chain, i.e. settling occurs unobservably:

Lemma 7.18

$$D{\frown}C \approx C{\frown}D$$
$$D{\frown}B \approx B.$$

Proof By expansion. In the second case, also use Lemma 7.16. □

Now we define

$$C_n \stackrel{\text{def}}{=} \overbrace{C{\frown}\cdots{\frown}C}^{n \text{ times}}{\frown}B$$

as the implementation of $Count_n$. We wish to show that the chains C_n satisfy the defining equations of $Count_n$; that is,

Lemma 7.19

$$C_0 \approx inc.C_1 + \overline{zero}.C_0$$
$$C_{n+1} \approx inc.C_{n+2} + \overline{dec}.C_n \,.$$

Proof The first equation follows directly from the defining equation of B, since $C_0 \overset{\text{def}}{=} B$ and $C_1 \overset{\text{def}}{=} B \frown B$. For the second equation we have

$$
\begin{aligned}
C_{n+1} &\equiv C \frown C_n && \text{by definition} \\
&\sim inc.(C \frown C \frown C_n) + \overline{dec}.(D \frown C_n) && \text{by expansion} \\
&\approx inc.C_{n+2} + \overline{dec}.C_n && \text{by Lemma 7.18 repeatedly.}
\end{aligned}
$$

Note that the step which expands $C \frown C_n$ requires no knowledge of C_n, beyond the fact that it cannot take part in any initial transition of $C \frown C_n$ because its only free names are $\{inc, zero, dec\}$.   □

It follows directly that C_n is indeed a correct implementation of $Count_n$; that is,

Theorem 7.20 $C_n \approx Count_n$.

Proof From Lemma 7.19, by the Unique Solution Theorem (Theorem 6.19).
                                                                                      □

Exercise 7.21 Do a corresponding proof that $C_n \approx Count_n$ for your modified design in Exercise 7.17. You will need a different lemma in place of Lemma 7.18.   ■

Exercise 7.22 Adapt the definitions of B, C and D so that C_v holds a value v in a finite value domain V; then if you define

$$C_{\vec{v}} \overset{\text{def}}{=} C_{v_1} \frown \cdots \frown C_{v_k} \frown B, \text{ where } \vec{v} = v_1, \ldots, v_k$$

the task is to prove that $C_{\vec{v}} \approx Stack_{\vec{v}}$. If you are energetic, prove this. It can be done along the same lines as the proof for the counter. Note that you need to generalise the linking operator to link families of ports indexed by V. ■

Exercise 7.23 Modify the defining equations for $Stack_{\vec{v}}$ so that they specify a queue (first-in-first-out) rather than a stack (last-in-first-out). Now adapt your modified counter design of Exercise 7.17 so that you obtain a correct implementation of a queue. Why does the original counter design not adapt easily for this purpose?   ■

7.6 Discussion

The examples which we have studied in this chapter are quite various; some are models of computing design, while others are models of real systems which are not primarily computational. The concept of communication, as a way of understanding how complex systems work, appears to have a wide range of applicability.

However, our method has been quite uniform; we have repeatedly used a equation of the form *System* $\approx$ *Specification* to represent correctness of behaviour. This is only one way in which one can represent correctness of behaviour, and the reader should not imagine that it is always appropriate. Much work over the last two or three decades has been devoted to rigorous methods of specification, both for sequential and for interactive systems; often a logical formalism is used to define the specification, while the system itself may be described in many ways – including a calculus such as ours.

In this book we confine ourselves to using equations to describe system properties. When they are appropriate, they do the job economically; they can also be supplemented by other methods.

Part II

The π-Calculus

8

What is Mobility?

We now introduce the π-calculus, as a model of the changing connectivity of interactive systems. As such, it can play two distinct rôles.

First, it models networking in the broad modern sense, in which messages are sent from site to site and may also contain links to active processes, or may even consist of processes which can be activated by the recipient and which will have links to other processes embedded in them.

Second, the π-calculus can be seen as a basic model of computation. Every basic model rests upon a small number of primitive notions; the π-calculus rests upon the primitive notion of *interaction*, just as Turing machines and régister machines rest upon the notion of reading and writing a storage medium, and just as recursive equations and the λ-calculus rest upon mathematical functions.

The capacity to change the connectivity of a network of processes is the crucial difference between the π-calculus and the communicating automata studied in Part I of this book. We should pause to reflect upon this capacity before plunging into detail. Is this changing connectivity what we really mean by *mobility* among processes? The first paper on the π-calculus, written in the late 1980s and published in 1992, was called *A calculus of mobile processes* [12], and the word 'mobility' is much more widely used now than it was then; this is largely due to the explosion in networking technology and the worldwide web. As normally happens in computer science, the word is used with many meanings, often inconsistent, and a mathematical theory such as ours must try to find something precise which those meanings share.

The various meanings differ in at least two respects: *what kind of entity moves*, and *in what space does it move*? There are several natural choices, for example

(A) *processes* move, in the physical space of *computing sites*;

77

(B) *processes* move, in the virtual space of *linked processes*;

(C) *links* move, in the virtual space of *linked processes*;

– and as soon as you see this list, you can probably think of more possible choices.

The π-calculus did not result from a full analysis of all such possibilities, because that would have been vague and inconclusive. But among these three, C was chosen for the following reason. First note that – at a suitable level of abstraction – the location of a process in a virtual space of processes is determined by the links which it has to other processes; in other words, your neighbours are those you can talk to. According to this way of thinking, the movement of a process can be represented entirely by the movement of its links; this means that choice B can be reduced to choice C. Moreover, choice C is more general – for you can move one link of a process P without moving all the others.

What about choice A? One might claim that it can be reduced to choice B, since a physical *computing site* can be modelled as a (virtual) process, and its *location* modelled as a link; that is, to be located at the site is to possess a link to it. Formally speaking, this can be done; the processes 'running' at a particular site are those that possess its location-link (much as a computer program can be supplied as data to an interpreter program). But this reduction of choice A to choice B is less convincing than the reduction of choice B to choice C.

The π-calculus adopts choice C, not because it is fundamental to all meanings of 'mobility' but because it is economical, flexible and (as we shall see) moderately simple. By pursuing this line, we hope to understand at least one kind of mobility better, and this may even yield a clearer definition of the other kinds. As we shall see below, the π-calculus only requires a single extension of the CCS model.

Before leaving this general discussion, it is worth discussing 'location' a little further. There have been many studies of the notion of (physical) location, some of them within the frame of CCS and/or the π-calculus. A promising recent study, highly motivated by the current technology of mobile computing, is the ambient calculus of Cardelli and Gordon [4]. An *ambient* is roughly a location for activity, and ambients can be nested; although the ambient calculus uses many of the same constructions as the π-calculus, it rests upon a strikingly different notion of primitive action: the basic act is not interaction but 'movement' from one ambient to another (named) ambient.

We now proceed to look at a few simple examples of changing connectivity, both in the external world and inside a computer. In doing so, we provide informally some examples of the π-calculus in action.

This chapter echoes Chapter 1, where we discussed how interactive processes may proliferate and die, and how this falls short of full *mobility* in the sense of choice C above – the capacity to relinquish existing links among processes, and to forge links which did not previously exist. We shall first revisit that discussion, in the light of the work of Part I. Then we shall illustrate the π-calculus informally through two examples of process mobility; one example (mobile phones) is from the modern world at large, and the other (an elastic buffer) is concerned with the fine detail of computing.

8.1 Limited mobility

In Chapter 4 we introduced concurrent processes which may interact, and may change their configuration in a limited way. Consider for example the following process

$$S \stackrel{\text{def}}{=} \text{new } c\,(A \mid C) \mid B$$

where A and B communicate with the external world via the ports a and b respectively.

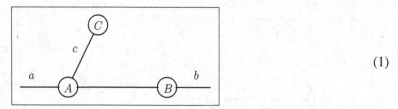

(1)

The processes of Chapter 4 can model two kinds of change in the shape of S. For example, suppose that

$$A \stackrel{\text{def}}{=} a.\text{new } d\,(A \mid A') + c.A''\,;$$

then A has two capabilities, the first of which is to interact with the environment at a, and then split into two components A and A' connected by a private channel d. The system then looks like this:

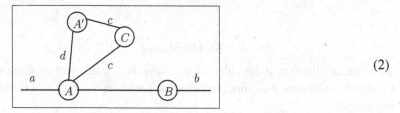

(2)

One interpretation of this change of configuration is that A is an agent for handling certain tasks transmitted along a, and cannot deal with them fast enough, so from time to time A creates a deputy A' to do some of the work.

Now suppose that $A' = c.0$. If C can perform $\bar{c}$ then, continuing our interpretation, we can think of this interaction as representing the handling of the task by A', which thereafter dies; the system then becomes

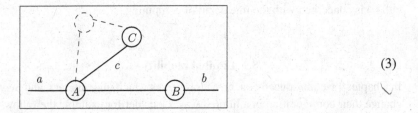

(3)

The two transitions $(1 \rightarrow 2)$, $(2 \rightarrow 3)$ illustrate how the communicating automata of Chapter 4 can both *proliferate* and *die*. But what they cannot do is to forge new links among existing components; for example, from (1) we can never reach the configuration

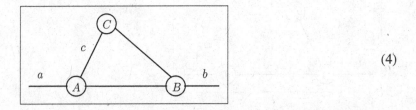

(4)

This is a significant limitation; many real systems do want to make transitions like $(1 \rightarrow 4)$. As we shall see, our calculus and its theory change markedly when we admit this possibility. In fact, the resulting calculus – the π-calculus – is more complex in some ways, but more simple in other ways. We take up this general discussion of mobility, as the π-calculus represents it, in Section 9.3.

8.2 Mobile phones

To appreciate the formal definition of the π-calculus, which will be given in Chapter 9, we present it at work in an example for which mobility is of central importance.

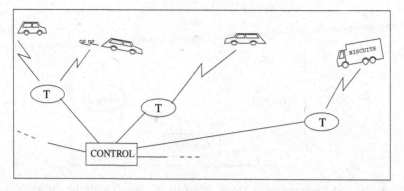

Imagine vehicles on the move, each connected by a unique wavelength to a single transmitter T. The transmitters all have fixed connections to a central control. On some event (e.g. signal fading) a vehicle may be switched to another transmitter. We should not confuse two kinds of movement; the physical movement of cars and the virtual movement of communication links between cars and transmitters. The two are of course interdependent; we see in this example that the physical movement of a car can give rise to the virtual movement of its link to a transmitter. We are mainly concerned here to understand virtual movement. After a car is switched to a new transmitter, the system may look like this:

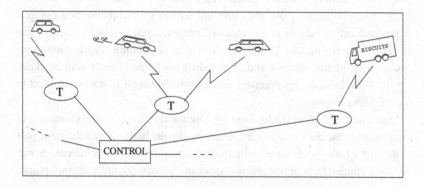

– and this switching needs a protocol, to work properly. We shall illustrate the π-calculus by describing this so-called 'hand-over' protocol.

For simplicity consider the case of only one vehicle and two transmitters; this allows us to concentrate upon the essential feature of the protocol.

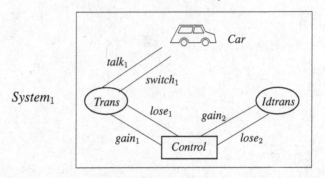

Consider first the transmitter *Trans*, which is in contact with the car and the central control. Showing its current links as parameters, we represent it by the expression

$$Trans\langle talk_1, switch_1, gain_1, lose_1\rangle$$

The car can talk ($talk_1$) via the transmitter, but at any time the transmitter can be told by the central control, *Control*, to lose the car ($lose_1$). As in Chapter 4 we use recursive equations to define the behaviour of a transmitter as follows:

$$Trans(talk, switch, gain, lose) \stackrel{\text{def}}{=} talk.\, Trans\langle talk, switch, gain, lose\rangle$$
$$+ lose(t, s).\, \overline{switch}\langle t, s\rangle.\, Idtrans\langle gain, lose\rangle$$
$$Idtrans(gain, lose) \stackrel{\text{def}}{=} gain(t, s).\, Trans\langle t, s, gain, lose\rangle\,.$$

The new ingredient here, compared with Chapter 4, is that reactions not only occur along channels, but also transmit names (= channels) as messages. A positive action like $lose(t, s)$ receives names, while a negative action like $\overline{switch}\langle t, s\rangle$ sends names. Thus $lose(t, s)$ is a name-binding construction; it introduces the bound names t and s. We shall consistently use round brackets, e.g. (t, s), to bind names received as input, while angle brackets are used to form tuples of names.

Note that *Control*, in telling *Trans* to lose the car, issues a new channel-pair to transmit to the car to replace its old channel-pair. It also issues the same pair to the other (idle) transmitter, which can thereby interact with the car. In our simple formulation, *Control* always issues one of two possible channel-pairs:

$$Control_1 \stackrel{\text{def}}{=} \overline{lose_1}\langle talk_2, switch_2\rangle.\, \overline{gain_2}\langle talk_2, switch_2\rangle.\, Control_2$$
$$Control_2 \stackrel{\text{def}}{=} \overline{lose_2}\langle talk_1, switch_1\rangle.\, \overline{gain_1}\langle talk_1, switch_1\rangle.\, Control_1\,.$$

Finally, the car can either talk or if requested switch to a new channel-pair:

$$Car(talk, switch) \stackrel{\text{def}}{=} \overline{talk}.\, Car\langle talk, switch\rangle + switch(t, s).\, Car\langle t, s\rangle\,.$$

We now consider how to assemble the whole system as a process. This is a familiar task; we just form a restricted composition of four processes:

$$System_1 \; \stackrel{\text{def}}{=} \; \text{new} \; talk_1, switch_1, gain_1, lose_1, talk_2, switch_2, gain_2, lose_2$$
$$(Car\langle talk_1, switch_1\rangle \mid Trans_1 \mid Idtrans_2 \mid Control_1)$$

where we use the auxiliary definitions

$$Trans_i \; \stackrel{\text{def}}{=} \; Trans\langle talk_i, switch_i, gain_i, lose_i\rangle$$
$$Idtrans_i \; \stackrel{\text{def}}{=} \; Idtrans\langle gain_i, lose_i\rangle \qquad\qquad (i = 1, 2).$$

We shall later give evidence that this protocol is correct. When we have introduced the reaction rules of the π-calculus we shall be able to verify that the hand-over does indeed occur, i.e. that the transition

$$System_1 \; \rightarrow^* \; System_2$$

occurs, where $System_2$ is just $System_1$ with the indices 1 and 2 exchanged:

$$System_2 \; \stackrel{\text{def}}{=} \; \text{new} \; talk_1, switch_1, gain_1, lose_1, talk_2, switch_2, gain_2, lose_2$$
$$(Car\langle talk_2, switch_2\rangle \mid Trans_2 \mid Idtrans_1 \mid Control_2) \, .$$

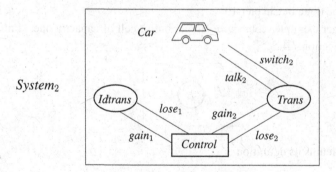

8.3 Other examples of mobility

Consider a multiprocessor system running many programs concurrently, possibly controlled by an operating system. Such a system often consists of active components which we may call *clients* and passive components called *resources*. (This active/passive dichotomy is not essential to the π-calculus, but it is useful and natural in many applications.)

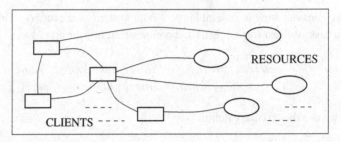

Clients may be linked to each other, and also linked to resources; a link of the latter kind means that the client is currently using the resource. Both clients and resources may proliferate or die, and links may move; the system's structure may therefore be highly mobile. But we may wish to verify that there is some discipline in the mobility; for example, that the resources are *uniquely handled*, by which we mean that at every moment each resource is used by (i.e. linked to) at most one client.

It will turn out that in the π-calculus we can indeed enforce such disciplines, by imposing simple constraints upon the formal presentation of the system. Each discipline is akin to a type system in a friendly programming language. But here, instead of ensuring proper treatment of *values* (which is the usual purpose of a type system), it ensures a certain pattern of *behaviour* – not for a single system, but for the family of systems which respect that discipline. This work will be done in Chapter 10.

As another example, consider a simple buffer cell of capacity one, similar to *Cell* in Section 7.4.

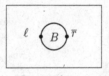

In the π-calculus its definition is

$$B(\ell, r) \stackrel{\text{def}}{=} \ell(x).\, C\langle x, \ell, r\rangle$$
$$C(x, \ell, r) \stackrel{\text{def}}{=} \overline{r}\langle x\rangle.\, B\langle \ell, r\rangle\,.$$

Note the new treatment of the 'datum' parameter x; in Section 7.4 we considered data to be in some arbitrary value domain, but here they are represented just by names. Later, we shall see that an *actual* datum (whether an integer, or an array, or anything else) is treated in the π-calculus as just a special kind of process – and the name x which represents it is actually a channel for communicating with the datum.

For now, recall the way we make a chain of n buffer cells:

Writing B for $B\langle \ell, r \rangle$, this system is defined by linking as in Example 4.11:

$$B^{(n)} \stackrel{\text{def}}{=} \overbrace{B \frown \cdots \frown B}^{n \text{ times}} .$$

Of course this chain $B^{(n)}$ has fixed capacity n. If we want a buffer with *unbounded* capacity, we can use a technique very similar to the counter or stack of Section 7.5 – creating a new cell whenever a new datum is inserted in the buffer. But this buffer would just grow in size and never shrink!

How can we get an *elastic* buffer – one which shrinks when it has too little data to fill it? We might like an empty cell $B\langle \ell, r \rangle$ to be able to cut itself out of the chain and die. To do this properly it must first link its left and right neighbours together. Thinking back to mobile phones, we need an extra channel between neighbours to carry this linking information. Then indeed we achieve true mobility – another instance of the last transition in Section 8.1.

To be more specific, let us define $B'(\ell_1, \ell_2, r_1, r_2)$

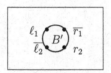

so that whenever B' finds itself as the right neighbour of a full cell C', then instead of receiving a datum from C' it links C' to its own right neighbour, and dies.

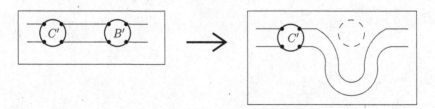

The full cell C' must therefore have the extra capability to receive this new link; so if we write $\vec{\ell}$ for $\ell_1,\ \ell_2$ and $\vec{r}$ for $r_1,\ r_2$ the new definitions are

$$B'(\vec{\ell},\vec{r}) \stackrel{\text{def}}{=} \overline{\ell_2}\langle \vec{r}\rangle$$
$$C'(x,\vec{\ell},\vec{r}) \stackrel{\text{def}}{=} \overline{r_1}\langle x\rangle.\ B'\langle\vec{\ell},\vec{r}\rangle + r_2(\vec{r'}).\ C'\langle x,\vec{\ell},\vec{r'}\rangle\ .$$

8.4 Summary

With a succession of examples, from mobile phones to a simple buffer, we have shown that mobility occurs on both a large and a small scale. These examples motivate the formal definition of the π-calculus, which now follows.

9

The π-Calculus and Reaction

In this chapter we define the π-calculus formally with its dynamics, i.e. its reaction rules. We begin with the *monadic* version of the calculus, in which a message consists of exactly one name. Then in Section 9.4 we derive the polyadic version which we have illustrated already and shall use thereafter.

9.1 Names, actions and processes

We shall assume that there exists an infinite set $\mathcal{N}$ of names. Lower case letters, usually $x, y, z, \ldots$, range over $\mathcal{N}$.

The *action prefixes* π of the π-calculus are a generalisation of the actions introduced at the end of Section 4.2; an action prefix represents either sending or receiving a message (a name), or making a silent transition. The syntax is

$$\pi \quad ::= \quad \begin{array}{ll} x(y) & \text{receive } y \text{ along } x \\ \overline{x}\langle y \rangle & \text{send } y \text{ along } x \\ \tau & \text{unobservable action} \end{array}$$

We now define processes, analogously with Section 4.3:

Definition 9.1 The π-calculus *The set $\mathcal{P}^\pi$ of π-calculus process expressions is defined by the following syntax:*

$$P \quad ::= \quad \sum_{i \in I} \pi_i.P_i \ \mid \ P_1 \mid P_2 \ \mid \ \text{new } a \, P \ \mid \ !P$$

where I is any finite indexing set. The processes $\sum_{i \in I} \pi_i.P_i$ are called summations *or* sums.

Slight extensions of the summation construction will be given in Sections 9.4 and 12.1. Composition and restriction are just as in Section 4.3.

In a sum $\sum_{i \in I} \pi_i.P_i$ we often say that P_i is *guarded* by π_i, since the action represented by π_i must occur before P_i becomes active. As previously, 0 is the empty sum; we often omit it after an action, writing for example $\overline{x}\langle y\rangle.0$ as $\overline{x}\langle y\rangle$.

The restriction new y and the input action $x(y)$ both bind the name y; on the other hand y is free in the output action $\overline{x}\langle y\rangle$. In this book we consistently use round brackets, (y), for the binding occurrence of a parametric name (one that may be instantiated by another name), and angle brackets $\langle y\rangle$ (or no brackets) for non-binding occurrences of a name. Another use of the convention is in process definitions, such as the definition of *Car* in Section 8.2. It is not a standard mathematical convention, but the π-calculus is unusual in its employment of names.

Note that, in comparison with Definition 4.1, process identifiers $A, B \ldots$ with their defining equations $A \overset{\text{def}}{=} P_A, \ldots$ are not part of the basic π-calculus; instead, it has a new construction $!P$, called *replication*. We shall see that replication, together with the passing of names as messages, provides all the power of defining parametric processes explicitly by recursive equations. This simplifies the theory considerably.

Example 9.2 Illustrating reaction Before presenting formal rules for reaction, we illustrate it with an example. Let

$$P = \text{new } z\left(\left(\overline{x}\langle y\rangle + z(w).\overline{w}\langle y\rangle\right) \mid x(u).\overline{u}\langle v\rangle \mid \overline{x}\langle z\rangle\right).$$

(In passing note that x, y and v are the only names free in P.) We say that a pair of positive and negative actions using the same channel, such as $\overline{x}\langle y\rangle$ and $x(u)$, are *complementary*. If – as here – both are unguarded and not in the same summation (i.e. not alternatives to each other) then they constitute a *redex*; the *firing* of this redex constitutes a *reaction* $P \to P'$, which invokes a substitution – here $\{y/u\}$.

In the example P has two redexes; the pair $\overline{x}\langle y\rangle$, $x(u)$ and the pair $x(u), \overline{x}\langle z\rangle$. So there are two possible reactions $P \to P_1$ and $P \to P_2$, where

$$P_1 = \text{new } z\left(0 \mid \overline{y}\langle v\rangle \mid \overline{x}\langle z\rangle\right)$$
$$P_2 = \text{new } z\left(\left(\overline{x}\langle y\rangle + z(w).\overline{w}\langle y\rangle\right) \mid \overline{z}\langle v\rangle \mid 0\right).$$

There is no further redex in P_1, but there is one in P_2 – the pair $z(w), \overline{z}\langle v\rangle$; it arose from the substitution $\{z/u\}$ invoked by the first reaction. So we have $P_2 \to P_3$, where

$$P_3 = \text{new } z\left(\overline{v}\langle y\rangle \mid 0 \mid 0\right). \qquad \blacksquare$$

Exercise 9.3 Write down a process Q such that $Q|P_1$ has a redex but $Q|P_2$ has no redex except that in P_2. $\qquad \blacksquare$

It is helpful to have a way of pronouncing process expressions. We have adopted the notations $x(y)$ and $\overline{x}\langle z \rangle$ for receiving and sending messages, and it is natural to pronounce them 'in x y' and 'out x z'. Indeed, although we shall not do so in this book, some readers and authors may like to adopt the formal notations 'in $x(y)$' and 'out $x\langle z \rangle$'; for example the expression P_2 above would be written

$$P_2 = \text{new } z\left((\text{out } x\langle y \rangle + \text{in } z(w).\text{out } w\langle y \rangle) \mid \text{out } z\langle v \rangle \mid 0\right).$$

We now proceed to define reaction formally.

9.2 Structural congruence and reaction

Just as in Section 4.4, before defining reaction we need a structural congruence relation. For this purpose, we must first generalise the notion of process context and process congruence in the natural way.

Definition 9.4 Process context *Process contexts* C *are given by the syntax*

$$C ::= \; [\,] \; \mid \; \pi.C + M \; \mid \; \text{new } a\, C \; \mid \; C \mid P \; \mid \; P \mid C \; \mid \; !C\,.$$

$C[Q]$ *denotes the result of filling the hole* $[\,]$ *in the context* C *with the process* Q. *The* elementary *contexts are* $\pi.[\,]+M$, $\text{new } a\,[\,]$, $[\,]\mid P$, $P\mid[\,]$ *and* $![\,]$.

Definition 9.5 Process congruence *Let* $\cong$ *be an equivalence relation over* $\mathcal{P}$. *Then* $\cong$ *is said to be a* process congruence *if it is preserved by all elementary contexts; that is, if* $P \cong Q$ *then*

$$
\begin{aligned}
\pi.P + M &\cong \pi.Q + M \\
\text{new } x\, P &\cong \text{new } x\, Q \\
P \mid R &\cong Q \mid R \\
R \mid P &\cong R \mid Q \\
!P &\cong !Q\,.
\end{aligned}
$$

The following is again an easy consequence:

Proposition 9.6 *An arbitrary equivalence relation* $\cong$ *is a process congruence if and only if, for all process contexts* C, $P \cong Q$ *implies* $C[P] \cong C[Q]$.

We are now ready for structural congruence. Compared with Definition 4.7 there are two differences. First, alpha-conversion can occur for a name bound either by restriction or by an input action. Second, the law for defined parametric processes is replaced by a simple law for replication, which reflects the intuition that $!P$ stands for an unlimited number of copies of P able to run concurrently.

Definition 9.7 Structural congruence *Two process expressions P and Q in the π-calculus are* structurally congruent, *written $P \equiv Q$, if we can transform one into the other by using the following equations (in either direction):*

(1) *Change of bound names (alpha-conversion)*
(2) *Reordering of terms in a summation*
(3) $P \mid 0 \equiv P$, $P \mid Q \equiv Q \mid P$, $P \mid (Q \mid R) \equiv (P \mid Q) \mid R$
(4) $\text{new } x\,(P \mid Q) \equiv P \mid \text{new } x\,Q$ *if* $x \notin \text{fn}(P)$
    $\text{new } x\, 0 \equiv 0$, $\text{new } xy\, P \equiv \text{new } yx\, P$
(5) $!P \equiv P \mid {!P}$.

Exercise 9.8 Prove for Example 9.2 that

$$P \equiv x(u).\overline{u}\langle v\rangle \mid \text{new } z\,\big((\overline{x}\langle y\rangle + z(w).\overline{w}\langle y\rangle) \mid \overline{x}\langle z\rangle\big) \text{ and } P_3 \equiv \overline{v}\langle y\rangle . \quad \blacksquare$$

Exercise 9.9 Prove that if x is not free in Q then $\text{new } x\, Q \equiv Q$. $\quad\blacksquare$

Exercise 9.10 If $Q_1 \equiv Q_2$ show that Q_1 and Q_2 have the same free names. (It is enough to show this separately for each of the laws of structural congruence.) $\quad\blacksquare$

Exercise 9.11 Show that every process not containing a replication can be put in the standard form

$$P \equiv \text{new } x_1 \cdots x_m\,(N_1 \mid \cdots \mid N_n)$$

where each N_i is a sum. See Theorem 4.9. $\quad\blacksquare$

Because of replication, the standard form for the π-calculus differs a little from that of Definition 4.8:

Definition 9.12 Standard form *A process expression*

$$\text{new } \vec{a}\,(M_1 \mid \cdots \mid M_m \mid !Q_1 \mid \cdots \mid !Q_n)$$

is said to be in standard form *if each M_i is a non-empty sum, and each Q_j is itself in standard form. (If $m = n = 0$ then the form is $\text{new } \vec{a}\, 0$; if $\vec{a}$ is empty then there is no restriction.)*

Proposition 9.13 *Every process is structurally congruent to a standard form.*

Proof For any restriction $\text{new } a$ not inside a summation, we can bring it to the outermost by using alpha-conversion (if necessary) followed by the rule $P \mid \text{new } a\, Q \equiv \text{new } a\,(P \mid Q)$ and other laws of structural congruence. This leaves a parallel composition of zero or more terms, each of which must be either a summation or a replication; then the body of each replication can be treated similarly. $\quad\square$

Exercise 9.14 (For logicians) Prove that if neither P nor Q contains replication then it is decidable if $P \equiv Q$. ∎

Exercise 9.15 (For experienced logicians) Is $P \equiv Q$ decidable in general? ∎

We are now ready to give the reaction rules for the π-calculus. The following definition is analogous to Definition 4.13; as there, structural congruence is used in one of the rules.

Definition 9.16 Reaction *The reaction relation* → *over* $\mathcal{P}^\pi$ *contains exactly those transitions which can be inferred from the rules in the table below:*

REACTION RULES

TAU : $\tau.P + M \to P$

REACT : $(x(y).P + M) \mid (\overline{x}\langle z\rangle.Q + N) \to \{z/y\}P \mid Q$

PAR : $\dfrac{P \to P'}{P \mid Q \to P' \mid Q}$ RES : $\dfrac{P \to P'}{\mathsf{new}\, x\, P \to \mathsf{new}\, x\, P'}$

STRUCT : $\dfrac{P \to P'}{Q \to Q'}$ *if* $P \equiv Q$ *and* $P' \equiv Q'$

Exercise 9.17 Show how the three transitions $P \to P_1$, $P \to P_2$ and $P_2 \to P_3$ in Example 9.2 can be inferred by the reaction rules. ∎

Note that there is no specific reaction rule for replication. All that is needed to give the required behaviour is the fourth rule of structural congruence.

Exercise 9.18 By using structural congruence, exhibit the redex in

$$x(z).\overline{y}\langle z\rangle \mid !(\mathsf{new}\, y)\overline{x}\langle y\rangle.Q$$

and give the result of the reduction. ∎

9.3 Mobility

We now wish to explain the mobility of the π-calculus in graphical terms. First, let us reconsider our diagrammatic convention. In Section 4.1 we emphasized the distinction between transition graphs and flowgraphs, and thereafter we respected the distinction by drawing a rectangle around every flowgraph. But transition graphs are less helpful in the π-calculus, because they do not easily indicate the passage of messages; so we shall not use them. We shall still draw flowgraphs, but not necessarily in rectangles. Also, we shall not usually label ports with names or co-names; instead, we often label an arc with a name x to indicate that the processes at each end of the arc both use x in some way; and of course in the π-calculus x can be used not only as an input channel $x(\ )$ or output channel $\overline{x}(\ )$, but also as the content of a message, $\langle x \rangle$.

Proceeding to mobility, consider the composition $P|R|Q$, drawn as follows:

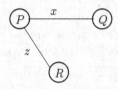

This means that z is free in both P and R, and x is free in both P and Q. If the name z is restricted to P and R, let us draw new $z\,(P|R)\mid Q$ as

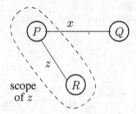

We may think of P as having exclusive access to R along z. Now suppose $P = \overline{x}\langle z \rangle.P'$; this means that P wishes to send z along x to Q. Further, if z is not free in P' then P will thereby lose its link to R. Suppose also $Q = x(y).Q'$. Then we truly have the transition

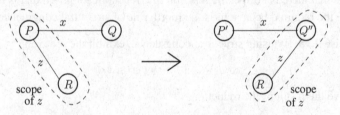

$$\mathsf{new}\,z\,(P \mid R) \mid Q \;\to\; P' \mid \mathsf{new}\,z\,(R \mid Q'')$$

where $Q'' = \{z/y\}Q'$. The new scope of new z is justified by structural congruence.

Exercise 9.19 Verify this transition, from the rules of reaction and structural congruence.　■

Exercise 9.20 We tacitly assumed that z is not free in Q. But suppose it is; e.g. $Q = x(y).\overline{z}\langle y \rangle$. Then what is the transition?

Hint: Consider which structural congruence rule must first be applied. ∎

One way to interpret the above transition is that 'R has moved from P to Q'. But it is more accurate to say that '*a link to R* has moved from P to Q', because there may be other links to R. For example, suppose R is a person, z is his telephone number, and the other links to R are physical (e.g. R's front door). Has R moved, just because P tells Q the telephone number and then forgets it herself?

Alternatively, it could be that z is the physical link, P being Edinburgh and Q being Cambridge; in physically 'moving' from Edinburgh to Cambridge R may keep his phone number, and then people who phone him need not know he has physically moved.

A close analogy is that a process may physically move within a distributed system (e.g. it may be shifted to another processor), but still preserve its logical links with other processes.

It appears more appropriate to talk of movement of *access*, or change of *contiguity*, than movement of *processes* themselves.

9.4 The polyadic π-calculus

We clearly wish to send messages consisting of more than one name, as in the output action $\overline{switch}\langle t, s \rangle$ which occurred in Section 8.2. So we want to allows the forms

$$x(y_1 \cdots y_n).P \text{ and } \overline{x}\langle z_1 \cdots z_n \rangle.Q$$

(where all the y_i are distinct) for any $n \geq 0$. This can be encoded in the monadic π-calculus, but not in the obvious way. The obvious attempt is to encode these forms as

$$x(y_1).\cdots.x(y_n).P \text{ and } \overline{x}\langle z_1 \rangle.\cdots.\overline{x}\langle z_n \rangle.Q .$$

But consider the example

$$x(y_1 y_2).P \mid \overline{x}\langle z_1 z_2 \rangle.Q \mid \overline{x}\langle z_1' z_2' \rangle.Q' ; \qquad\qquad (*)$$

we probably expect that the pair $y_1 y_2$ will be replaced either by $z_1 z_2$ or $z_1' z_2'$. But the obvious encoding yields

$$x(y_1).x(y_2).P \mid \overline{x}\langle z_1 \rangle.\overline{x}\langle z_2 \rangle.Q \mid \overline{x}\langle z_1' \rangle.\overline{x}\langle z_2' \rangle.Q'$$

which allows mix-ups; for example $y_1 y_2$ can be replaced by $z_1' z_1$, which was not intended.

Exercise 9.21 Show how this mix-up happens.   ∎

For a correct encoding, we have to ensure that there can be no interference
on the channel along which a composite message is sent. To send the message
$\langle z_1 \cdots z_n \rangle$, we first send a *fresh* name w along x, then send the components z_i
one by one along w. So we translate the multiple action prefixes as follows:

$$x(y_1 \cdots y_n).P \quad \longmapsto \quad x(w).w(y_1).\cdots.w(y_n).P$$
$$\overline{x}\langle z_1 \cdots z_n \rangle.Q \quad \longmapsto \quad \mathsf{new}\, w\, (\overline{x}\langle w\rangle.\overline{w}\langle z_1\rangle.\cdots.\overline{w}\langle z_n\rangle.Q)\,.$$

Exercise 9.22 Apply this encoding to $(*)$; do enough reductions to convince
yourself that only the 'right' replacements occur.   ∎

This encoding justifies us in taking the monadic calculus as basic. It also
gives a striking example of the power of restricted names. The reader will
not be surprised to learn that the π-calculus can be used as the basis for a
model for cryptographic communication protocols; restricted names provide
the power to represent hidden keys. Abadi and Gordon [1] have devised an
extension of the π-calculus called the 'spi calculus' for this purpose.

From now on we shall freely use the *polyadic* π-calculus, which admits
the multiple action prefixes $x(\vec{y})$ and $\overline{x}\langle\vec{z}\rangle$. Note in particular that it admits
the cases $x(\ )$ and $\overline{x}\langle\ \rangle$ where $\vec{y}$ and $\vec{z}$ are empty; we write these content-free
actions as just x and $\overline{x}$.

To allow us to take the transmission of compound messages as primitive, we
extend the main reaction rule to the following:

$$\text{REACT}: \quad (x(\vec{y}).P + M) \mid (\overline{x}\langle\vec{z}\rangle.Q + N) \rightarrow \{\vec{z}/\vec{y}\}P \mid Q$$

in which the vectors $\vec{y}$ and $\vec{z}$ must have the same length.

9.5 Recursive definitions

Our examples of π-calculus processes in Sections 8.2 and 8.3 indicate how
useful it is to define processes parametrically, in the form

$$A(\vec{x}) \stackrel{\text{def}}{=} Q_A\,,$$

where A is a process identifier, the names $\vec{x}$ are distinct, and Q_A a process
expression which may contain 'calls' of A and other parametric processes.

Such a mechanism for recursive definitions was taken as basic in Section 4.3,
and to deal with its semantics we introduced the structural congruence law
$A\langle\vec{y}\rangle \equiv \{\vec{y}/\vec{x}\}Q_A$.

However, in the basic π-calculus we have no need for process identifiers and
recursive definition, since we can derive the same effect using replication. This

may seem surprising since the syntax of replication is so simple. The key to the derivation is to use message-passing to model the passing of parameters to A, replication to model the multiple activations of A, and restriction to model the scope of the definition of A.

Suppose, for example, we want to encode in the π-calculus the definition

$$A(\vec{x}) \stackrel{\text{def}}{=} Q_A \,, \text{ where } Q_A = \cdots A\langle\vec{u}\rangle \cdots A\langle\vec{v}\rangle \cdots$$

and where the scope of the definition is supposed to be some process

$$P = \cdots A\langle\vec{y}\rangle \cdots A\langle\vec{z}\rangle \cdots .$$

(We have exhibited some typical calls of A, both from P and from Q_A.) Then we can translate the definition into a use of replication as follows:

(1) Invent a new name, say a, to stand for A;
(2) For any process R, denote by $\widehat{R}$ the result of replacing every call $A\langle\vec{w}\rangle$ in R by $\overline{a}\langle\vec{w}\rangle$;
(3) Replace P, and the accompanying definition of A, by

$$\widehat{P} \stackrel{\text{def}}{=} \text{new } a\,(\widehat{P} \mid !a(\vec{x}).\widehat{Q_A}) \,.$$

This translation generalises easily to the case of several processes defined by mutual recursion; $\widehat{\widehat{P}}$ will contain a replicated component for each such definition.

Exercise 9.23 Consider the buffer defined in Section 8.3:

$$\begin{aligned}
B(\ell, r) &\stackrel{\text{def}}{=} \ell(x).\, C\langle x, \ell, r\rangle \\
C(x, \ell, r) &\stackrel{\text{def}}{=} \overline{r}\langle x\rangle.\, B\langle\ell, r\rangle \,,
\end{aligned}$$

and call the two right-hand sides Q_B, Q_C. Write down $\widehat{Q_B}$ and $\widehat{Q_C}$.

Now suppose we want the scope of the definition to be

$$P = \overline{\ell}\langle x_1\rangle.\overline{\ell}\langle x_2\rangle.\overline{\ell}\langle x_3\rangle \mid B_2 \mid r(y_1).r(y_2).r(y_3)$$

where B_2 is the two-place buffer defined by

$$B_2 \stackrel{\text{def}}{=} \text{new } m\,(B\langle\ell, m\rangle \mid B\langle m, r\rangle) \,.$$

Write down $\widehat{P}$, and satisfy yourself that it behaves essentially as you would expect P to behave – but with more τ transitions. ∎

It is interesting to reflect upon this encoding of recursive definitions. Is it natural, or contrived? If you are familiar with implementing procedures of a high-level language you may find it quite natural. You can think of $!a(\vec{x}).\widehat{Q_A}$ as the compiled code corresponding to the precedure A, and each call $\overline{a}\langle\vec{y}\rangle$

occurring within $\widehat{Q_A}$ or elsewhere as a command to create a new 'activation record' of the procedure.

9.6 Abstractions

You may have noticed that there are three ways to bind names. In the basic calculus we have $x(y).P$ and new $y\,P$, while in defining parametric processes we use $A(\vec{x}) \stackrel{\text{def}}{=} Q_A$.

It is useful to have a single basic way of binding a name x in a process P. We shall write it $(x).P$, and call it an *abstraction* with *arity* 1; more generally

$$(x_1). \cdots (x_n).P$$

is an abstraction with arity n. As always, we allow alpha-conversion of these bound names. We shall use the letters $F, G, \ldots$ to stand for abstractions. If F has arity n we write $F : n$. Note that a process P is just an abstraction with arity 0.

Clearly, if $F : n$ then $(x).F : n+1$. We can also apply an abstraction to a name; if $F : n+1$ then $F\langle x \rangle : n$. We define

$$((x).F)\langle y \rangle \stackrel{\text{def}}{=} \{y/x\}F \ .$$

We use the abbreviations

$$(x_1 \cdots x_n).F \quad \stackrel{\text{def}}{=} \quad (x_1). \cdots (x_n).F \qquad (x_1, \ldots, x_n \text{ distinct})$$
$$F\langle y_1 \cdots y_n \rangle \quad \stackrel{\text{def}}{=} \quad (\cdot\cdot (F\langle y_1 \rangle)\langle y_2 \rangle \cdots)\langle y_n \rangle \ ,$$

from which we deduce that

$$((\vec{x}).F)\langle \vec{y} \rangle = \{\vec{y}/\vec{x}\}F \tag{*}$$

for vectors $\vec{x}, \vec{y}$ of equal length.

Returning to our three kinds of binding, we can now consider them all as convenient 'sugared' notation for different uses of abstractions. We can think of

$$\begin{aligned}
x(\vec{y}).P \quad &\text{as} \quad x((\vec{y}).P) \\
\text{new } x\,P \quad &\text{as} \quad \text{new } ((x).P) \\
A(\vec{x}) \stackrel{\text{def}}{=} Q \quad &\text{as} \quad A \stackrel{\text{def}}{=} (\vec{x}).Q \ .
\end{aligned}$$

We also gain expressive power by defining new operations which act upon abstractions, not only upon processes.

Example 9.24 Linking In Example 4.11 we defined the linking of two processes P and Q with respect to a left port ℓ and a right port r thus :

$$P \frown Q \stackrel{\text{def}}{=} \text{new } m\,(\{m/r\}P \mid \{m/\ell\}Q) \ .$$

But this is specific to ℓ and r; it is cleaner to define linking as an operator on processes *parametric* upon two ports, i.e. upon abstractions of arity 2. Thus, for $F : 2$ and $G : 2$ we define

$$F^\frown G \stackrel{\text{def}}{=} (\ell, r).\, \text{new}\, m\, (F\langle \ell, m \rangle \mid G\langle m, r \rangle)\,.$$

Let us apply this to the buffer processes B and C of Section 8.3. We have $B : 2$ and $C : 3$; also $C\langle x \rangle : 2$. So the chain $J = C\langle x_1 \rangle ^\frown B ^\frown C\langle x_2 \rangle$ is itself an abstraction of arity 2, parametric on its input port and output port, while $J\langle in_1, out_4 \rangle$ is a process with these ports fixed. ∎

Exercise 9.25 Prove the structural congruence

$$F^\frown(G^\frown H) \equiv (F^\frown G)^\frown H\,.$$

You will need $(*)$ above, and some alpha-conversions. ∎

Exercise 9.26 Sequential Composition In a similar way, in Example 5.27 we defined sequential composition of two processes, assumed to terminate by performing a specific action $\overline{done}$, as

$$P; Q \stackrel{\text{def}}{=} \text{new}\, start\, (\{ start/done \} P \mid start.Q)\,.$$

Instead, define sequential composition $F; G$ as an operation on abstractions F, G of arity 1 – parametric upon the terminating action. Then prove that it is associative, i.e.

$$F; (G; H) \sim (F; G); H\,.$$

You need only assume that strong equivalence ($\sim$) satisfies two properties: (1) $P \equiv Q$ implies $P \sim Q$, and (2) if $x \neq y$ then $x.\text{new}\, y\, (P|y.Q) \sim \text{new}\, y\, (x.P|y.Q)$. ∎

9.7 Summary

We have defined the π-calculus, which possesses four constructions: summation (or choice), parallel composition, restriction and replication. We have given its reaction rules and explained how they represent the mobility of links and processes. We have found useful a notion of structural congruence, under which certain syntactic forms are regarded as indistinguishable; the syntax is thus made to reflect the non-sequentiality of the processes which it represents.

Before proceeding to deal with the behavioural equivalence of processes in Chapter 13, we examine in the next two chapters some examples which demonstrate how reactions work, and a type discipline which helps considerably in understanding applications.

10

Applications of the π-Calculus

In this chapter we look at some ways of using the π-calculus which depend on no more theory than we already have.

We focus on two applications. The first shows how the calculus can impose a discipline on the degree of mobility in a system. The second shows that data structures, of the ordinary kind present in high-level programming languages, can be seen as just a special kind of process. This applies both to read-only data, such as is handled in functional programming languages, and also to data structures which may be updated.

10.1 Simple systems

To prepare the way for our first application, we look at certain properties of π-calculus processes which are *invariant under reaction*; this means that if P has the property and $P \to P'$ then P' has the property. Such invariant properties often help in analysing systems. We shall consider a special class of systems called *simple* systems, which satisfy three conditions S1, S2 and S3.

We shall consider systems which can (using structural congruence) be expressed in the form

$$P \equiv \mathsf{new}\ \vec{z}\,(M_1 \mid \cdots \mid M_m \mid !N_1 \mid \cdots \mid !N_n)\,. \tag{$*$}$$

Now this is a special case of the standard form of Definition 9.12; so our first property S1 of a process P is

$S1(P)$: P is structurally congruent to a standard form $(*)$ in which all the replicated components are summations.

Not *every* process P satisfies property S1; a simple counter-example is $!(\overline{x}\langle y\rangle \mid \overline{x}\langle y\rangle)$, since it replicates a non-summation. Also note that property S1 is not invariant under reaction; for example

$$P = \overline{w}\langle x\rangle.Q \mid w(z).!(\overline{z}\langle y\rangle|\overline{z}\langle y\rangle)$$

satisfies S1, but reduces to $Q \mid !(\overline{x}\langle y\rangle|\overline{x}\langle y\rangle)$ which does not satisfy S1.

Let us now add another condition for a process P to be simple:

S2(P): P satisfies $(*)$ and no M_i or N_j contains a replication (!).

It turns out that the conjunction S1 $\wedge$ S2 is invariant under reaction.

Exercise 10.1 Prove this in a special case; suppose $P = \text{new } z \,(M|!N)$, and suppose that $P \to P'$ results from an instance $M|N \to Q$ of the REACT rule, so that $P' \equiv \text{new } z \,(Q|!N)$. Note that Q cannot contain a replication. Now apply Exercise 9.11 to Q, to show that P' satisfies both S1 and S2, i.e. that S1 $\wedge$ S2 holds for P'. ∎

Finally, we shall add a further condition for P to be simple:

S3(P): P satisfies $(*)$ and no M_i or N_j contains a composition ($|$).

It is easy to show that S1 $\wedge$ S2 $\wedge$ S3 is reaction-invariant. We shall call a system *simple* if it satisfies this conjunction.

Exercise 10.2 Show that *simplicity* of a system, defined in this way, is another property invariant under reaction. ∎

Some useful systems are simple. For example:

Example 10.3 Buffers are simple Consider the chain

$$J = C\langle x_1\rangle \frown B \frown C\langle x_2\rangle$$

of three buffer processes, given in Example 9.24 to illustrate abstraction. Then $J\langle \ell, r\rangle$ is a buffer process. It rests on the recursive definitions of B and C given in Section 8.3, but these can be translated away according to the method of Section 9.5, and what we get is a simple system. ∎

Exercise 10.4 Show that the translation of $J\langle \ell, r\rangle$ is as follows:

$$\text{new } bcm_1m_2 \quad (\overline{c}\langle x_1, \ell, m_1\rangle \mid \overline{b}\langle m_1, m_2\rangle \mid \overline{c}\langle x_2, m_2, r\rangle$$
$$\mid \,!b(i, o).i(x).\overline{c}\langle x, i, o\rangle \mid !c(y, i, o).\overline{o}\langle y\rangle.\overline{b}\langle i, o\rangle)$$

which is clearly simple. ∎

Another example of a simple system is the mobile phone system of Section 8.2 (when recursion is translated away). Roughly speaking, a process will be simple if it is a restricted composition of components which are sequential, involving recursive definitions whose right-hand sides are sequential,

We shall now look at further reaction-invariant conditions, which express useful limitations on the mobility of a process.

10.2 Unique handling

Many questions can be asked about the behaviour of systems like the one in Exercise 10.4. Sometimes the answers are intuitively 'obvious', because we can appeal to the intuition which we used in designing the process. For example, in the mobile phones example in Section 8.2 it is fairly clear that the car will never be connected to more than one transmitter at any one time. But can we check this rigorously from the process definitions? To do so we would seem to need a detailed flow analysis, and the mobility of the system may make this difficult. Moreover we would like to be able to carry out such a flow analysis for a wide class of systems. We look for theorems about the π-calculus, which assert that if a system P has a certain syntactic property, then it is guaranteed to have a certain dynamic property. This section gives an example of such a theorem, about simple systems.

Imagine that a resource R (a process) is accessed by sending a message along x to it. For example, we might have $R = !x(u).R'$, if R is a replicated resource. We would often like to know, of a system P representing a community of processes including R, that at any given time no more than one member of the community has access to R. (Consider, for example, a distributed operating system.) We shall formulate precisely what this means, and will find sufficient conditions on P which guarantee the property.

Let us say that P *handles* x if P has a free occurrence of x in an action prefix of the form $\overline{x}\langle\cdots\rangle$ or $\overline{v}\langle\cdots x \cdots\rangle$. Note that this is a purely syntactic property, which tells us little about the future behaviour of P. At least it is clear that if P does not handle x then it cannot *immediately* either send a message along x or send x as a message. But after some other interactions it may be able to do so; for example if $P = a(z).\overline{z}\langle v \rangle$ then P may receive x along channel a from a partner, and then it can execute $\overline{x}\langle v \rangle$.

Note that this property of P is preserved by structural congruence, i.e. if $P \equiv Q$ and P handles x then so does Q. When defining syntactic properties we must always ensure that structural congruence preserves them, since we wish to consider structurally congruent expressions as standing for the same process, and we are interested in properties of *processes*, not expressions.

Definition 10.5 Unique handling *Let P be a simple system, in the form* $(*)$. *Say that P uniquely handles x if at most one of the M_i, and none of the N_j, handles x.*

Exercise 10.6 Convince yourself that this property is preserved by structural congruence. Is this true of the property 'at most one of the M_i and N_j handles x'? ∎

If $P \rightarrow P'$, can we be sure that P' uniquely handles x? Clearly not! Suppose for example

$$P_1 = \overline{a}\langle x \rangle.\overline{x}\langle u \rangle \mid a(z).\overline{z}\langle v \rangle \ ;$$

then $P_1 \rightarrow \overline{x}\langle u \rangle | \overline{x}\langle v \rangle$, in which two components handle x.

But we would like the unique handling of x to be a property invariant under reaction, for some class of simple systems. What conditions should we add? To avoid the above counter-example, we could demand that P satisfies the following property:

Definition 10.7 Forgetfulness *A term P is x-forgetful if in any subterm of the form $\overline{a}\langle \vec{u}x\vec{v} \rangle.Q$, neither $\vec{u}$ nor $\vec{v}$ contains x and Q does not handle x.*

Note that in the monadic calculus this condition simplifies to: *in any subterm of the form $\overline{a}\langle x \rangle.Q$, Q does not handle x.* This rules out the example P_1, but is still not enough! We may have P simple and x-forgetful, but if $P \rightarrow P'$ then P' may not be x-forgetful. For example, take the simple system

$$P_2 = \overline{b}\langle x \rangle \mid b(y).\overline{a}\langle y \rangle.\overline{y}\langle u \rangle \mid a(z).\overline{z}\langle v \rangle \ ;$$

then $P_2 \rightarrow P_1$, and P_2 is indeed x-forgetful but P_1 is not (as we observed). The problem is that the first reaction causes x to be substituted for the bound name y in a term which is not y-forgetful, making it into a term which is not x-forgetful. So, backs-to-the-wall, let us make a third condition that, for every subterm of the form $z(\vec{y}).Q$, Q is y-forgetful for each $y \in \vec{y}$. This condition rules out our second counter-example P_2, and we now have sufficient conditions for an invariant:

Theorem 10.8 Unique handling *Let P be simple, and satisfy the following conditions for some x:*

(1) *it uniquely handles x;*

(2) *it is x-forgetful;*

(3) *for every subterm of form $z(\vec{y}).Q$, Q is y-forgetful for each $y \in \vec{y}$.*

Further, let $P \rightarrow P'$. Then P' is simple and also satisfies (1), (2) and (3).

Proof We shall do the proof for the monadic calculus; the adaptation for the polyadic calculus is not hard. Let

$$P = \mathsf{new}\ \vec{z}\,(M_1 \mid M_2 \mid \cdots \mid M_m \mid !N_1 \mid \cdots \mid !N_n).$$

Since we can expand a replication by $!N \equiv N|!N$, we can assume without loss of generality that the redex of the reaction $P \to P'$ is $M_1|M_2$, where

$$M_1 \equiv \cdots + \overline{u}\langle v \rangle.\mathsf{new}\ \vec{z_1}\,M_1', \quad M_2 \equiv \cdots + u(w).\mathsf{new}\ \vec{z_2}\,M_2'$$

with $w, \vec{z_1}$ and $\vec{z_2}$ all different from x and v, and

$$P' \equiv \mathsf{new}\ \vec{z}\vec{z_1}\vec{z_2}\,(M_1' \mid \{v\!/w\}M_2' \mid \cdots \mid !N_1 \mid \cdots \mid !N_n).$$

Note that since P is simple, the terms M_1' and M_2' can be assumed to be sums. (The restrictions new $\vec{z_1}$ and new $\vec{z_2}$ may of course be empty.) We now prove

(1′) *P' uniquely handles x.* From (1), it is enough to show that P has at least as many components which handle x as P' does. Now if M_1' handles x, then M_1 does since it has M_1' as a subterm. If $\{v\!/w\}M_2'$ handles x then there are two cases; either $v \neq x$ and M_2' does, hence M_2 does, or $v = x$ and hence M_1 does, but from (2) M_1' does not.

(2′) *P' is x-forgetful.* From (2), M_1', M_3, ..., $!N_1$,..., $!N_n$ are all x-forgetful; it remains to show that $\{v\!/w\}M_2'$ is x-forgetful. Now M_2', being a subterm of M_2, is x-forgetful, so if $v \neq x$ then also $\{v\!/w\}M_2'$ is x-forgetful. On the other hand if $v = x$ then M_1 handles x, so from (1) M_2' does not; so $\{x\!/w\}M_2'$ will be x-forgetful provided that M_2' is w-forgetful; but the latter holds by (3) because M_2' is bound by (w) in M_2.

(3′) *In any subterm $z(y).Q$ of P', Q is y-forgetful.* From (3), it is enough to consider subterms of $\{v\!/w\}M_2'$, since all others occur also in P. If $\{v\!/w\}M_2'$ has a subterm $z'(y)Q'$ we can assume that $v, w \neq y$ (by alpha-conversion); then M_2' has a subterm $z(y).Q$ with $Q' = \{v\!/w\}Q$, and since Q is y-forgetful it follows by (3) that Q' also is so.   □

In adapting the proof to the polyadic case, the exact conditions required by Definition 10.7 for a system to be x-forgetful are important, as the following exercise shows.

Exercise 10.9 Suppose that the condition that *neither $\vec{u}$ nor $\vec{v}$ contains x* is dropped from Definition 10.7. Under this weaker definition, for example $\overline{a}\langle xx \rangle.M$ is x-forgetful as long as M doesn't handle x. Show now that Theorem 10.8 will not hold under the weaker definition, by finding summations M, N for which

$$P = \overline{a}\langle xx \rangle.M \mid a(uv).N$$

satisfies the three conditions of the theorem, but that

$$P \rightarrow P', \text{ where } P' = M \mid \{xx/uv\}N$$

and P' is not x-forgetful. ∎

Exercise 10.10 Show that the system of Exercise 10.4 satisfies the condition of the theorem, with x_1 for x, provided that $x_1 \neq x_2$. ∎

The last example suggests that our theorem is likely to apply to many systems. In fact such invariants have been used in verifying the behaviour of transfer protocols such as the one in Section 8.2.

Later, when we study sorting disciplines, we shall see how to relax the rather strong condition (3), so that it need not be applied to all input-bound names but only those of the same sort as x.

10.3 Data revisited

In Section 7.4 we introduced data structures such as a buffer $Buff^{(n)}_{v_1,\dots,v_k}$, holding k values from a data domain V. For this purpose we had to extend our language of concurrent processes to allow parameters which range over arbitrary values. This extension of language is fine for many practical purposes, but the need for it shows that the formalism is not complete in itself. Moreover we had to constrain V to be finite, and this is unsatisfactory.

In the π-calculus, rudimentary data values i.e. *names* – form the content of messages. It is not obvious that this gives us the power to represent all data. But we announced in Section 8.3 that we would treat all data as special kinds of process, using names as the channels via which they are manipulated. This has a great advantage; it means that in one treatment we can unite mathematical values with mutable data structures. They are all processes, but differ in their discipline of interaction.

In the next few sections we show how this works. Let us begin with *ephemeral* data, values which don't persist beyond a single use. We hardly think about them, but they correspond closely to what we might call a *copy* or *instance* of a value. For example there are two copies of 12 in the expression

$$12 \times (x + 12) ;$$

once we are told that $x = 3$ then we calculate the value of the expression to be

180, and there is nothing left of the two 12s. On the other hand the value of x should persist, because we expect to use it again in other calculations. As you can guess, we shall use replication to make data persist; but for now we shall stay with ephemeral data.

Let us start with the simplest useful data domain, the truth values $\{true, false\}$. Statically, that's all a truth value is: a member of this set. But dynamically – which is how we *use* values – it is a switch telling us which of two ways to proceed. ('Proceeding' is what processes do!) The simplest possible switch that one might think of in the π-calculus is the abstraction $(tf).\bar{t}$ which, given a two-item menu of channels, will transmit on the first one; similarly $(tf).\bar{f}$ will transmit on the second. This pair of abstractions is the essence of our encoding of the truth values; but we want to locate them somewhere, at ℓ say, and moreover we would like to make them parametric on the location ℓ.

Definition 10.11 Truth values (ephemeral) *The ephemeral truth values in the π-calculus are the abstractions*

$$True(\ell) \stackrel{\text{def}}{=} \ell(tf).\bar{t}, \quad False(\ell) \stackrel{\text{def}}{=} \ell(tf).\bar{f}.$$

Now, what is a menu? Suppose we want $True\langle\ell\rangle$, $False\langle\ell\rangle$ to switch control into P, Q respectively. Then we provide at $\bar{\ell}$ a menu consisting of a pair of 'buttons' $\langle t'f'\rangle$, together with the process $t'.P + f'.Q$ representing the actions which result from pressing the buttons. (In Chapter 12 we shall find that menus are a special case of *concretions*, which are dual to *abstractions*.)

In order that a menu can interact with a value (or switch), the two must be co-located. If we locate *True* at ℓ and the menu at $\bar{\ell}$, we then have the reactions

$$True\langle\ell\rangle \mid \bar{\ell}\langle t'f'\rangle.(t'.P + f'.Q) \quad \rightarrow^* \quad P$$
$$False\langle\ell\rangle \mid \bar{\ell}\langle t'f'\rangle.(t'.P + f'.Q) \quad \rightarrow^* \quad Q.$$

In what follows we shall treat the values in all standard data types as switches in this way. For example, the members of the enumerated value domain

$$\{Monday, Tuesday, Wednesday, Thursday, Friday, Saturday, Sunday\}$$

are represented by abstractions which expect a seven-item menu, e.g.

$$Monday(\ell) \stackrel{\text{def}}{=} \ell(mo, tu, we, th, fr, sa, su).\overline{mo}, \quad \dots$$

With this convention, every value is a *unary* abstraction, independently of the domain to which it belongs. This means that we can give polymorphic definitions of data *structures* such as lists, to work in the same manner whether the list-members are truth values, days-of-the-week or even other lists.

To match the located truth values, we also define conditional processes para-metric upon their co-locations as follows:

$$Cond(P,Q)(\ell) \stackrel{\text{def}}{=} (\text{new}\, t f)\overline{\ell}\langle t f\rangle.(t.P + f.Q)\,,$$

where we ensure that ℓ, t, f are not free in P, Q. The restriction on the 'buttons' t and f ensures that interactions with different menus cannot be confused.

Exercise 10.12 Show the following reactions:

$$True\langle\ell\rangle \mid Cond(P,Q)\langle\ell\rangle \quad \rightarrow^* \quad P$$
$$False\langle\ell\rangle \mid Cond(P,Q)\langle\ell\rangle \quad \rightarrow^* \quad Q\,.$$

∎

Notice that *Cond* is a derived operator upon processes; we have met such de-rived operators before, e.g. the linking operator $\frown$ of Example 9.24. As we introduce more derived operators, we shall come close to defining functional programming over data types within the π-calculus.

Now, what is a data type in general? We shall consider all those which are defined by a set of constants and constructors; examples are

A truth value is	either *True*	or *False*;
An integer is	either *Zero*	or *Succ* of an integer;
A list is	either *Nil*	or *Cons* of a value and a list;
A tree is	...

Of course a constant is just a nullary constructor. The data type of truth values is especially simple because both constructors are constants. Consider lists; there are two constructors, one nullary and one binary. So we define

$$Nil(k) \stackrel{\text{def}}{=} k(nc).\overline{n}\,, \quad Node(kv\ell) \stackrel{\text{def}}{=} k(nc).\overline{c}\langle v\ell\rangle\,.$$

Thus $Nil\langle k\rangle$ is a copy of the empty list, located at k. But $Node\langle kv\ell\rangle$ is not yet a whole list (so we have not called it *Cons*); it is just a list connector:

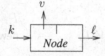

It's a generalised switch; you give it a menu at k and it selects the c option – and also sends its two links along c. This allows you to walk down a list and inspect its members by conducting a dialogue with the list.

We shall now show how to represent elements of any data type by unary abstractions, taking lists as an example. Let V range over a data type already represented in this way, and let L range over lists (so represented).

Definition 10.13 Lists (ephemeral)   *The constant Nil, the construction Cons(V, L) and a list of n values are defined as follows:*

$$Nil \stackrel{\text{def}}{=} (k).k(nc).\overline{n}$$

$$Cons(V, L) \stackrel{\text{def}}{=} (k).\text{new } v\ell \, (Node\langle kv\ell \rangle \mid V\langle v \rangle \mid L\langle \ell \rangle)$$

$$\text{where } Node(kv\ell) \stackrel{\text{def}}{=} k(nc).\overline{c}\langle v\ell \rangle$$

$$[V_1, \ldots, V_n] \stackrel{\text{def}}{=} Cons(V_1, Cons(\cdots Cons(V_n, Nil) \cdots)) .$$

Note that values so defined have no free names. To place a copy of a value L at some location k, we form $L\langle k \rangle$. Here is a picture of $[\mathit{True}, \mathit{False}]\langle k \rangle$:

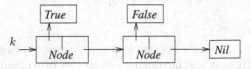

Exercise 10.14 Write out this π-calculus term in full, unwinding the definitions.   ■

10.4 Programming with lists

We now illustrate how to do functional programming with lists inside the π-calculus. First, to switch according to whether a list is a *Cons* or *Nil*, by analogy with *Cond* we define

$$Listcases(P, F)(k) \stackrel{\text{def}}{=} (\text{new } nc)\overline{k}\langle nc \rangle.(n.P + c.F) ,$$

where we expect F to be a binary abstraction which will accept the names of the head and tail of a list. $Listcases(P, F)\langle k \rangle$ provides a menu for use by any list which is co-located at k. The following is easy to prove, by analogy with Exercise 10.12:

Proposition 10.15

$$Listcases(P, F)\langle k \rangle \mid Nil\langle k \rangle \qquad \rightarrow^* \quad P$$
$$Listcases(P, F)\langle k \rangle \mid Cons(V, L)\langle k \rangle \quad \rightarrow^* \quad \text{new } v\ell \, (F\langle v\ell \rangle \mid V\langle v \rangle \mid L\langle \ell \rangle) .$$

Exercise 10.16 Prove this. In each case there are two reactions.   ■

$Listcases(P, F)\langle k \rangle$ can be written in a sugared form, using the familiar programming notation for a case statement (e.g. in Standard ML). If $F = (v\ell)Q$, we write it as

$$\text{case } k \text{ of } \quad Nil? \qquad \Rightarrow P$$
$$Cons?(v\ell) \Rightarrow Q .$$

As a first example of programming, here is a recursively defined process which copies a list from location l to location m:

$$Copy\langle \ell m\rangle \quad \overset{\text{def}}{=} \quad \begin{array}{l} \text{case } \ell \text{ of} \\ \quad Nil? \qquad\qquad \Rightarrow Nil\langle m\rangle \\ \quad Cons?\,(v\ell') \quad \Rightarrow \text{new } m'\,(Node\langle mvm'\rangle \mid Copy\langle \ell'm'\rangle)\,. \end{array}$$

Note that the expression $Copy\langle \ell m\rangle$ does not *contain* the list to be copied; but if placed alongside a list L co-located at ℓ, it will copy L by walking down it. (In doing so, it will destroy $L\langle \ell\rangle$!)

Proposition 10.17

$$L\langle \ell\rangle \mid Copy\langle \ell m\rangle \;\rightarrow^*\; L\langle m\rangle\,.$$

Proof Note first that $Copy\langle \ell m\rangle = Listcases(P, F)\langle \ell\rangle$, where

$$\begin{aligned} P &= Nil\langle m\rangle \\ F(v\ell') &= \text{new } m'\,(Node\langle mvm'\rangle \mid Copy\langle \ell'm'\rangle)\,. \end{aligned}$$

We prove the result by induction on the structure of the list L. The base case is

$$Nil\langle \ell\rangle \mid Copy\langle \ell m\rangle \;\rightarrow^*\; Nil\langle m\rangle$$

which follows directly from the first part of Proposition 10.15. For the inductive step, we assume the proposition as stated and must prove

$$Cons(V, L)\langle \ell\rangle \mid Copy\langle \ell m\rangle \;\rightarrow^*\; Cons(V, L)\langle m\rangle\,.$$

Starting with a use of the second part of Prop 10.15, we proceed thus:

$$\begin{aligned} &Cons(V, L)\langle \ell\rangle \mid Copy\langle \ell m\rangle \\ \rightarrow^* \quad &\text{new } v\ell'\,(F\langle v\ell'\rangle \mid V\langle v\rangle \mid L\langle \ell'\rangle) \\ \equiv \quad &\text{new } v\ell'm'\,(Node\langle mvm'\rangle \mid Copy\langle \ell'm'\rangle \mid V\langle v\rangle \mid L\langle \ell'\rangle) \quad \text{by expanding } F \\ \rightarrow^* \quad &\text{new } vm'\,(Node\langle mvm'\rangle \mid V\langle v\rangle \mid L\langle m'\rangle) \qquad\qquad\qquad \text{by induction} \\ \equiv \quad &Cons(V, L)\langle m\rangle \qquad\qquad\qquad\qquad\qquad\qquad\quad \text{by Def'n 10.13}\,, \end{aligned}$$

as required. □

Note that $Copy\langle \ell m\rangle$ is close to being a function; if we 'give it' a list L located at ℓ then it will copy it to m. It only operates on one list, but it has *two* parameters, the second of which is the location for the result.

In similar fashion we define the concatenating operator $Join\langle k\ell m\rangle$ which, given two lists located at k and ℓ, will concatenate them and place the result at m. It walks down the first list, copying its elements one by one, and then copies the whole second list to join on the end of the first.

$$Join(k\ell m) \quad \overset{\text{def}}{=} \quad \text{case } k \text{ of}$$
$$\begin{aligned} Nil? &\quad \Rightarrow Copy\langle \ell m \rangle \\ Cons?\,(vk') &\quad \Rightarrow \text{new } m'\,(Node\langle mvm' \rangle \mid Join\langle k'\ell m' \rangle)\,. \end{aligned}$$

Now we would like to show that *Join* works properly. To formulate this, suppose $K = [U_1, \ldots, U_r]$ and $L = [V_1, \ldots, V_s]$; then we define their concatenation to be $K \oplus L = [U_1, \ldots, U_r, V_1, \ldots, V_s]$. The operator $\oplus$ satisfies obvious properties such as

$$\begin{aligned} Nil \oplus L &= L \\ Cons(V, K \oplus L) &= Cons(V, K) \oplus L\,. \end{aligned}$$

We can now prove the following:

Proposition 10.18

$$K\langle k \rangle \mid L\langle \ell \rangle \mid Join\langle k\ell m \rangle \;\to^*\; (K \oplus L)\langle m \rangle\,.$$

Proof We follow the same strategy as in the previous proposition; this time we do induction on the structure of K. The base case will use Proposition 10.17. In the step case, the above obvious properties of $\oplus$ are needed.   □

Exercise 10.19 Fill in the details of this proof.   ■

Although *Copy* and *Join* are *nearly* like functions, there is a difference. Consider a system

$$S = Join\langle k\ell m \rangle \mid K_1\langle k \rangle \mid K_2\langle k \rangle \mid L\langle \ell \rangle$$

where K_1 and K_2 are different lists. Then Prop 10.18 tells us that two different reactions are possible:

$$\begin{aligned} S &\to^* K_1\langle k \rangle \mid (K_2 \oplus L)\langle m \rangle \\ S &\to^* K_2\langle k \rangle \mid (K_1 \oplus L)\langle m \rangle\,; \end{aligned}$$

this is because *Join* has a choice of two operands, both located at k. What must be done to determine an operand unambiguously? The answer is to use restriction. We now define two new derived operations, *Move* and *Append*, which really do behave as functions. Unlike *Copy* and *Join*, they operate directly on list abstractions, of which they make a copy accessible only to themselves:

$$\begin{aligned} Move(L) &\quad \overset{\text{def}}{=} \quad (m).\text{new } \ell\,(L\langle \ell \rangle \mid Copy\langle \ell m \rangle) \\ Append(K, L) &\quad \overset{\text{def}}{=} \quad (m).\text{new } k\ell\,(K\langle k \rangle \mid L\langle \ell \rangle \mid Join\langle k\ell m \rangle)\,. \end{aligned}$$

With this definition we really *have* captured functional programming on lists. In fact, when we have defined observation equivalence ($\approx$) in Chapter 13 we shall be able to prove:

Theorem 10.20

$$Move(L) \approx L$$
$$Append(K, L) \approx K \oplus L \,.$$

The proof will be no harder than for Props 10.17 and 10.18.

10.5 Persistent and mutable data

Hitherto our values have been ephemeral, and we would have to take special care if we tried to define a function which needs to use its argument twice. For example, we might like to define $Double(\ell m)$ so that

$$L\langle \ell \rangle \mid Double\langle \ell m \rangle \rightarrow^* (L \oplus L)\langle m \rangle \,.$$

It would be no use to try the definition $Double\langle \ell m \rangle \stackrel{\text{def}}{=} Join\langle \ell \ell m \rangle$, because $Join\langle \ell \ell m \rangle$ will destroy the list $L\langle \ell \rangle$ on its first pass through it.

Of course, one can be careful to make enough copies. But we may also adopt the general solution of making data values *persistent*, by adding replication to the definitions of constructors. We now give the analogues of Definitions 10.11 and 10.13 for truth values and lists, using an asterisk (*$True$, *$False$, ...) to distinguish the persistent constructors.

Definition 10.21 Truth values (persistent) *The persistent truth values in the* π-*calculus are*

$$*True(\ell) \stackrel{\text{def}}{=} \;!\ell(tf).\bar{t} \,, \quad *False(\ell) \stackrel{\text{def}}{=} \;!\ell(tf).\bar{f} \,.$$

For a constructor like *Cons*, we do not replicate whole constructions like $Cons(V, L)$; this leads to difficulties. Instead, we replicate just the list connector on which it is based. Thus, we used the right-hand of the following pair:

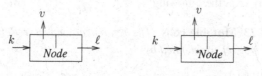

$$Node\langle kv\ell \rangle = k(nc).\bar{c}\langle v\ell \rangle \quad *Node\langle kv\ell \rangle = \;!k(nc).\bar{c}\langle v\ell \rangle \,.$$

Definition 10.22 Lists (persistent) *The constant* *Nil, *the construction* *Cons(V, L) *and a list of n values are defined as follows:*

$$*Nil \quad \overset{\text{def}}{=} \quad (k).!k(nc).\overline{n}$$

$$*Cons(V, L) \quad \overset{\text{def}}{=} \quad (k).\text{new } v\ell \; (*Node\langle kv\ell \rangle \mid V\langle v \rangle \mid L\langle \ell \rangle)$$

$$\text{where } *Node(kv\ell) \overset{\text{def}}{=} !k(nc).\overline{c}\langle v\ell \rangle$$

$$*[V_1, \ldots, V_n] \quad \overset{\text{def}}{=} \quad *Cons(V_1, *Cons(\cdots *Cons(V_n, *Nil)\cdots)) \, .$$

In terms of these definitions, we can also define *Copy, *Join, *Move and *Append which are just like *Copy, ..., Append* except that they use the replicated *Node connector instead of *Node*. It turns out that the analogue of Theorem 10.20 still holds. We shall not pursue the details of persistent data further here.

However, once data structures are persistent it makes sense to ask whether their members could be not just values, but *mutable* data cells. (It would not make sense with ephemeral structures, because it is no use changing something that you will not be able to access again!) What is a mutable cell? We imagine that

- either it is empty or it contains a value;
- it can be tested for this state, yielding up its value if any;
- it can be emptied, or assigned a new value.

A definition along our standard lines for data types would satisfy the first two conditions, as follows: we would define

$$Nullref(r) \quad \overset{\text{def}}{=} \quad r(nc).\,\overline{n}.Nullref\langle r \rangle$$

$$Ref(rv) \quad \overset{\text{def}}{=} \quad r(nc).\,\overline{c}\langle v \rangle.Ref\langle rv \rangle \, .$$

For the third condition – mutability – we add options for the two channels c, n to be used positively as well as negatively, i.e. for reading as well as for writing. We arrive at the following:

Definition 10.23 Mutable cells *The reference connector Ref and the null reference cell Nullref are defined by*

$$Nullref(r) \quad \overset{\text{def}}{=} \quad r(nc).\,(\overline{n}.Nullref\langle r \rangle + c(v').Ref\langle rv' \rangle + n.Nullref\langle r \rangle)$$

$$Ref(rv) \quad \overset{\text{def}}{=} \quad r(nc).\,(\overline{c}\langle v \rangle.Ref\langle rv \rangle + c(v').Ref\langle rv' \rangle + n.Nullref\langle r \rangle) \, ;$$

further, a mutable cell holding a value V is defined by

$$Store(V) \stackrel{\text{def}}{=} (r).\text{new } v \, (Ref\langle rv \rangle \mid V\langle v \rangle) .$$

This structure, being a unary abstraction, can be a member of a list just as a value can. Here is an example:

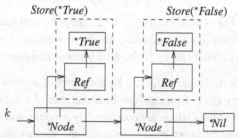

Unlike the arrows out of **Node*, the arrows out of *Ref* are mobile, and can be swung to point at anything else. So the above represents a list whose elements may be changed, i.e. we can change the value accessed from a node. (But we cannot change the structure of the list; this would need *Ref* pointers inserted between the nodes). In the notation of Definition 10.22, this list structure – located at k – is just

$$^*[\, Store(^*True), Store(^*False) \,]\langle k \rangle \, ;$$

compare it with $[\, True, False \,]\langle k \rangle$ shown after Definition 10.13.

What program constructions might operate upon storage cells, analogous to *Listcases* for analysing list structures? Here are three possible:

$$Refcases(P, F) \stackrel{\text{def}}{=} (r).(\text{new } nc)\overline{r}\langle nc \rangle.(n.P + c.F)$$
$$Nullify(P) \stackrel{\text{def}}{=} (r).(\text{new } nc)\overline{r}\langle nc \rangle.\overline{n}.P$$
$$Assign(P) \stackrel{\text{def}}{=} (rv).(\text{new } nc)\overline{r}\langle nc \rangle.\overline{c}\langle v \rangle.P .$$

The first will analyse the contents of the storage cell named r, just as *Listcases* analyses lists; the third will replace the contents (if any) of the storage cell named r by the value named v, and then proceed to P; the second is similar. The following are easy to prove, and they state formally what we have just described:

Exercise 10.24 Verify the following reactions:

$$
\begin{array}{rcl}
Refcases(P, F)\langle r \rangle \mid Nullref\langle r \rangle & \to^* & P \mid Nullref\langle r \rangle \\
Refcases(P, F)\langle r \rangle \mid Ref\langle rv \rangle & \to^* & F\langle v \rangle \mid Ref\langle rv \rangle \\
Nullify(P)\langle r \rangle \mid Ref\langle rv \rangle & \to^* & P \mid Nullref\langle r \rangle \\
Assign(P)\langle rv' \rangle \mid Ref\langle rv \rangle & \to^* & P \mid Ref\langle rv' \rangle .
\end{array}
$$

■

Once again, a programming language may adopt sugared notation for these constructions. For example $Refcases(Assign(P)\langle ru \rangle, (v).Q)\langle r \rangle$ might appear as follows:

$$
\begin{array}{llll}
\text{refcase } r \text{ of} & Empty? & \Rightarrow & r := u;\ P \\
& Contents?\,(v) & \Rightarrow & Q\,.
\end{array}
$$

Exercise 10.25 The cells of Definition 10.23 are persistent structures; this was achieved by defining them recursively, not by replication. Use the technique of Section 9.5 to define them by replication without recursion.   ∎

Having seen how storage cells can be members of a list structure, we can easily see that *any* kind of process can be a member of a data structure. This even applies to processes which are concurrently running, and processes which have free names which support other interactions. We can imagine, for example, a tree of active processes; the tree structure provides a way in which a user – or another process – can interact with them while they are running.

In summary, we have explored data structures in some depth; we proved some rigorous results about ephemeral data, and to a lesser extent (because this chapter should not be too long) for both persistent and mutable data. The purpose has not been to make it easy to program with such structures – many languages do that – but to show that the π-calculus can express their behaviour and analyse their properties.

11

Sorts, Objects, and Functions

This chapter introduces a simple type system for the π-calculus. We shall find that all our examples obey the discipline, and that the use of so-called *sorts* and *sortings* is a real help in understanding applications.

The discipline will help us to classify the 'sorts' of information which can be transmitted in an interaction. We have already seen that we can get the effect of transmitting the values of standard data types, by passing their names; we shall now see that our sorting discipline is quite closely linked to the hierarchy of data types.

If the π-calculus gives us the effect of sending *data* as messages, we may also ask whether it gives us the effect of sending arbitrary *processes* as messages. We shall show that this is so. In fact we show how both *objects* of object-oriented programming and the *functions* of functional programming can be transmitted; thus the π-calculus can express both these programming disciplines.

11.1 A hierarchy of channel types?

In programming we usually *think* in types, even if the language doesn't impose them upon us. Most languages have basic types like BOOL, INTEGER and STRING; for example we write u : STRING and v : INTEGER to indicate the types of values (or variables) u and v. From this, it is a short step to using *type constructors*; for example, the Cartesian product '$\times$' allows us to write STRING $\times$ INTEGER as the type of all pairs of a string and an integer. Another useful type constructor is LIST; for any type τ, LIST(τ) is the type of sequences or lists whose members are of type τ. For example, a dictionary which associates strings with values of type τ can be represented by an 'association list' of type LIST(STRING $\times \tau$). There are other type constructors, and expressions built from these constructors give us what is called a *type hierarchy*.

Is there a type hierarchy for the π-calculus and its channels? Consider a channel in the mobile phone example of Section 8.2, say the channel $lose_1$. Looking at the equation defining $Control_1$, we see that $lose_1$ carries a pair of names such as $talk_2$ and $switch_2$. We may be led to introduce a type constructor CHAN which can take a sequence of types; in this example, if $talk_2$ has type τ and $switch_2$ has type σ then we may assign to $lose_1$ the type $\text{CHAN}(\tau, \sigma)$. We can define a type hierarchy of all types that can be built by CHAN and sequencing; for example

$$\text{CHAN}(\,)\,,\quad \text{CHAN}(\text{CHAN}(\text{CHAN}(\,)), \text{CHAN}(\,))\,,\quad \ldots$$

Strikingly, this is not enough. For if $switch_i$ has type σ, then since it can carry the pair $\langle talk_1, switch_1 \rangle$ we may like to say that the type σ must satisfy the equation

$$\sigma = \text{CHAN}(\tau, \sigma)\,;$$

but a hierarchy cannot allow an item to be a component of itself! We shall now adopt an approach which allows such circularities, though not in the form of equations.

11.2 Sorts and sortings

Assume a basic collection Σ of *sorts*. (For each application we may have a different such collection.) To every name x is assigned a sort σ, and we write $x : \sigma$. This is done in such a way that each $\sigma \in \Sigma$ is assigned to infinitely many names.

A *sort list* over Σ, as its name implies, is just a finite sequence $\vec{\sigma} = \sigma_1, \ldots, \sigma_n$ of sorts. Σ^* is the set of all sort lists over Σ.

Sort lists classify sequences of names; if $x_i : \sigma_i$ $(1 \leq i \leq n)$ and $\vec{x} = x_1 \cdots x_n$ then we write $\vec{x} : \sigma_1, \ldots, \sigma_n$. They also classify abstractions; if $F = (\vec{x})P$ and $\vec{x} : \vec{\sigma}$ then we write $F : \vec{\sigma}$. Note especially that all processes have the empty sort list, i.e. $P : \epsilon$.

We could have used the term 'type' instead of 'sort'. But we prefer to keep the former available for classifying *processes*, rather than the names which they use. (We do not attempt such a classification in this book.)

The main point of classifying names by sort is to ensure that when a process receives a name it uses it properly. Consider for example

$$P = x(y).\overline{y}\langle uv \rangle\,,\quad Q = \overline{x}\langle y' \rangle.y'(w).Q'\,. \tag{$*$}$$

We do not want $P|Q$ to be a legitimate construction, since P uses the bound name y for a channel which carries a *pair* of values, while Q uses y' to carry a *single* value, yet the communication will substitute y' for y. To help to enforce a suitable discipline, we define the notion of sorting as follows:

Definition 11.1 Sorting *Given a set Σ of sorts, a* sorting *over Σ is a partial function*

$$ob \; : \; \Sigma \rightharpoonup \Sigma^*$$

and we say that a process or family of processes respects *ob if, for every sub-term of the form $x(\vec{y}).P$ or $\overline{x}\langle\vec{y}\rangle.P$,*

$$if\; x:\sigma \;then\; \vec{y} : ob(\sigma)\; .$$

Example 11.2 Sorting can be impossible In $(*)$ above, there is no sorting respected by both P and Q. For suppose $x:\sigma$; then since the actions $x(y)$ and $\overline{x}\langle y'\rangle$ occur, $ob(\sigma)$ must be of the form τ with $y:\tau$ and $y':\tau$. But $\overline{y}\langle uv\rangle$ and $y'(w)$ occur, so the sequences uv and w must have the same sort $ob(\tau)$, which is impossible. ∎

Example 11.3 Sorting for mobile phones For the system of Section 8.2 let us choose

$$\Sigma = \{\text{TALK}, \text{SWITCH}, \text{GAIN}, \text{LOSE}\}\;,$$

with

$$talk_i:\text{TALK}, \;\; switch_i:\text{SWITCH}, \;\; gain_i:\text{GAIN}, \;\; lose_i:\text{LOSE} \qquad (i=1,2)\;.$$

Then the only sorting ob respected by the system is such that

$$ob: \begin{cases} \text{TALK} & \mapsto & \epsilon \\ \text{SWITCH} & \mapsto & \text{TALK}, \text{SWITCH} \\ \text{GAIN} & \mapsto & \text{TALK}, \text{SWITCH} \\ \text{LOSE} & \mapsto & \text{TALK}, \text{SWITCH}\;. \end{cases}$$

We could choose instead $\Sigma = \{\text{TALK}, \text{SWITCH}\}$, equating the sorts GAIN and LOSE with SWITCH, thus giving $gain_i$, $lose_i$ and $switch_i$ all the same sort. There is freedom in how much we choose to distinguish names by their sorts. ∎

Exercise 11.4 What sorting ob is respected by the elastic buffer system at the end of Section 8.3? If $x:V$ in that system, is it necessary for $ob(V)$ to be defined? ∎

The following is important, and is easy to prove:

Proposition 11.5 *Sorting is preserved by structural congruence and reaction; that is, if $P \equiv P'$ or $P \to P'$ and P respects ob then P' respects ob.*

If a sorting is respected, it constrains the pattern of interaction. This can help in analysing behaviour.

Example 11.6 Sorting assists analysis Suppose a process $P|Q$ has free names x_i : A, y_i : B, u_i : C, v_i : D, and that it respects a sorting ob under which

$$A \mapsto B, \ B \mapsto \epsilon, \ C \mapsto D, \ D \mapsto \epsilon \ .$$

Now suppose that P contains only the x_i free (no y_i, u_i or v_i); then P may at some time receive y_i from Q, and use it, but it will never receive any of the u_i or v_i.   ∎

One can see here the germ of a proof that, if we are computing with data values and the appropriate sorting is respected, than we can never receive (say) a boolean value when we expect an integer.

Example 11.7 Unique handling revisited Recall the sufficient conditions for unique handling derived in Theorem 10.8. To ensure unique handling of a particular name x at all future times in a system S, we required a strong condition: that in *every* subterm of the form $z(\vec{y}).Q$, Q must be y-forgetful for each $y \in \vec{y}$. We need not recall exactly what 'y-forgetful' means; the point is that we had to impose this condition on every input-bound name y, simply because it might at some time be instantiated to the particular name x. But if S respects some sorting with x : A and y : B, and A $\neq$ B, then y could never be instantiated to x, and we need impose no condition on the use of y. In fact, Theorem 10.8 can be improved to the following theorem.   ∎

Theorem 11.8   Unique handling (sorted) *Let S be simple, respecting a sorting, and let S satisfy the following conditions for some x : A; (1) it uniquely handles x; (2) it is x-forgetful; (3) for every subterm of form $z(\vec{y}).Q$, Q is y-forgetful for each $y \in \vec{y}$ for which y : A. Further, let $S \rightarrow S'$. Then S' is simple and also satisfies (1), (2) and (3).*

The proof is a simple adaptation of the earlier proof. It also depends on the fact that sorting is preserved by reaction, Prop 11.5.

11.3 Extending the sort language

Already we see that a sorting tells us something about the pattern of interaction in a system. Consider now the pattern of interaction with data types, as we presented them in Section 10.3. The following table shows again the abstractions which represent truth values and lists, together with sortings which they respect:

$$True(b) \stackrel{\text{def}}{=} b(tf).\bar{t} \qquad\qquad Nil(\ell) \stackrel{\text{def}}{=} \ell(nc).\bar{n}$$

$$False(b) \stackrel{\text{def}}{=} b(tf).\bar{f} \qquad\qquad Node(\ell) \stackrel{\text{def}}{=} (v\ell').\ell(nc).\bar{c}\langle v\ell'\rangle$$

b:BOOL, t:TRUE, f:FALSE $\qquad\qquad$ ℓ:LIST, n:NIL, c:CONS, v:VAL

$$\begin{cases} \text{BOOL} \mapsto \text{TRUE, FALSE} \\ \text{TRUE} \mapsto \epsilon \\ \text{FALSE} \mapsto \epsilon \end{cases} \qquad \begin{cases} \text{LIST} \mapsto \text{NIL, CONS} \\ \text{CONS} \mapsto \text{VAL, LIST} \\ \text{NIL} \mapsto \epsilon \end{cases}$$

This scheme can clearly be generalised to all data types. But it has two shortcomings.

First, we may not want to distinguish among the sorts TRUE, FALSE and NIL; channels of these sorts simply carry the empty message and it may be convenient to use a standard sort for such channels. The natural thing, then, is to bring back the constructor CHAN which we discussed in Section 11.1; we shall now call it a *sort constructor*, and decree that for any sort list $\vec{\sigma}$ there is a sort CHAN($\vec{\sigma}$) for channels along which messages of sort $\vec{\sigma}$ may be sent. Then, if we wish, we can replace all the sorts TRUE, FALSE and NIL by the single sort CHAN(ϵ).

The second shortcoming is that the generic nature of the sort LIST is not made evident; we would like to have a sort LIST(σ) parametric in the sort σ of values. Now, what kinds of message can travel along a channel of sort LIST(σ)? The answer is that along a channel of this sort we can send a pair of channels, the first of which (e.g. n) can carry empty messages and the second of which (e.g. c) can carry messages consisting of a channel of sort σ and a channel of sort LIST(σ). So a channel of sort LIST(σ) carries messages having the sort list

$$\text{CHAN}(\epsilon), \text{CHAN}(\sigma, \text{LIST}(\sigma)).$$

This means that the appropriate sorting function *ob* should satisfy

$$ob: \text{LIST}(\sigma) \mapsto \text{CHAN}(\epsilon), \text{CHAN}(\sigma, \text{LIST}(\sigma));$$

for any sort σ.

So both our shortcomings can be got over by allowing sort constructors, and having sorts which are not just atomic but can be any expressions built out of sort constructors (a sort hierarchy, if you like); we also require that our sorting functions behave in a certain manner for each such sort constructor. The following definition makes all this precise.

Definition 11.9 Sort language *A sort language Σ is generated by a set Γ of sort constructors, each with a rank ≥ 0. The language Σ consists of sorts σ of the form*

$$C(\sigma_1, \ldots, \sigma_n)$$

where $C \in \Gamma$ has rank n and $\sigma_1, \ldots, \sigma_n$ are sorts. A sorting over Σ is a partial function

$$ob : \Sigma \rightharpoonup \Sigma^*$$

determined as follows. To each sort constructor $C \in \Gamma$ corresponds at most one sorting rule of the form

$$ob : C(s_1, \ldots, s_n) \mapsto \rho_1, \ldots, \rho_m$$

where $s_1, \ldots, s_n$ are sort variables which may appear in the sorts ρ_i. Thus, for any sorts $\sigma_1, \ldots, \sigma_m$ the sort list $ob(C(\sigma_1, \ldots, \sigma_n))$ is obtained by substituting $\vec{\sigma}$ for $\vec{s}$ in $\rho_1, \ldots, \rho_m$. We may omit the parentheses around the argument(s) of a sort constructor when it does not lead to ambiguity.

The most important sort constructor of all is the *channel* sort constructor $CHAN_n$, of rank n, with the sorting rule

$$CHAN_n(s_1, \ldots, s_n) \mapsto s_1, \ldots, s_n .$$

Thus a channel whose sort is $CHAN_n\vec{\sigma}$ carries messages of size n having sort $\vec{\sigma}$. We shall always omit the subscript n from CHAN.

Example 11.10 Sorting for buffer cell The buffer cell $B \stackrel{\text{def}}{=} \ell(x).\overline{r}\langle x\rangle.B$ respects this sorting rule, with (say) $x : \text{BOOL}$, $\ell : \text{CHAN BOOL}$, $r : \text{CHAN BOOL}$.

∎

Note that the new sort discipline is just a refinement of what we had before; all that we have done is to allow the set Σ, which we previously called *basic* sorts, to have a hierarchical structure – and to require that any sorting function *ob* respects this structure by treating each sort constructor uniformly. We can still we have basic sorts, such as SWITCH and TALK, as sort constructors of rank 0, with the same sorting rules as before:

$$\text{SWITCH} \mapsto \text{TALK}, \text{SWITCH}, \quad \text{TALK} \mapsto \epsilon .$$

Example 11.11 Sorting for reference cells Consider the reference cell $Ref\langle rv\rangle$ defined in Section 10.5. To avoid special sorts for c and n, the constructor names, we define a sort constructor REF of rank 1, with the sorting rule

$$\text{REF}\, s \mapsto \text{CHAN}\, \epsilon, \text{CHAN}\, s .$$

It is easy to check that *Ref*⟨*rv*⟩ respects this sorting rule, with $v : \sigma$, $r : \text{REF}\,\sigma$ for any sort σ. ∎

Example 11.12 Sorting for lists We introduce the sort constructor LIST of rank 1, which we have already discussed, with the sorting rule

$$\text{LIST}\,s \;\mapsto\; \text{CHAN}\,\epsilon,\; \text{CHAN}(s, \text{LIST}\,s) .$$ ∎

Exercise 11.13 A multi-level list, essentially a binary tree with values at its leaves, is defined informally thus:

> A bintree is either *Leaf* of a value
> or *Pair* of a bintree and a bintree.

Define its constructors in the style of Definition 10.13, and define the corresponding sort constructor BINTREE of rank one. ∎

We shall take advantage of sort constructors in the next section, where we see how to represent object-oriented programming in the π-calculus.

In future, instead of assuming a fixed assignment of sorts to names, we shall freely adopt the convention of introducing new bound names with their sorts. For example, we may write

$$Node(\ell : \text{LIST}\,\sigma) \stackrel{\text{def}}{=} (v\ell').\ell(nc).\bar{c}\langle v\ell' \rangle .$$

11.4 Object-oriented programming

Though the π-calculus was developed for other purposes, it elegantly captures the way in which objects interact in a concurrent object-oriented language. This is not surprising. A central idea in such a language is that objects, or rather their 'identities' (i.e. their names), can be passed from object to object and new objects created on the fly; this is just what the π-calculus is good at.

We now proceed to show how to represent objects in the π-calculus. We shall illustrate how name-passing in the π-calculus represents object interactions, but in particular we shall show how the sorting discipline helps to organise the representation. What follows is a simplified account of work by David Walker [20], one of the originators of the π-calculus, to whom I am indebted.

In a certain simple language, a program consists just of a sequence of class declarations followed by an initiating statement, while a class declaration indicates the local variables and methods which belong to each object of the class.

The syntax is

$$program \quad ::= \quad class\text{-}dec \cdots class\text{-}dec \,; \; statement$$

$$class\text{-}dec \quad ::= \quad \text{class } A$$
$$\text{var } V_1 : B_1, \ldots, V_m : B_m$$
$$method\text{-}dec \cdots method\text{-}dec$$

$$method\text{-}dec \quad ::= \quad \text{method } M(X_1 : A_1, \ldots, X_n : A_n) : A \; = \; statement$$

$$statement \quad ::= \quad \cdots \cdots .$$

Here $A, A_1, \ldots, B, B_1, \ldots$ are class names, $V_1, \ldots, V_m$ are names of variables (i.e. reference cells holding objects), $X_1, \ldots, X_n$ are object parameter names, and M is a method name. We choose not to specify the syntax of statements. As an example of a class declaration, here is the class of a priority queues (with numbers as members) having methods for adding and removing a single member.

```
class Queue
    var V : NAT, P : Queue
    method Add (X : NAT) =
        return ;
        if V = nil then (V := X ; P := fresh(Queue))
        else if V < X then P.Add (X) else (P.Add (V) ; V := X)
    method Rem ( ) : NAT =
        return V ;
        if not(V = nil) then (V := P.Rem ( ) ; if V = nil then P := nil)
```

Note that a method can return before finishing its work; this is what gives rise to concurrent activity.

Let us see how a program would be represented in the π-calculus. To organise the presentation we shall use the sort constructors CHAN and REF introduced in Section 11.3. We also need two other sort constructors, CLASS and METHOD; their sorting rules are:

$$\text{CLASS } s \quad \mapsto \quad s$$
$$\text{METHOD}(s_1, \ldots, s_n, s') \quad \mapsto \quad s_1, \ldots, s_n, \text{CHAN } s' .$$

(Strictly speaking there is a sort constructor METHOD_n of rank n for each $n \geq 0$.) We shall not go so far as a full formal translation, but far enough to see how it would work. Consider the following class declaration:

$$class\text{-}dec_A \;\; = \;\; \textbf{class}\; A$$
$$\textbf{var}\; V_1 : A,\; V_2 : B$$
$$\textbf{method}\; M_1(X_1 : B) : A \;=\; S_1$$
$$\textbf{method}\; M_2(X_1 : A, X_2 : A) : B \;=\; S_2$$

where we shall not detail the statements S_1 and S_2; but note that S_1 is expected to return a member of the object class A, and S_2 a member of class B. Corresponding to this particular class declaration, we introduce a sort constructor A of rank 0; its sorting rule is

$$A \;\mapsto\; \text{METHOD}(B, A),\; \text{METHOD}(A, A, B) \,.$$

Thus the sort list $ob(A)$ of any member of the class A is just the sequence of its (two) method sorts.

In translating this class declaration we shall use a variety of π-calculus names, sorted as follows:

k_A	: CLASS A	unique name of class A
$v_1, \ldots$	: REF A	variables over class A
$x_1, \ldots$	: A	method parameters of class A
r	: CHAN A	method result of class A
a	: A	name of any object of class A
m_1	: METHOD(B, A)	name of method M_1
m_2	: METHOD(A, A, B)	name of method M_2 .

The translation of $class\text{-}dec_A$ will be

$$[\![class\text{-}dec_A]\!] \;\stackrel{\text{def}}{=}\; !\;\textbf{new}\; a \; \overline{k_A}\langle a\rangle . Object_A\langle a\rangle \,,$$

which delivers a new object with a new unique name a whenever accessed at k_A. The only names free in this generic process are the names k_C of all classes C in the program.

Each new object $Object_A\langle a\rangle$ must contain reference cells representing its own variables V_1 and V_2, and must provide the methods for repeated use. So

$$Object_A(a) \;\stackrel{\text{def}}{=}\; \textbf{new}\; v_1 : \text{REF A},\; v_2 : \text{REF B}$$
$$(Nullref\langle v_1\rangle \mid Nullref\langle v_2\rangle \mid !Methods_A\langle a\rangle)$$

where v_1, v_2 may occur free in $Methods_A\langle a\rangle$. Note that a reference cell is initially empty.

It is important that each object of the class has its own copy of the methods. One reason for this is that each method may refer to the variables associated with the particular object to which it belongs. Also, the method may wish to refer to this very object itself (using the keyword self), and this will be represented by the unique name a of the object. (In some languages one can replace the methods in an object, and this is another reason why each object must keep its own set of methods.)

Finally we define

$$Methods_A(a) \quad \overset{\text{def}}{=} \quad \text{new } m_1 : \text{METHOD}(B, A), \; m_2 : \text{METHOD}(A, A, B)$$
$$\overline{a}\langle m_1 m_2 \rangle.(m_1(x_1 : B, \; r : \text{CHAN A}).[\![S_1]\!]$$
$$+ \; m_2(x_1 : A, x_2 : A, \; r : \text{CHAN B}).[\![S_2]\!]) \; .$$

Thus when invoked at a, $Object_A\langle a \rangle$ delivers its menu of methods, one of which will be selected by the invoking agent.

Having seen how to represent classes, objects, methods and variables as π-calculus processes, let us now discuss briefly how to translate individual statements. We shall adopt the convention of Example 5.27 in which each statement terminates with the action $\overline{done}$, allowing an easy definition of sequential composition.

As a first example, suppose that the method M_1 in our example contains the statement

$$\text{return } V_1 \; .$$

The required action is in three phases: get the contents of V_1, signalling error if the cell is empty; send this value along the result channel r; then signal $\overline{done}$. Noting that v_1 is the location of V_1, and using the *Refcases* construction of Section 10.5, we get

$$Refcases(Error, \; (a).\overline{r}\langle a \rangle. \overline{done})\langle v_1 \rangle \; .$$

We shall not trouble to define the *Error* process to be invoked when V_1 is empty.

Exercise 11.14 Suppose that the method M_2 in our example contains the statement

$$V_1 \; ::= \; X_2.M_1(\text{fresh}(B)) \; .$$

This means: get a new object of class B; then apply the first method of X_2 (which is an object of class A) to this new object; then assign the result to the cell V_1 of the current object. What is the translation of this statement? *Hint*: Use the operation *Assign* from Section 10.5.   ■

This short section does not, of course, do justice to object-oriented programming. In particular, we have not dealt with the possibility that, given a class A, we may wish to define a class A' whose objects possess the same methods as A and possibly more besides. Such a class A' is called a *subclass* of A. It is also common to allow that if a method M is defined for class A, the corresponding method M for the subclass A' is re-defined; this is known as 'method override'. Our translation would need adaptation to accommodate subclasses. A related but different feature is 'method update', where one is allowed to change the method M for a *particular object* in a class, as opposed to method override which re-defines M for a whole subclass. Method update can be accommodated with a minor change to our translation; all that is needed is to access methods via reference cells, just as for variables. However, the sorting discipline will only be respected if the new and old methods have the same sort.

Nor do we claim that object-oriented programming should be done directly in the π-calculus. But we hope to have shown that the π-calculus can explain and formalise many of the important concepts of object-oriented programming; moreover, we have thereby given a non-trivial example of our sorting discipline in action.

11.5 Processes and abstractions as messages

An obvious question arises about sorts: what 'sorts' of message should be allowed? Why do we allow just names as messages; why not processes themselves? One answer is that we purposely set out to study a lean calculus, to see what power it has. If we throw everything in at the start, we never discover whether we need all of it.

Of course, it would add convenience if we could send processes as messages. Let us see what extension to the π-calculus is necessary for this. The main change needed is in the action prefixes, π. We must add *variables* $p, q, r, \ldots$ over processes, to use in input actions; and we must also allow process expressions to appear as messages in output actions. Then we can write e.g.

$$P = \overline{x}\langle R\rangle.P', \qquad Q = x(r).(r \mid r \mid Q') . \tag{1}$$

Here Q is willing to receive any process and then 'run' two copies of it alongside Q'. So we would expect the reaction

$$P \mid Q \rightarrow P' \mid R \mid R \mid Q' . \tag{2}$$

Of course, this goes beyond the syntax of the π-calculus. But in fact there is no need (except for convenience) to extend the π-calculus at all to get an equivalent effect. Restricted names and replication give us all the power we need. To get the effect of (1) we write

$$\widehat{P} = (\text{new } z)\overline{x}\langle z\rangle.(!z.R \mid P') , \qquad \widehat{Q} = x(z).(\overline{z} \mid \overline{z} \mid Q') . \qquad (3)$$

Then with the π-calculus as it stands we get the reaction (2) almost exactly, in three steps.

Exercise 11.15 Perform these three steps. Why is the result not *exactly* as in (2)? Use the result of Exercise 12.20 to argue that it is exact enough. ∎

Note how replication in (3) allows for multiple use of the transmitted process. Well then, why should we not allow multiple use with different instantiations, i.e. allow the transmitted process to be *parametric*? Of course, this just means passing *abstractions* as messages; as a generalisation of (1) we would allow

$$P = \overline{x}\langle F\rangle.P' , \qquad Q = x(f).(f\langle u\rangle \mid f\langle v\rangle \mid Q') , \qquad (4)$$

where we are using f as a variable over abstractions, and we allow the datum F in the action $\overline{x}\langle F\rangle$ to be an abstraction. The term $f\langle u\rangle$ just means 'run f with parameter u'.

This generalisation causes no difficulty; in the π-calculus, in place of (3), we write

$$\widehat{P} = (\text{new } z)\overline{x}\langle z\rangle.(!zF \mid P') , \qquad \widehat{Q} = x(z).(\overline{z}\langle u\rangle \mid \overline{z}\langle v\rangle \mid Q') . \qquad (5)$$

Exercise 11.16 Check that the intended reaction of $P|Q$, with the definition of (4), is matched by (5). ∎

We have to be careful about the scope of names when we pass processes or abstractions as messages, just as we have to be careful in conventional programming when we pass functions or procedures as parameters. When a process is received as a message, its free names should 'mean' what they meant to the sender, not what they might happen to mean to the receiver. For example, suppose instead of (1) we have

$$P = (\text{new } w)\overline{x}\langle R\rangle.P' , \qquad Q = x(r).(r \mid r \mid Q') , \qquad (6)$$

where w is a private name representing a link between the sender P' and the message process R. The reaction

$$P \mid Q \;\rightarrow\; \text{new } w\, P' \mid R \mid R \mid Q'$$

would be faulty, since it has reduced the scope of new w to contain just P'; R has 'escaped' from the scope of new w, so any w in R will be wrongly equated with any free w which Q' may contain.

But our translation into the π-calculus does achieve the correct effect, which is

$$P \mid Q \;\rightarrow\; \mathsf{new}\, w \,(P' \mid R \mid R) \mid Q' \,.$$

Exercise 11.17 Write down the translation of (6) into the π-calculus, by analogy with (1). Check that in three reactions it achieves essentially the correct effect. ∎

11.6 Functional computing as name-passing

If we claim that the π-calculus is a general computational model, then we must be able to simulate other models within it. We shall do this now for the λ-calculus, the essence of functional programming.

The terms $M, N, \ldots$ of the λ-calculus are built from variables $x, y, \ldots$ by the following very simple syntax:

$$M \;::=\; x \;\mid\; (\lambda x\, M) \;\mid\; (M\, N)\,,$$

the last two forms being called λ-*abstraction* and *application* respectively. The essential computation rule is

$$\lambda\,\mathrm{REDUCTION}: \quad ((\lambda x\, M)\, N) \rightarrow \{{}^{N}\!/\!x\} M \,.$$

In practical computing, when we 'pass' a procedure or function as a parameter to another, what we actually transmit is a name – a reference or address of the code of the procedure. In simulating the λ-calculus we use this idea, which is of course central to the π-calculus.

How does a λ-term M compute? For simplicity, we consider the case in which M has no free names. Such a term has to consist of a λ-abstraction $M_0 = \lambda x_1\, M_1$ applied to a sequence of arguments, i.e.

$$M \;=\; M_0 N_1 \cdots N_k \,,$$

which is an abbreviation for $(\cdots ((M_0 N_1) N_2) \cdots N_k)$. The simplest regime for λ-calculus computation proceeds as follows:

- Reduce $(\lambda x_1\, M_1) N_1$ to $\{{}^{N_1}\!/\!x_1\} M_1$;
- Compute this term by reduction;
- If and when it becomes a λ-abstraction $\lambda x_2\, M_2$, then reduce $(\lambda x_2\, M_2) N_2$, and so on.

To encode this procedure we shall represent the linkage from M_0 to its sequence of arguments by 'nodes' $\overline{v_i}\langle x_i v_{i+1}\rangle$, rather like the list nodes of Section 10.3 (but simpler). The following diagram shows the structure of the computation:

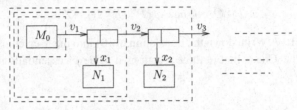

The π-calculus term corresponding to any M has to know where to find its argument-list. So we translate M into a unary abstraction $[\![M]\!]$ of π-calculus; we apply this to $\langle u \rangle$ if the arguments are to be found at u. Now:

- What does it mean for $[\![M]\!]\langle u \rangle$ to 'find its arguments' at u? It means that 'when ready' it will consume the node $\bar{u}\langle xv \rangle$, thus finding the name x of the first argument and a link v to the remainder.

- What does 'x names an argument' mean? If the argument is N, it means that there exists a replicated resource

$$!x[\![N]\!] \, .$$

- What does '$[\![M]\!]\langle u \rangle$ is ready' mean? It means that M has become an abstraction $\lambda x\, M'$. So the π-calculus term $[\![\lambda x\, M']\!]\langle u \rangle$ has to be able to perform an input action at u.

With these hints, we now define the unary abstraction $[\![M]\!]$ by induction on the structure of M. We use two kinds of names: $x, y, z, \ldots$ for arguments, and $u, v, w, \ldots$ for *lists* of arguments.

Definition 11.18 Translation of λ-calculus *The translation $[\![M]\!]$ of an arbitrary λ-term M into π-calculus is a unary abstraction $[\![M]\!]$, defined inductively as follows:*

$$
\begin{aligned}
\textit{variable}: \quad & [\![x]\!](u) \; \overset{\text{def}}{=} \; \bar{x}\langle u \rangle \\
\lambda\textit{-abstraction}: \quad & [\![\lambda x\, M]\!](u) \; \overset{\text{def}}{=} \; u(xv).[\![M]\!]\langle v \rangle \\
\textit{application}: \quad & [\![(M\,N)]\!](u) \; \overset{\text{def}}{=} \; \mathsf{new}\, v\,([\![M]\!]\langle v \rangle \mid \mathsf{new}\, x\,(\bar{v}\langle xu \rangle \mid !x[\![N]\!]))
\end{aligned}
$$

where, in the third equation, x is chosen not free in N.

In the first equation, the translation of a variable x is a messenger; it sends the argument-list named u to function named x. The second equation represents the readiness of a λ-abstraction to receive a first argument named x, and the name v of a further argument-list. In the final equation, when M becomes ready it will receive along the channel v both the private name x of its first argument $[\![N]\!]$, and the name u of its further argument-list. It is helpful to compare the third equation to the diagram.

Note that the names $x, y, \ldots$ (but not $u, v, \ldots$) are used both in λ-terms and in their translations. In fact we can show

Proposition 11.19 *The free names of $[\![M]\!]$ are exactly the free variables of M.*

Proof An easy induction on the structure of M. $\qquad\qquad\qquad\qquad$ □

It is worth 'evaluating' a few translations, to see that the reactions of π-calculus simulate reductions in λ-calculus.

Example 11.20 Illustrating λ-reduction Consider the reduction $(\lambda x\, x)N \to N$. For the translation we have

$$[\![\lambda x\, x]\!]\langle v\rangle \;=\; v(xw).\overline{x}\langle w\rangle \,,$$

and hence

$$[\![(\lambda x\, x)N]\!]\langle u\rangle \;=\; \mathsf{new}\, v\, (v(xw).\overline{x}\langle w\rangle \mid \mathsf{new}\, y\, (\overline{v}\langle yu\rangle \mid \,!y[\![N]\!]))\,.$$

Now we easily find that

$$[\![(\lambda x\, x)N]\!]\langle u\rangle \;\to^*\; [\![N]\!]\langle u\rangle \mid \mathsf{new}\, y\, !y[\![N]\!]\,,$$

and in Chapter 12, where we study the strong congruence relation $\sim$, we shall find that $\mathsf{new}\, y\, !yF \sim 0$ for any abstraction F. (See Exercise 12.20.) So we may write

$$[\![(\lambda x\, x)N]\!]\langle u\rangle \;\to^*\!\sim\; [\![N]\!]\langle u\rangle\,,$$

which of course matches the λ-reduction. $\qquad\qquad\qquad\qquad\qquad\blacksquare$

Exercise 11.21 Show similarly that the reduction $(\lambda x\, (xy))(\lambda z\, z) \to^* y$ is properly simulated by the reaction sequence

$$[\![(\lambda x\, (xy))(\lambda z\, z)]\!]\langle v\rangle \;\to^*\!\sim\; \overline{y}\langle v\rangle\,. \qquad\qquad\qquad\blacksquare$$

In any decent interpretation of the λ-calculus, we find that the terms $(\lambda x\, M)N$ and $\{N\!/x\}M$ denote the same entity. This is what is meant by saying that the interpretation *respects* reduction. So it is natural to ask in what sense the translations of these two terms into π-calculus are equivalent. We should not be too hasty in answering this, because in the λ-calculus the substitution $\{N\!/x\}$ can instantly create any finite number of copies of N (which may be a term of any size), while reaction in the π-calculus only induces substitution of *names* for names. However, in Chapter 13 we shall introduce the *weak* equivalence relation $\approx$, and we shall be able to prove the following:

Theorem 11.22 The λ-translation is sound $[\![(\lambda x\, M)N]\!] \approx [\![\{^N\!/x\}M]\!]$.

Having translated the λ-calculus, we naturally ask whether the translated terms $[\![M]\!]$ respect any sorting discipline. We may expect not, since we have translated the *type-free* λ-calculus, i.e. we have assumed no type discipline for the λ-terms M. (Thus we can cheerfully write terms like the self-application (xx), which have questionable meaning.) However, the translations $[\![M]\!]$ do indeed respect an elegant sorting, as the following theorem shows.

Theorem 11.23 The λ-translation is sorted   *Let* $\Gamma = \{\text{CHAN}, \text{FUN}\}$, *and let ob be the sorting*

$$\text{CHAN}\, s \;\mapsto\; s$$
$$\text{FUN} \;\mapsto\; \text{CHAN}(\text{FUN}),\ \text{FUN}\ ;$$

also ascribe sorts $u, v, w, \ldots$: FUN *and* $x, y, z, \ldots$: CHAN(FUN). *Then for every λ-term* M, *the abstraction* $[\![M]\!]$ *respects ob and has sort* FUN.

Proof By induction on the structure of M.

Case $M = x$. Then $[\![M]\!] = (u).\overline{x}\langle u\rangle$. This clearly respects *ob* and has the sort of u, namely FUN.

Case $M = (\lambda x M')$. Then $[\![M]\!] = (u).u(xv).[\![M]\!]\langle v\rangle$. By induction $[\![M]\!]$ respects *ob* and has sort FUN. Hence also $[\![M]\!]\langle v\rangle$ respects *ob*; so also does the action prefix $u(xv)$, and the result follows.

Case $M = (M_1 M_2)$. Then $[\![M]\!] = \mathsf{new}\,v\,([\![M_1]\!]\langle v\rangle\,|\,\mathsf{new}\,x\,(\overline{v}\langle xu\rangle\,|\,!x[\![M_2]\!]))$. By induction $[\![M_2]\!]$ respects *ob* and has sort FUN, so the process $!x[\![M_2]\!]$ respects *ob*. The rest of the argument is similar to the previous two cases.

□

After this mild surprise, it is natural to ask what sorting is respected by the translations of terms of a *typed* λ-calculus. For the simplest such calculus, aptly called the *simply-typed* λ-calculus, the answer is elegant; we get a refinement of the sorting presented above. We shall not give the details.

The two theorems in this section indicate that the semantic theory of mobile processes, while not highly developed, promises to be consistent with the theory of functional computation.

12

Commitments and Strong Bisimulation

This chapter is modelled on Chapter 5. The *commitments* of the π-calculus correspond to the transitions of CCS. But before introducing the commitment rules we need to enlarge the π-calculus just slightly.

We then present the commitment rules which fully define the dynamic behaviour of the π-calculus. Several properties are proved, closely analogous to properties of the transition relation in Chapter 5. This leads naturally to the treatment of strong bisimulation for the π-calculus. We then show that strong bisimulation is a congruence in an appropriate sense, and finish by deriving some congruence properties of the replication operator.

12.1 Abstractions and concretions

In Section 5.1 we introduced the transitions $P \xrightarrow{\alpha} P'$ for concurrent processes. We can look upon each such transition as a *commitment* of P to take part in a reaction involving α. Consider

$$P \mid Q = (\cdots + a.P') \mid (\cdots + \overline{a}.Q') ;$$

the reaction $P|Q \to P'|Q'$ requires two complementary commitments, $P \xrightarrow{a} P'$ and $Q \xrightarrow{\overline{a}} Q'$. But no data passes in this reaction. In the π-calculus, data does pass in a reaction; we therefore have to revise the notion of transition. Now consider

$$P \mid Q = (\cdots + x(\vec{y}).P') \mid (\cdots + \overline{x}\langle\vec{z}\rangle.Q') ;$$

two complementary commitments along x may occur, leaving the 'residues' $(\vec{y}).P'$ and $\langle\vec{z}\rangle.Q'$ of P and Q respectively. The first residue is an *abstraction*, which we have already met; we call the second a *concretion*. Think of them as a positive and a negative *ion*; these ions combine to give us the reaction

$$P \mid Q \rightarrow \{\vec{z}/\vec{y}\}P' \mid Q' \, .$$

Thus concretions are a kind of dual to abstractions. It smooths the theory of equivalence if we admit these dual entities. In fact, concretions have an extra twist which abstractions don't have; we can see this by looking again at the menus offered to data values as described in Section 10.3. We saw there that the conditional construction *Cond* offers the menu $\langle tf \rangle.(t.P + f.Q)$ to a truth value; this menu is of course a concretion, but it is also subject to the restriction new tf. These 'exported' restrictions are an essential part of the π-calculus; they represent controlled mobility. So we shall allow restricted concretions such as

$$\text{new } tf \, \langle tf \rangle.(t.P + f.Q)$$

to make clear that the names t, f are shared only between the message $\langle tf \rangle$ (to be received elsewhere) and the continuation process $(t.P + f.Q)$.

Another example of a concretion is the menu of methods offered by an object, in the representation of object-oriented programming which we explored in Section 11.4. We can rewrite the definition of *Methods*$_\text{A}$ given in that section as follows (omitting the sorts):

$$\begin{aligned} Methods_\text{A}(a) &\stackrel{\text{def}}{=} \bar{a}C \, , \text{ where} \\ C &\stackrel{\text{def}}{=} \text{new } m_1 m_2 \, \langle m_1 m_2 \rangle. \, (m_1(x_1 r).[\![S_1]\!] + m_2(x_1 x_2 r).[\![S_2]\!]) \, . \end{aligned}$$

We now define abstractions and concretions formally, together with certain operations upon them.

Definition 12.1 Abstractions and concretions *An* abstraction *of arity $n \geq 0$ takes the form $(\vec{x}).P$, where $|\vec{x}| = n$. We use the letters $F, G, \dots$ to stand for abstractions. Two abstractions are structurally congruent ($\equiv$) if, up to alpha-conversion, their bound names $\vec{x}$ are identical and their process parts P are structurally congruent.*

A concretion *of arity $n \geq 0$ takes the form* new $\vec{x}\langle \vec{y} \rangle.P$, *where $|\vec{y}| = n$ and $\vec{x} \subseteq \vec{y}$. The letters C, D will stand for concretions. Two concretions are structurally congruent if, up to alpha-conversion and re-ordering of restricted names, their prefixes* new $\vec{x}\langle \vec{y} \rangle$ *are identical and their process parts P are structurally congruent.*

An agent *is an abstraction or a concretion. We denote the set of agents by $\mathcal{A}^\pi$, and used the letters A, B for arbitrary agents.*

Note that processes are agents; a process is both an abstraction and a concretion, having arity 0.

We must now make a slight generalisation of the summation forms $\sum \pi_i.P_i$ introduced in Definition 9.1. In the polyadic calculus we already allow a summand like $\overline{x}\langle y_1 y_2 \rangle.P$, which is a special case of $\overline{x}C$ where C is a concretion. We now find it convenient to allow a summand $\overline{x}C$ where C is *any* concretion, even with a restriction; and example is $\overline{x}(\text{new } y_1 \langle y_1 y_2 \rangle.P)$. So we now consider a summation form to be $\sum \alpha_i A_i$, where each summand can be of the form xF, $\overline{x}C$ or τP.

Definition 12.2 Application and reaction *The* application $F@C$ *of an abstraction and concretion of equal arity is defined as follows, assuming $\vec{z}$ not free in $(\vec{x}).P$:*

$$(\vec{x}).P @ \text{ new } \vec{z}\,\langle \vec{y} \rangle.Q \stackrel{\text{def}}{=} \text{new } \vec{z}\,(\{\vec{y}/\vec{x}\}P \mid Q)$$

To allow for the extended form of summation, the REACT *rule of Definition 9.16 is extended to*

$$\text{REACT}: \quad (xF + M) \mid (\overline{x}C + N) \to F@C.$$

Note that the application $F@C$ is actually a process, because the positive and negative charges on the ions have neutralised each other, leaving behind a substitution and a shared restriction.

Exercise 12.3 Show that when C has no restriction, so that the old REACT rule applies, the new REACT rule gives the same result. ■

For the purpose of defining commitment rules in the next section, we need to extend restriction and composition to operate upon all agents. In forming either new $z\,A$ or $A \mid Q$, which will be abstractions or concretions of the same arity as A, we essentially move the charge on the ion A to the outermost. More precisely:

Definition 12.4 *The operations* new $z\,A$ *and* $A \mid Q$ *(for arbitrary agent A and process Q) are defined as follows, using alpha-conversion where necessary to avoid clash of names. For an abstraction $A = (\vec{x}).P$, assuming $z \notin \vec{x}$ and $\vec{x}$ not free in Q:*

$$\text{new } z\,((\vec{x}).P) \stackrel{\text{def}}{=} (\vec{x}).\text{new } z\,P$$
$$((\vec{x}).P) \mid Q \stackrel{\text{def}}{=} (\vec{x}).(P \mid Q).$$

For a concretion $A = \text{new } \vec{x}\,\langle \vec{y} \rangle.P$, again assuming $z \notin \vec{x}$ and $\vec{x}$ not free in Q:

$$\text{new } z\,(\text{new } \vec{x}\,\langle \vec{y} \rangle.P) \stackrel{\text{def}}{=} \begin{cases} \text{new } z\vec{x}\,\langle \vec{y} \rangle.P & \text{if } z \in \vec{y} \\ \text{new } \vec{x}\,\langle \vec{y} \rangle.\text{new } z\,P & \text{otherwise} \end{cases}$$
$$(\text{new } \vec{x}\,\langle \vec{y} \rangle.P) \mid Q \stackrel{\text{def}}{=} \text{new } \vec{x}\,\langle \vec{y} \rangle.(P \mid Q).$$

From this definition we derive some useful structural congruences:

Proposition 12.5

$$(1) \qquad A \mid (P \mid Q) \;\equiv\; (A \mid P) \mid Q$$

$$(2) \qquad \mathsf{new}\, x\,(A \mid Q) \;\equiv\; \begin{cases} A \mid \mathsf{new}\, x\, Q & (x\ not\ free\ in\ A) \\ \mathsf{new}\, x\, A \mid Q & (x\ not\ free\ in\ Q) \end{cases}$$

$$(3) \quad (F \mid P)\,@\,(C \mid Q) \;\equiv\; (F@C) \mid P \mid Q$$

$$(4) \qquad \mathsf{new}\, x\,(F@C) \;\equiv\; \begin{cases} F\,@\,\mathsf{new}\, x\, C & (x\ not\ free\ in\ F) \\ \mathsf{new}\, x\, F\,@\,C & (x\ not\ free\ in\ C) \end{cases}$$

Proof Straightforward, using Definitions 12.1 and 12.4, and the laws of structural congruence. $\qquad\qquad\qquad\qquad\qquad\qquad\qquad\qquad\qquad\qquad\qquad\qquad\quad\Box$

We are now ready to define commitment rules.

12.2 Commitment rules

We have seen that the commitments $P \xrightarrow{x} F$, $P \xrightarrow{\overline{x}} C$ are the proper generalisations for the π-calculus of the transitions $P \xrightarrow{a} P'$, $P \xrightarrow{\overline{a}} P'$. We now give the formal rules of commitment, analogous to the formal transition rules given in Definition 5.1. The rules do not employ structural congruence, but alpha-conversion is allowed.

Definition 12.6 Commitment *The commitments of a process are exactly those which can be inferred from the four rules in the table below, together with alpha-conversion:*

COMMITMENT RULES

$$\text{SUM}_\text{C}: \quad M + \alpha A + N \xrightarrow{\alpha} A$$

$$\text{L-REACT}_\text{C}: \quad \frac{P \xrightarrow{x} F \qquad Q \xrightarrow{\overline{x}} C}{P \mid Q \xrightarrow{\tau} F@C} \qquad\qquad \text{R-REACT}_\text{C}: \quad \frac{P \xrightarrow{\overline{x}} C \qquad Q \xrightarrow{x} F}{P \mid Q \xrightarrow{\tau} F@C}$$

$$\text{L-PAR}_\text{C}: \quad \frac{P \xrightarrow{\alpha} A}{P \mid Q \xrightarrow{\alpha} A \mid Q} \qquad\qquad \text{R-PAR}_\text{C}: \quad \frac{Q \xrightarrow{\alpha} A}{P \mid Q \xrightarrow{\alpha} A \mid P}$$

$$\text{RES}_\text{C}: \quad \frac{P \xrightarrow{\alpha} A}{\mathsf{new}\, x\, P \xrightarrow{\alpha} \mathsf{new}\, x\, A} \ \ if\ \alpha \notin \{x, \overline{x}\} \qquad\qquad \text{REP}_\text{C}: \quad \frac{P \mid\, !P \xrightarrow{\alpha} A}{!P \xrightarrow{\alpha} A}$$

The rules L-PAR$_\text{C}$, R-PAR$_\text{C}$ and RES$_\text{C}$ allow a commitment to occur in the context of a parallel composition or restriction, and they use the operations defined in 12.4. REP$_C$ is the only rule which infers transitions for a replicated process; hence $!P$ and $P|!P$ have exactly the same transitions.

Here is an example of inferring a commitment, laid out as a tree:

$$\cfrac{\cfrac{\rule{4cm}{0.4pt}}{\overline{y}\langle x\rangle.Q + \overline{w}\langle v\rangle.R \xrightarrow{\overline{y}} \langle x\rangle.Q}\ \text{SUM}_C}{}$$

$$\cfrac{\rule{2.5cm}{0.4pt}}{y(z).P \xrightarrow{y} (z).P}\ \text{SUM}_C \qquad \cfrac{\text{new}\,x\,(\overline{y}\langle x\rangle.Q + \overline{w}\langle v\rangle.R) \xrightarrow{\overline{y}} \text{new}\,x\,\langle x\rangle.Q}{}\ \text{RES}_C$$

$$\cfrac{\rule{9cm}{0.4pt}}{y(z).P\ |\ \text{new}\,x\,(\overline{y}\langle x\rangle.Q + \overline{w}\langle v\rangle.R) \xrightarrow{\tau} \text{new}\,x\,(\{x\!/\!z\}P\ |\ Q)}\ \text{L-REACT}_C$$

At each node of the tree there is a commitment, together with the name of the rule by which it was inferred from its 'children'.

Exercise 12.7 For the process P of Example 9.2, infer the commitments $P \xrightarrow{\tau} P_1$, $P \xrightarrow{\tau} P_2$ and $P_2 \xrightarrow{\tau} P_3$ using the commitment rules. Compare the inference with the one of Exercise 9.17, using the reaction rules. Also infer the commitment

$$P \xrightarrow{\overline{x}} \langle y\rangle.\text{new}\,z\,(0\ |\ x(u).\overline{u}\langle v\rangle\ |\ \overline{x}\langle z\rangle)\,,$$

and discover the other two commitments $P \xrightarrow{\alpha} A$ with $\alpha \neq \tau$. ∎

As in Section 5.1 we can prove a simple relationship between our commitment relation and structural congruence:

Theorem 12.8 *If* $P \xrightarrow{\alpha} A$ *and* $P \equiv Q$, *then there exists* B *such that* $Q \xrightarrow{\alpha} B$ *and* $A \equiv B$. *Hence* $\equiv$ *is a strong bisimulation (see Definition 12.13).*

The proof follows the lines of Proposition 5.2 and Theorem 5.13. We now proceed to show that the reaction relations $\rightarrow$ and the silent commitment relation $\xrightarrow{\tau}$ coincide up to $\equiv$, and also that if $P \xrightarrow{\lambda} A$ then P and A have a close syntactic connection. The results are exact analogues of those in Section 5.1, and we omit the proofs.

Lemma 12.9 *If* $P \rightarrow P'$ *then* $P \xrightarrow{\tau}\equiv P'$.

Lemma 12.10 *Let* $P \xrightarrow{\lambda} A$. *Then* P *and* A *can be expressed, up to structural congruence, in the form*

$$\begin{aligned} P &\equiv\ \text{new}\,\vec{z}\,((\lambda B + M)\ |\ Q) \\ A &\equiv\ \text{new}\,\vec{z}\,(B\ |\ Q) \end{aligned}$$

where λ *is not restricted by* new $\vec{z}$.

Theorem 12.11 $P \xrightarrow{\tau}\equiv P'$ *if and only if* $P \rightarrow P'$.

Proposition 12.12

(1) *Given P, there are only finitely many commitments $P \xrightarrow{\alpha} A$.*

(2) *If $P \xrightarrow{\alpha} A$ then $\mathrm{fn}(A, \alpha) \subseteq \mathrm{fn}(P)$.*

(3) *If $P \xrightarrow{\alpha} A$ and σ is any substitution then $\sigma P \xrightarrow{\sigma\alpha} \sigma A$.*

12.3 Strong bisimulation, strong equivalence

Hitherto the analogy between commitments in the π-calculus and the transition relation of Chapter 5 has been very close. In proceeding to deal with bisimulation, we now have to deal properly with the fact that the target A of a commitment $P \xrightarrow{\alpha} A$ is not a process, but an agent (i.e. an abstraction or concretion). So we have to bring agents into the picture in defining what bisimulation means.

We shall be using binary relations over $\mathcal{P}^{\pi}$. For any such relation $\mathcal{S}$, we shall consider it extended to a relation over $\mathcal{A}^{\pi}$; it is defined to hold between two abstractions and between two concretions of like arity, as follows:

FSG means for all $\vec{y}$, $F\langle\vec{y}\rangle \, \mathcal{S} \, G\langle\vec{y}\rangle$ (where $F, G : n$ and $|\vec{y}| = n$)

CSD means $C \equiv \mathrm{new}\,\vec{z}\,\langle\vec{y}\rangle.P$ and $D \equiv \mathrm{new}\,\vec{z}\,\langle\vec{y}\rangle.Q$ such that $P\mathcal{S}Q$.

Then we define simulation exactly as one would expect, by analogy with Definition 3.3:

Definition 12.13 Strong simulation *A binary relation $\mathcal{S}$ over $\mathcal{P}^{\pi}$ is a strong simulation if, whenever $P\mathcal{S}Q$,*

if $P \xrightarrow{\alpha} A$ then there exists B such that $Q \xrightarrow{\alpha} B$ and $A\mathcal{S}B$.

If both $\mathcal{S}$ and its converse are strong simulations then $\mathcal{S}$ is a strong bisimulation. Two agents A and B are strongly equivalent, written $A \sim B$, if the pair (A, B) is in some strong bisimulation.

Note one point in particular. If $F = (\vec{x}).P$ and $G = (\vec{x}).Q$ are two abstractions, to ensure that $F \sim G$ it is not sufficient simply that $P \sim Q$; we must have $\{\vec{y}/\vec{x}\}P \sim \{\vec{y}/\vec{x}\}Q$ for all $\vec{y}$. An example to illustrate this difference will be found in Section 12.4.

Proposition 12.14 $\sim$ *is an equivalence relation, and is itself a strong bisimulation.*

The notion of bisimulation up to $\equiv$ can be justified, and used, just as it was in Section 5.2:

Definition 12.15 Strong bisimulation up to $\equiv$ *A binary relation $\mathcal{S}$ over $\mathcal{P}$*

is a strong simulation up to ≡ *if, whenever PSQ,*

if $P \xrightarrow{\alpha} A$ *then there exists* B *such that* $Q \xrightarrow{\alpha} B$ *and* $A \equiv S \equiv B$.

S *is a* strong bisimulation up to ≡ *if its converse also has this property.*

Proposition 12.16 *If* S *is a strong bisimulation up to* ≡ *and PSQ, then* $P \sim Q$.

As before, we can show that every process is strongly bisimilar to a summation:

Proposition 12.17 *For all processes* $P \in \mathcal{P}^\pi$, $P \sim \Sigma\{\alpha A \mid P \xrightarrow{\alpha} A\}$.

From this result, an expansion law analogous to Proposition 5.23 can be derived, but we omit it.

Example 12.18 Equivalent summation Let us express R as a summation, up to $\sim$, where

$$R = \mathsf{new}\, x \, \overbrace{(x(y).P_1}^{P} \mid \overbrace{\mathsf{new}\, z \, (\overline{x}\langle z\rangle.Q_1 + y(w).Q_2))}^{Q} .$$

(Assume that z, w are not free in P.) Informally, it is easy to see that there is one possible reaction – i.e. a τ commitment involving the channel x, and that (since x in restricted) there is only one other commitment, namely along the y channel. Let us see how this works formally. First, using the commitment rulers we find that P has one commitment and Q has two:

$$P \xrightarrow{x} (y)P_1$$

$$Q \quad \begin{cases} \xrightarrow{\overline{x}} & \mathsf{new}\, z \, \langle z\rangle.Q_1 \\ \xrightarrow{y} & (w).\mathsf{new}\, z \, Q_2 . \end{cases}$$

This yields four commitments for $P|Q$:

$$P \mid Q \quad \begin{cases} \xrightarrow{x} & (y).P_1 \mid Q \\ \xrightarrow{\overline{x}} & \mathsf{new}\, z \, \langle z\rangle.Q_1 \mid P \\ \xrightarrow{y} & (w).\mathsf{new}\, z \, Q_2 \mid P \\ \xrightarrow{\tau} & (y).P_1 \,@\, \mathsf{new}\, z \, \langle z\rangle.Q_1 \end{cases}$$

which can be reduced by Definition 12.4 to

$$P \mid Q \quad \begin{cases} \xrightarrow{x} & (y).(P_1 \mid Q) \\ \xrightarrow{\overline{x}} & \mathsf{new}\, z \, \langle z\rangle.(Q_1 \mid P) \\ \xrightarrow{y} & (w).(\mathsf{new}\, z \, Q_2 \mid P) \\ \xrightarrow{\tau} & \mathsf{new}\, z \, (\{z/y\}P_1 \mid Q_1) . \end{cases}$$

From this we deduce only two commitments for R:

$$R \begin{cases} \xrightarrow{y} & (w).\text{new } x \, (\text{new } z \, Q_2 \mid P) \\ \xrightarrow{\tau} & \text{new } xz \, (\{z/y\}P_1 \mid Q_1) \, . \end{cases}$$

It therefore follows by Prop 12.17 that

$$R \sim y(w).\text{new } x \, (P \mid \text{new } z \, Q_2) + \tau. \text{new } xz \, (\{z/y\}P_1 \mid Q_1) \, . \qquad \blacksquare$$

Exercise 12.19 Where have we used the assumption that z, w are not free in P? $\qquad \blacksquare$

Exercise 12.20 Prove that

$$(\text{new } x)xF \sim 0 \, , \quad (\text{new } x)\overline{x}C \sim 0$$

and also that

$$(\text{new } x)!xF \sim 0 \, , \quad (\text{new } x)!\overline{x}C \sim 0 \, .$$

These are important properties; they say that 'inaccessible processes may be garbage-collected'! $\qquad \blacksquare$

Exercise 12.21 Recall $System_1$ of Section 8.2. Show the structural congruence

$$\begin{aligned} System_1 &\equiv \text{new } \vec{\ell_2} \, (S \mid Idtrans_2) \, , \text{ where} \\ S &\equiv \text{new } \vec{\ell_1} \, (Car_1 \mid Trans_1 \mid Control_1) \, . \end{aligned}$$

($\vec{\ell_i}$ is short for $gain_i, lose_i, talk_i, switch_i$ and $Car_1 \stackrel{\text{def}}{=} Car\langle talk_1, switch_1 \rangle$.) Next, show that the only commitments of S are $S \xrightarrow{\tau} S$ and $S \xrightarrow{\tau} S'$ for a certain S'. (The first represents talk between Car_1 and $Trans_1$.) Then show that for a certain $System'$

$$System_1 \sim \tau.System_1 + \tau.System' \, . \qquad \blacksquare$$

12.4 Congruence

We now prepare to show that $\sim$ is a congruence relation. We must be careful to see what this means, as the following example indicates.

Example 12.22 Substitution can negate equivalence First note that if $x \neq y$ then

$$\overline{x} \mid y \sim \overline{x}.y + y.\overline{x} \, .$$

To prove this, we show that $\mathcal{S} = \{(\overline{x}|y, \ \overline{x}.y+y.\overline{x}), \ (y,y), \ (\overline{x},\overline{x}), \ (0,0)\}$ is a strong bisimulation. The only difficulty could be with the first pair. But note that the only commitments of $\overline{x}|y$ are $\overline{x}|y \xrightarrow{y} \overline{x}$ and $\overline{x}|y \xrightarrow{\overline{x}} y$, and of the other member are $\overline{x}.y+y.\overline{x} \xrightarrow{y} \overline{x}$ and $\overline{x}.y+y.\overline{x} \xrightarrow{\overline{x}} y$, and these are identical commitments. On the other hand if we substitute x for y we destroy the equivalence, since $\overline{x}|x \not\sim \overline{x}.x+x.\overline{x}$. ∎

Exercise 12.23 Why is $\overline{x}|x \not\sim \overline{x}.x+x.\overline{x}$?
Hint: Find a τ commitment which distinguishes them. ∎

What this shows is that we can have $P \sim Q$, but for some substitution $\sigma P \not\sim \sigma Q$, and so $(y).P \not\sim (y).Q$. Therefore we can have $P \sim Q$ but $z(\overline{y}).P \not\sim z(y).Q$.

Thus there is a process context, namely $z(y).[\ ]$, which does not preserve strong equivalence; hence, according to Definition 9.5 strong equivalence is not a process congruence. Nevertheless, we can claim that $\sim$ is a congruence in a new sense, provided that we think of $z(y).P$ as zF where F is the abstraction $(y).P$. This is consistent with our new view of process summations as $\alpha_1 A_1 + \cdots + \alpha_n A_n$ rather than $\pi_1.P_1 + \cdots + \pi_n.P_n$. The following definition makes the new kind of congruence precise:

Definition 12.24 Agent congruence *An equivalence relation $\cong$ over $\mathcal{A}^\pi$ is an* agent congruence *if it is preserved by contexts in the following sense:*

(1) *If $A \cong B$ then $\alpha A + M \cong \alpha B + M$ (where M is any sum)*
(2) *If $P \cong Q$ then* new $a\,P \cong$ new $a\,Q$, $P|R \cong Q|R$, $R|P \cong R|Q$, $!P \cong !Q$ *and for concretions* new $\vec{x}\,\langle\vec{y}\rangle.P \cong$ new $\vec{x}\,\langle\vec{y}\rangle.Q$
(3) *For abstractions, if $\{\vec{y}/\vec{x}\}P \cong \{\vec{y}/\vec{x}\}Q$ for all $\vec{y}$, then $(\vec{x}).P \cong (\vec{x}).Q$.*

The notion of agent congruence is more complex than process congruence. This is the necessary price we pay for the passage of messages in reactions. In particular, congruence of abstractions is analogous to the equivalence of procedures in a conventional programming language. Consider two procedure declarations in such a language, procedure $F(x_1,\ldots,x_n)$; P and procedure $G(x_1,\ldots,x_n)$; Q. Their respective procedure bodies P and Q employ the formal parameters $\vec{x}$, and for F and G to be considered equivalent we would naturally require their bodies P and Q to be equivalent for *all* possible values $y_1,\ldots,y_n$ of the formal parameters.

We now have what we want:

Proposition 12.25 Strong congruence *Strong equivalence $\sim$ in the π-calculus is an agent congruence.*

We omit the proof. This result shows that strong equivalence is a practically useful equivalence relation.

12.5 Basic congruence properties of replication

Clearly if $P \equiv Q$ then $P \sim Q$. We have seen several cases where $P \not\equiv Q$ but $P \sim Q$. The main difference between the two congruences is that $P \sim Q$ may hold even when P and Q are very different with respect to concurrent composition. (The simplest example is $x \mid y \sim x.y + y.x$.)

There are also some strong congruences between different replication patterns. Of course we have the *structural* congruence $!P \equiv P|!P$; but intuitively, replication 'ought to' satisfy more equations than this one.

First, perhaps surprisingly, it turns out that $!P \not\equiv !P|!P$. (It is quite hard to prove this; in fact it is often hard, given a set of axioms, to demonstrate that something *does not* follow from them.) Yet these two expressions surely ought to be equivalent in some sense; our intuition is that they both provide as many copies of P as you like, and to have two such copy-generators cannot be better than having one. In fact, they are strongly congruent:

Proposition 12.26 $!P \sim !P \mid !P$.

Proof We might expect to show that $\{ (!P, !P|!P) \mid P \in \mathcal{P}^\pi \}$ is a bisimulation, but actually we have to work a bit harder. We need to include some more pairs. In fact, we shall show that

$$\mathcal{S} \overset{\text{def}}{=} \{ (!P|Q, \ !P|!P|Q) \mid P, Q \in \mathcal{P}^\pi \}$$

is a strong bisimulation up to $\equiv$. The result follows by taking $Q = 0$.

Consider first all the possible commitments $!P|!P|Q \overset{\alpha}{\to} B$ of the right-hand member of a pair. By analysis of the commitment rules, we find that they can arise only in five ways as follows:

(1) $!P \overset{\alpha}{\to} B'$ with $B \equiv B' \mid !P \mid Q$;

(2) $Q \overset{\alpha}{\to} B'$ with $B \equiv B' \mid !P \mid !P$;

(3) $\alpha = \tau$ and $!P \overset{x}{\to} F, !P \overset{\overline{x}}{\to} C$ such that $A \equiv F@C \mid Q$;

(4) $\alpha = \tau$ and $!P \overset{x}{\to} F, Q \overset{\overline{x}}{\to} C$ such that $A \equiv F@C \mid !P$;

(5) The latter with $!P, Q$ interchanged.

We wish to match each of these by a commitment $!P|Q \overset{\alpha}{\to} A$ of the left-hand member, with $A\mathcal{S}B$. We shall just consider case (3); the others are no harder. So we have

$$\alpha = \tau, \ !P \overset{x}{\to} F, \ !P \overset{\overline{x}}{\to} C, \ \text{and } B \equiv F@C \mid Q .$$

Now these transitions can only be inferred by the commitment rules if for some F' and C' there are transitions

$$P \overset{x}{\to} F' \text{ and } P \overset{\overline{x}}{\to} C', \ \text{where } F \equiv F' \mid !P \text{ and } C \equiv C' \mid !P .$$

Tracing back through these equations, we find that the original commitment was of the form

$$!P \mid !P \mid Q \xrightarrow{\alpha} \overbrace{!P \mid !P \mid F'@C' \mid Q}^{B},$$

and since $!P \equiv !P|P|P$ we can match this with the commitment

$$!P \mid Q \xrightarrow{\alpha} \overbrace{!P \mid F'@C' \mid Q}^{A}$$

of the left-hand member; by taking $Q' = F'@C'|Q$ we then see that $A\mathcal{S}B$ up to $\equiv$, as required.

It is somewhat easier to show that each commitment of the left-hand member is matched by the right-hand member. □

The other principle congruence property of replication is as follows:

Proposition 12.27 $!!P \sim !P$.

We shall leave the proof as an exercise.

Exercise 12.28 Find a strong bisimulation which will prove this proposition. *Hint*: Just as in the previous result, some extra pairs must be present in the bisimulation. Find them by experiment. ∎

Finally, we note that neither of the last two results holds for structural congruence:

Proposition 12.29

(1) $!P \not\equiv !P \mid !P$;
(2) $!!P \not\equiv !P$.

The proof is left as quite a hard exercise.

Exercise 12.30 Prove this proposition. We shall not need it for any other purpose, but the logically-minded may enjoy it as a puzzle.
Hint: Consider (2) first, as it's easier. Define the *replication depth* (rd) of a process expression to be the maximum depth of nesting of replication within it; for example, the rd of $!(!!0|!0)$ is 3. If $Q \equiv R$ is provable by just one use of any rule of structural congruence, what can you say about the rd's of Q and R? What can you say about the rd's of $!!P$ and $!P$? Once you have settled (2), try to find an attribute of process expressions, like replication depth but more refined, which will settle (1). ∎

12.6 Replicated resources

Our next property of replication is more subtle. In previous chapters we have many times met the construction $!xF$, where the replication is so to speak controlled by the channel x. Indeed, if a system contains

$$\text{new}\, x \,(P \mid !xF)$$

then we can think of $!xF$ as a private resource of P.

Now suppose $P = P_1 | P_2$ in the above. Then P_1 and P_2 share the private resource; either of them may activate a copy by executing a commitment $\overline{x}C$. Well then, is it true that

$$\text{new}\, x \,(P_1 \mid P_2 \mid !xF) \;\sim\; \text{new}\, x \,(P_1 \mid !xF) \mid \text{new}\, x \,(P_2 \mid !xF) \,?$$

That is, does it make any difference if P_1 and P_2 *each* have identical private resources?

Yes, in general, there is a difference. But it only arises if P_1 and P_2 use x not only in the form $\overline{x}C$, but also in other ways e.g. to communicate with each other. For example if $P_1 = x$ and $P_2 = \overline{x}$ then you should be able to find an F for which the above equation does not hold.

Exercise 12.31 Do this. F can be very simple indeed. ∎

To exclude this we make a definition:

Definition 12.32 *An agent A is* negative *on x if its only free occurrences of x are in the form $\overline{x}C$.*

Thus if P is negative on x it can only send messages on x; it cannot receive them on x, nor can it transmit x itself as a message. Negativity is preserved by commitment:

Proposition 12.33 *If P is negative on x and $P \xrightarrow{\alpha} A$, then A is negative on x.*

Intuitively, if P_1, P_2 and F are all negative on x then P_1 and P_2 can never communicate with each other on that channel – not even by acquiring a copy of F. Therefore it cannot change their behaviour to enclose them in separate restrictions $\text{new}\, x$. The following elegant result makes the intuition precise:

Theorem 12.34 *Let P_1, P_2 and F be negative on x. Then*

$$\text{new}\, x \,(P_1 \mid P_2 \mid !xF) \;\sim\; \text{new}\, x \,(P_1 \mid !xF) \mid \text{new}\, x \,(P_2 \mid !xF) \,.$$

Proof We shall not carry out the proof in detail. It consists of proving that the set of all pairs

$$\text{new } \vec{y} \text{ new } x \, (P_1 \mid P_2 \mid !xF) \, , \quad \text{new } \vec{y} \, (\text{new } x \, (P_1 \mid !xF) \mid \text{new } x \, (P_2 \mid !xF))$$

such that P_1, P_2 and F are negative on x is a bisimulation up to $\equiv$. $\qquad\square$

Exercise 12.35 Consider the encoding of recursion by replication, given in Section 9.5. Recall that we can replace a recursive definition $A(\vec{x}) \stackrel{\text{def}}{=} Q_A$ by a construction based on replication, by defining a certain translation $\widehat{P}$ for any process P which uses A. Use Theorem 12.34 to prove that

$$\widehat{P_1 \mid P_2} \sim \widehat{P_1} \mid \widehat{P_2} \, . \qquad\blacksquare$$

This shows that, as we would expect, having one copy of a recursive definition around is just the same as having many copies.

The last theorem says that the construction $\text{new } x \, (\text{-} \mid !xF)$ can be 'pushed inside' or 'distributed over' a parallel composition. The next theorem says that it can also be pushed inside a replication. This should not surprise us, because a replication $!P$ is just a multiple parallel composition, so to push the resource inside it means that every copy of P gets its own copy of the resource – which should not make any difference.

Theorem 12.36 *Let P and F be negative on x. Then*

$$\text{new } x \, (!P \mid !xF) \, \sim \, ! \, \text{new } x \, (P \mid !xF) \, .$$

We omit the proof; again we have to exhibit an appropriate bisimulation, and we also have to use the previous result.

We shall need both these theorems when in Chapter 13 we prove that our interpretation of the λ-calculus in the π-calculus is sound.

12.7 Summary

We have defined bisimulation of π-calculus processes in terms of the notion of *commitment*, a refinement of the notion of transition. This led to the strong congruence relation $\sim$, analogous to that of Chapter 5. The replication operator ($!$) was studied in some detail, partly for its own importance (since it is the only way to define infinitely proceeding processes in the π-calculus), and partly as a source of good examples of strong congruence.

In the following chapter, by analogy with Chapters 6 and 7, we proceed to study the weak congruence relation $\approx$ which is insensitive to the internal behaviour of processes.

13

Observation Equivalence and Examples

This chapter corresponds to Chapters 6 and 7 in Part I. We first extend the notion of observation equivalence to deal with the added refinement that links are passed in reactions; then we present examples, all of which involve systems studied earlier in Part II.

13.1 Experiments

In Chapter 6 observation equivalence was defined in terms of the notion of *experiment*. An atomic experiment was represented by the relation $\overset{\lambda}{\Rightarrow}$, defined to mean $\Rightarrow\overset{\lambda}{\rightarrow}\Rightarrow$, for λ of the form a or $\overline{a}$. In the absence of message-passing there was complete symmetry between positive and negative experiments.

We have already seen the asymmetry in the π-calculus between positive and negative actions, in our treatment of strong bisimulation; it was represented by the contrast between abstractions and concretions. We must now confront another aspect of the asymmetry.

Input experiments In the commitment $P \overset{x}{\rightarrow} (\vec{y}).P'$, no account is taken of the actual message $\vec{z}$ supplied on the x channel. Indeed, the point of the abstraction $(\vec{y}).P'$ is to represent all the possible paths which P' may follow, depending upon the message $\vec{z}$ received. We shall now understand an atomic input experiment to consist of a commitment *together with* the supply of a particular message $\vec{z}$; the experiment will not only allow silent transitions to occur *before* the commitment to $(\vec{y}).P'$, but will also allow silent transitions of $\{\vec{z}/\vec{y}\}P'$ to occur *after* the commitment, in a manner possibly dependent upon $\vec{z}$. As a simple example, suppose

$$P = x(y).P', \quad \text{where } P' = \overline{y} \mid z.Q \mid w.R \,;$$

142

then after the respective messages $\overline{z}$, $\overline{w}$ there are different silent transitions

$$\{z/y\}P' \to Q \mid w.R \text{ and } \{w/y\}P' \to z.Q \mid R .$$

These considerations lead to the formal definition of input experiments below.

Output experiments In the commitment $P \xrightarrow{\overline{x}}$ new $\vec{z}\,\langle\vec{y}\rangle.P'$, we understand that the observer receives the message $\vec{y}$ (some of whose names may be restricted), and – in contrast with an input experiment – the observation has no influence on the subsequent behaviour of P'. Thus, apart from the use of a concretion to comprise such messages, there is little difference from Chapter 6 in the notion of output experiment.

Definition 13.1 Atomic experiment *The transition relation* $\xrightarrow{x\langle\vec{y}\rangle}$ *over* $\mathcal{P}^\pi$ *is defined as follows:*

$$P \xrightarrow{x\langle\vec{y}\rangle} P' \text{ if, for some } F, P \xrightarrow{x} F \text{ and } F\langle\vec{y}\rangle \equiv P' .$$

An atomic input experiment *is an instance of the relation* $\xrightarrow{x\langle\vec{y}\rangle}$, *defined as follows:*

$$P \overset{x\langle\vec{y}\rangle}{\Longrightarrow} P' \text{ iff } P \Rightarrow \xrightarrow{x\langle\vec{y}\rangle} \Rightarrow P' .$$

An atomic output experiment *is an instance of the relation* $\overset{\overline{x}}{\Rightarrow}$, *defined as follows:*

$$P \overset{\overline{x}}{\Rightarrow} \text{ new } \vec{z}\,\langle\vec{y}\rangle.P' \text{ if, for some } P'', P \Rightarrow \xrightarrow{\overline{x}} \text{ new } \vec{z}\,\langle\vec{y}\rangle.P'' \text{ and } P'' \Rightarrow P' .$$

It may be thought preferable to write $P \overset{\overline{x}}{\Rightarrow}$ new $\vec{z}\,\langle\vec{y}\rangle.P'$ in the form $P \overset{\overline{x}(\text{new }\vec{z})\langle\vec{y}\rangle}{\Longrightarrow} P'$, by analogy with $P \overset{x\langle\vec{y}\rangle}{\Longrightarrow} P'$. But this would obscure the fact that the scope of the restriction new $\vec{z}$ includes P' as well as $\langle\vec{y}\rangle$.

13.2 Weak bisimulation and congruence

In terms of atomic experiments, we readily define the following by analogy with Definition 6.2:

Definition 13.2 Weak simulation *A binary relation* $\mathcal{S}$ *over* $\mathcal{P}^\pi$ *is a* weak simulation *if, whenever* $P\mathcal{S}Q$,

    if $P \Rightarrow P'$ *then there exists* Q' *such that* $Q \Rightarrow Q'$ *and* $P'\mathcal{S}Q'$;
    if $P \overset{x\langle\vec{y}\rangle}{\Longrightarrow} P'$ *then there exists* Q' *such that* $Q \overset{x\langle\vec{y}\rangle}{\Longrightarrow} Q'$ *and* $P'\mathcal{S}Q'$;
    if $P \overset{\overline{x}}{\Rightarrow} C$ *then there exists* D *such that* $Q \overset{\overline{x}}{\Rightarrow} D$ *and* $C\mathcal{S}D$.

If both S and its converse are weak simulations then S is a weak bisimulation. Two agents A and B are weakly equivalent *or* observation equivalent, *written $A \approx B$, if the pair (A, B) is in some weak bisimulation.*

Just as with strong equivalence, the weak equivalence $F \approx G$ of two abstractions means that $F\langle \vec{y} \rangle \approx G\langle \vec{y} \rangle$ for all $\vec{y}$. Thus the assertion that $(\vec{x}).P \approx (\vec{x}).Q$ is stronger than $P \approx Q$; it asserts not only that $P \approx Q$ but also that $\{\vec{y}/\vec{x}\}P \approx \{\vec{y}/\vec{x}\}Q$ for all $\vec{y}$.

It is easy to show, by analogy with Proposition 6.3, that in order to establish S as a weak simulation it is only necessary to check single transitions:

Proposition 13.3 *A binary relation S is a weak simulation if and only if, whenever PSQ,*

> *if $P \to P'$ then there exists Q' such that $Q \Rightarrow Q'$ and $P'SQ'$;*
> *if $P \overset{x\langle\vec{y}\rangle}{\to} P'$ then there exists Q' such that $Q \overset{x\langle\vec{y}\rangle}{\Rightarrow} Q'$ and $P'SQ'$;*
> *if $P \overset{\overline{x}}{\to} C$ then there exists D such that $Q \overset{\overline{x}}{\Rightarrow} D$ and CSD .*

We now summarise some properties of weak equivalence which we shall need.

Proposition 13.4

> (1) *$\approx$ is an equivalence relation, and is itself a weak bisimulation;*
> (2) *$P \sim Q$ implies $P \approx Q$;*
> (3) *$P \approx \tau.P$.*

For completeness, we shall record that the notion of weak bisimulation up to $\equiv$ is valid here, just as it was in Section 6.2. We restate the appropriate definition and proposition.

Definition 13.5 Weak simulation up to $\sim$ *A binary relation S over $\mathcal{P}$ is a weak simulation up to $\sim$ if, whenever PSQ,*

> *if $P \to P'$ then there exists Q' such that $Q \Rightarrow Q'$ and $P' \sim S \sim Q'$;*
> *if $P \overset{x\langle\vec{y}\rangle}{\to} P'$ then there exists Q' such that $Q \overset{x\langle\vec{y}\rangle}{\Rightarrow} Q'$ and $P' \sim S \sim Q'$; if $P \overset{\overline{x}}{\to} C$ then there exists D such that $Q \overset{\overline{x}}{\Rightarrow} D$ and $C \sim S \sim D$.*

S is a weak bisimulation up to $\sim$ *if its converse also has this property.*

Proposition 13.6 *If S is a weak bisimulation up to $\sim$ and PSQ, then $P \approx Q$.*

As far as congruence is concerned, weak equivalence behaves just as well as strong equivalence (see Proposition 12.25):

Proposition 13.7 Observation congruence   *Observation equivalence is an agent congruence, that is:*

> (1) *If $A \approx B$ then $\alpha A + M \approx \alpha B + M$ (where M is any sum)*

(2) *If $P \approx Q$ then* new $a\,P \approx$ new $a\,Q$, $P|R \approx Q|R$, $R|P \approx R|Q$, $!P \approx$ $!Q$ *and for concretions* new $\vec{x}\,\langle\vec{y}\rangle.P \approx$ new $\vec{x}\,\langle\vec{y}\rangle.Q$

(3) *For abstractions, if $\{\vec{y}/\vec{x}\}P \approx \{\vec{y}/\vec{x}\}Q$ for all $\vec{y}$, then $(\vec{x}).P \approx (\vec{x}).Q$.*

13.3 Unique solution of equations

We shall now consider how we may generalise Theorem 6.19 which asserts that a family of equations over processes

$$X_i \approx \sum_j \alpha_{ij}.X_{k(i,j)} \qquad (i \in I)$$

has a unique solution up to $\approx$. In the π-calculus, where agents are usually parametric upon names, we want to solve equations for abstractions, not just for processes. We shall later give an illustration of this.

The following theorem asserts that uniqueness holds under similar conditions to Theorem 6.19.

Theorem 13.8 Unique solution *Let $\vec{X} = X_1, X_2, \ldots$ be a (possibly infinite) sequence of variables over abstractions. In the following formal equations*

$$\begin{aligned} X_1(\vec{x}_1) &\approx \alpha_{11}A_{11} + \cdots + \alpha_{1n_1}A_{1n_1} \\ X_2(\vec{x}_2) &\approx \alpha_{21}A_{21} + \cdots + \alpha_{2n_2}A_{2n_2} \\ &\cdots \qquad \cdots \;\cdots \end{aligned}$$

assume that each term αA on the right takes one of the two forms

xH, *where H is an abstraction of the form $(\vec{v}).X_k\langle\vec{w}\rangle$; or*

$\overline{x}C$, *where C is a concretion of the form* new $\vec{u}\,\langle\vec{v}\rangle.X_k\langle\vec{w}\rangle$.

Let the abstractions $\vec{F}$ and $\vec{G}$ be two solutions of the equations. (We can assume w.l.o.g. that their free names differ from any names bound in the formal equations.) Then

$$F_i \approx G_i, \;\text{ for all } i.$$

Proof For convenience, write $M_i[\vec{X}]$ for the right-hand side of the equation for X_i. We first prove a lemma:

Lemma If $R \approx F_i\langle\vec{t}\rangle$ or $R \approx G_i\langle\vec{t}\rangle$ and $R \Rightarrow R'$, then $R \approx R'$.

Proof For example $R \approx \{\vec{t}/\vec{x}_i\}M_i[\vec{F}]$, and the result follows since M_i admits no silent actions.

We shall show that

$$\mathcal{S} = \{(P,Q) \mid P \approx F_i\langle\vec{t}\rangle \text{ and } Q \approx G_i\langle\vec{t}\rangle \text{ for some } i \text{ and some } \vec{t}\}$$

is a weak bisimulation. So take an arbitrary pair $(P,Q) \in \mathcal{S}$. Let σ be the substitution $\{\vec{t}/\vec{x}_i\}$. Then we have $P \approx \sigma M_i[\vec{F}]$ and $Q \approx \sigma M_i[\vec{G}]$. Now consider all possible actions of P:

Case $P \to P'$. Then by the lemma $P \approx P'$, and by choosing $Q' = Q$ we have $Q \Rightarrow Q'$ with $(P', Q') \in \mathcal{S}$.

Case $P \xrightarrow{y\langle\vec{z}\rangle} P'$. Then $\sigma M_i[\vec{F}] \xrightarrow{y\langle\vec{z}\rangle} P'' \approx P'$. So M_i has a term $x(\vec{v}).X_k\langle\vec{w}\rangle$ with $\sigma x = y$ and

$$F_k\langle\rho\vec{w}\rangle \Rightarrow P'' \text{ where } \rho = \{\vec{z}/\vec{v}\}\sigma,$$

so by the lemma $P' \approx F_k\langle\rho\vec{w}\rangle$. But also $\sigma M_i[\vec{G}] \xrightarrow{y\langle\vec{z}\rangle} G_k\langle\rho\vec{w}\rangle$; hence there exists Q' such that $Q \xrightarrow{y\langle\vec{z}\rangle} Q' \approx G_k\langle\rho\vec{w}\rangle$, so $(P', Q') \in \mathcal{S}$ as required.

Case $P \xrightarrow{\overline{y}} C$. Then $\sigma M_i[\vec{F}] \xrightarrow{\overline{y}} C' \approx C$. So M_i has a term $\overline{x}$ new $\vec{u}\langle\vec{v}\rangle.X_k\langle\vec{w}\rangle$ with $\sigma x = y$ and

$$F_k\langle\sigma\vec{w}\rangle \Rightarrow C' \text{ with } C' \equiv \text{ new } \vec{u}\langle\sigma\vec{v}\rangle P',$$

so by the lemma $C \approx$ new $\vec{u}\langle\sigma\vec{v}\rangle F_k\langle\sigma\vec{w}\rangle$. But also $\sigma M_i[\vec{G}] \xrightarrow{\overline{y}}$ new $\vec{u}\langle\sigma\vec{v}\rangle.G_k\langle\sigma\vec{w}\rangle$; calling this D', there exists D such that $Q \xrightarrow{\overline{y}} D \approx D'$, and $(C, D) \in \mathcal{S}$ as required. $\square$

13.4 List programming

The following example illustrates weak equivalence, and employs the fact that it is an agent congruence.

Let us return to Section 10.4, where we worked with processes representing data structures, and in particular list structures. We shall justify the claim that our definitions of operations on lists are sound.

Theorem 10.20

$$\begin{aligned} Move(L) &\approx L \\ Append(K, L) &\approx K \oplus L. \end{aligned}$$

Proof We shall only do the first; the second follows the same pattern. We must show

$$\text{new } \ell \, (L\langle\ell\rangle \mid Copy\langle\ell m\rangle) \approx L\langle m\rangle, \tag{1}$$

for which we shall use induction on the structure of L. Recall that

$$Copy\langle\ell m\rangle = \text{new } nc \, (\overline{\ell}\langle nc\rangle \mid n.P + c.F) \tag{2}$$

where

$$F(v\ell') = \text{new } m' \, (Node\langle mvm'\rangle \mid Copy\langle\ell'm'\rangle) \text{ and } P = Nil\langle m\rangle. \tag{3}$$

Case $L = Nil$ (inductive basis). We have

$$\text{new}\,\ell\,(Nil\langle\ell\rangle \mid Copy\langle\ell m\rangle)$$
$$= \quad \text{new}\,\ell\,(\ell(nc).\bar{n} \mid \text{new}\,nc\,(\bar{\ell}\langle nc\rangle \mid n.P + c.F)) \qquad \text{from (2)}$$
$$\sim \quad \tau.\tau.P$$
$$\approx \quad Nil\langle m\rangle \qquad \text{from (3)}$$

as required.

Case $L = Cons(V, K)$ (inductive step). We have

$$\text{new}\,\ell\,(Cons(V, K)\langle\ell\rangle \mid Copy\langle\ell m\rangle)$$
$$= \quad \text{new}\,\ell\,(\text{new}\,v\ell'\,(\ell(nc).\bar{c}\langle v\ell'\rangle \mid V\langle v\rangle \mid K\langle\ell'\rangle)$$
$$\mid \text{new}\,nc\,(\bar{\ell}\langle nc\rangle \mid n.P + c.F)) \qquad \text{from (2)}$$
$$\sim \quad \tau.\tau.\text{new}\,v\ell'\,(F\langle v\ell'\rangle \mid V\langle v\rangle \mid K\langle\ell'\rangle)$$
$$\approx \quad \text{new}\,vm'\,(Node\langle mvm'\rangle \mid V\langle v\rangle \mid \text{new}\,\ell'\,(K\langle\ell'\rangle \mid Copy\langle\ell'm'\rangle))$$
$$\qquad\qquad\qquad \text{from (3)}$$
$$\approx \quad \text{new}\,vm'\,(Node\langle mvm'\rangle \mid V\langle v\rangle \mid K\langle m'\rangle) \qquad \text{by induction}$$
$$\equiv \quad Cons(V, K)\langle m\rangle\,.$$

This completes the proof that $Move(L) \approx L$. Note that, in substituting the inductive assumption in the last step but one, we have used the congruence property of weak equivalence. ◻

Exercise 13.9 Complete the proof of the theorem by proving the second equation. You will be able to follow the line of Exercise 10.19 in proving Prop 10.18. There, the transition relation $\rightarrow^*$ was used; here, because of the presence of a restriction, you will be able to strengthen the transition relation to weak equivalence ($\approx$). ∎

A proof of this kind is, of course, at a very low level. This is true for most proofs done from first principles in the π-calculus. Uniform proof techniques for reasoning about data structures can be derived which make proofs of this kind much less detailed.

13.5 Imperative programming

The constructions of Section 10.5 dealt with mutable reference cells, and with assigning values to them and testing them for emptiness. Such constructions would be useful in giving the formal semantics of a concurrent imperative programming language. We have no intention of embarking on this task; we would only remark that reference cells give the full power of *pointers* in the languages Pascal and C, for example. Here we use the reference cell constructions to provide two simple illustrations of weak equivalence.

Consider first the simple sequential 'program'

$$Prog_1 = new\, r\, (Assign(Refcases(Q, F)\langle r\rangle)\langle rv\rangle \mid Nullref\langle r\rangle)\,.$$

It means 'assign v to the empty cell r, then test r; if it is empty do Q, otherwise do F upon the contents of r'. Note that the register r is restricted, so no other program can interfere with it. You would therefore expect that this program is equivalent to 'do F upon the value v, with this value also stored in r', i.e.

$$Prog_1 \approx new\, r\, (F\langle v\rangle \mid Ref\langle rv\rangle)\,.$$

Exercise 13.10 Prove this result. You will need simple uses of Proposition 12.17, together with the property $\tau.P \approx P$. What weaker statement could you make if r were not restricted in $Prog_1$? ■

Now consider a concurrent program, with two threads sharing the use of a register r:

$$Prog_2 = new\, r\, (Assign(P)\langle rv\rangle \mid Refcases(Q, F)\langle r\rangle \mid Nullref\langle r\rangle)\,.$$

Here, there is contention for access to r; the test for whether to enter Q or F will have a different outcome, depending on whether or not the assignment of v to r has taken place. Let us make the simplifying assumption that there is no further use of r, i.e. that r is not free in P, Q or F. Then we expect the following, representing the nondeterminism inherent in the program:

$$Prog_2 \approx \tau.\,(P \mid Q) + \tau.\,(P \mid F\langle v\rangle)\,.$$

Exercise 13.11 Prove this result. ■

13.6 Elastic buffer

In this section we shall illustrate the use of the unique solution property in proving correct an implementation of an unbounded buffer.

In Section 7.4 we specified the behaviour of a buffer with fixed capacity n, and then verified its implementation by a chain of n cells, each capable of holding a single value. Let us begin here by specifying the behaviour of a buffer of infinitely variable capacity. In contrast with Section 7.4 note that the π-calculus allows us to represent the data by names, so that there is no limitation on the size or nature of the data domain.

Definition 13.12 *The states $Buff^{(n)}\langle x_1, \ldots, x_n\rangle$ of an unbounded buffer with* *input port ℓ_1 and output port r_1 are specified as follows:*

$$Buff^{(0)} \quad \stackrel{\text{def}}{=} \quad \ell_1(x).\,Buff^{(1)}\langle x \rangle$$

$$Buff^{(n+1)}(x_1, \dots, x_{n+1}) \quad \stackrel{\text{def}}{=} \quad \ell_1(x).\,Buff^{(n+2)}\langle x, x_1, \dots, x_{n+1} \rangle$$
$$+ \overline{r_1}\langle x_{n+1} \rangle.\,Buff^{(n)}\langle x_1, \dots, x_n \rangle\,.$$

Now we would like to implement this specification by a chain of cells which grows and shrinks according to the contents of the buffer. In Section 8.3 we introduced a buffer cell with two states B' and C' defined as follows (we drop the primes here):

$$B(\vec{\ell}, \vec{r}) \quad \stackrel{\text{def}}{=} \quad \overline{\ell_2}\langle \vec{r} \rangle$$

$$C(x, \vec{\ell}, \vec{r}) \quad \stackrel{\text{def}}{=} \quad \overline{r_1}\langle x \rangle.\,B\langle \vec{\ell}, \vec{r} \rangle + r_2(\vec{r'}).\,C\langle x, \vec{\ell}, \vec{r'} \rangle\,.$$

(Throughout this section we shall abbreviate $\ell_1 \ell_2$ and $r_1 r_2$ by $\vec{\ell}$ and $\vec{r}$.) In the empty state B the buffer cell can cut itself out of a chain of cells by passing the address of its right neighbour to its left neighbour along the channel ℓ_2; in the full state $C\langle x \rangle$ it can yield up its datum x or receive from its right neighbour, along the channel r_2, the address of a new right neighbour.

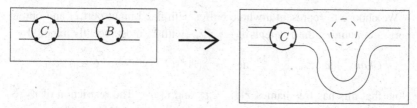

To make a chain of cells useful as a buffer we must be able to create new cells. So we introduces an agent A to reside at the left (joining) end of the buffer; each time A receives a new datum it creates a new C cell, and it also possesses the ability to change its right neighbour:

$$A(\vec{\ell}, \vec{r}) \quad \stackrel{\text{def}}{=} \quad \ell_1(x).\,(A \frown C\langle x \rangle)\langle \vec{\ell}, \vec{r} \rangle + r_2(\vec{r'}).\,A\langle \vec{\ell}, \vec{r'} \rangle\,.$$

Note that we use the linking operator of Example 9.24, on abstractions of arity 4. We first prove two simple properties which reflect the capacity for 'cut-out'.

Lemma 13.13 $C\langle x \rangle \frown B \approx C\langle x \rangle$ *and* $A \frown B \approx A$.

Proof For the first, for any $\vec{\ell}, \vec{r}$ we have

$$(C\langle x \rangle \frown B)\langle \vec{\ell}, \vec{r} \rangle \quad \equiv \quad \text{new } m_1 m_2 \,((\overline{m_1}\langle x \rangle.\,B\langle \vec{\ell}, \vec{m} \rangle$$
$$+ m_2(\vec{r}).\,C\langle x, \vec{\ell}, \vec{r} \rangle) \mid \overline{m_2}\langle \vec{r} \rangle)$$
$$\sim \quad \tau.\,C\langle x, \vec{\ell}, \vec{r} \rangle$$
$$\approx \quad C\langle x, \vec{\ell}, \vec{r} \rangle\,.$$

For the second, we show that for each particular $\vec{\ell}, \vec{r}$ the relation

$$\mathcal{S} \stackrel{\text{def}}{=} \{((A \frown B)\langle \vec{\ell}, \vec{r} \rangle, A \langle \vec{\ell}, \vec{r} \rangle)\} \cup \approx$$

is a weak bisimulation. (Notice that this relation is just $\approx$ augmented by one pair; in fact, we are showing that this pair is also in $\approx$.)

Since $(A \frown B)\langle \vec{\ell}, \vec{r} \rangle \rightarrow A \langle \vec{\ell}, \vec{r} \rangle$ every action of the right member of this pair can be matched by the left member; it remains to match the actions of the left member by those of the right.

The left member has only one action for any x, namely

$$(A \frown B)\langle \vec{\ell}, \vec{r} \rangle \stackrel{\ell_1 \langle x \rangle}{\rightarrow} ((A \frown C\langle x \rangle) \frown B)\langle \vec{\ell}, \vec{r} \rangle$$
$$\approx \quad (A \frown C\langle x \rangle)\langle \vec{\ell}, \vec{r} \rangle \qquad \text{by the first part}$$

where we have used the associativity of $\frown$, which was proved in Exercise 9.25. But this action can be matched in $\mathcal{S}$ by

$$A\langle \vec{\ell}, \vec{r} \rangle \stackrel{\ell_1 \langle x \rangle}{\rightarrow} (A \frown C\langle x \rangle)\langle \vec{\ell}, \vec{r} \rangle . \qquad \square$$

We choose to represent a whole buffer with fixed input port ℓ_1 and output port r_1 containing the elements $x_1, \ldots, x_n$ (with x_1 most recently joined) by

$$Chain^{(n)}(x_1, \ldots, x_n) \stackrel{\text{def}}{=} \text{new } \ell_2 r_2 \, (A \frown C\langle x_1 \rangle \frown \cdots \frown C\langle x_n \rangle)\langle \vec{\ell r} \rangle .$$

Note that this has free names $x_1, \ldots, x_n$ and ℓ_1, r_1. The restriction of r_2 removes the possibility that a user of the buffer can 'point' the buffer at a different client by transmitting a new interface $\vec{r'}$ at the port r_2. (Of course, a buffer which can be swung from client to client may be useful; but it will not meet our specification!) We shall now prove that these chains $Chain^{(i)}$ ($i \geq 0$) satisfy the equations which specify an unbounded buffer.

Theorem 13.14 *Assume that $\ell_1 \neq r_1$. Then for all n*

$$Chain^{(n)} \approx Buff^{(n)} .$$

Proof By Theorem 13.8, the unique solution theorem, it is enough to prove that the chaining abstractions $Chain^{(n)}$ satisfy the specifying equations for $Buff^{(n)}$, up to weak equivalence. For $n = 0$ we have

$$Chain^{(0)} \stackrel{\text{def}}{=} \text{new } \ell_2 r_2 \, A$$
$$\sim \quad \ell_1(x). \text{ new } \ell_2 r_2 \, (A \frown C\langle x \rangle)$$
$$\equiv \quad \ell_1(x). \, Chain^{(1)}\langle x \rangle$$

as required. For a non-empty buffer we have

$$Chain^{(n+1)}\langle x_1, \ldots, x_{n+1} \rangle$$
$$\overset{\text{def}}{=} \ \text{new } \ell_2 r_2 \, (A \frown C\langle x_1 \rangle \frown \cdots \frown C\langle x_{n+1} \rangle) \langle \vec{\ell r} \rangle$$
$$\sim \ \ell_1(x). \text{ new } \ell_2 r_2 \, (A \frown C\langle x \rangle \frown C\langle x_1 \rangle \frown \cdots \frown C\langle x_{n+1} \rangle) \langle \vec{\ell r} \rangle$$
$$+ \overline{r_1}\langle x_{n+1} \rangle. \text{ new } \ell_2 r_2 \, (A \frown C\langle x_1 \rangle \frown \cdots \frown C\langle x_n \rangle \frown B) \langle \vec{\ell r} \rangle$$
$$\approx \ \ell_1(x). \, Chain^{(n+2)}\langle x, x_1, \ldots, x_{n+1} \rangle$$
$$+ \overline{r_1}\langle x_{n+1} \rangle. \, Chain^{(n)}\langle x_1, \ldots, x_n \rangle \, ,$$

where at the last step we have used one or other case of Lemma 13.13, depending on whether $n > 0$ or $n = 0$. Again, this is the required equation, and the proof is complete. $\qquad\qquad\Box$

Note that the theorem does not hold if $\ell_1 = r_1$, and it is interesting to see why. This equality of input and output ports would cause feedback from the final cell in $Chain^{(n+1)}$ to its initial A cell, causing endless circulation within the buffer! The point at which the proof would fail is the second step for $Chain^{(n+1)}$, which is an expansion with two terms. There would be a third term, a τ action, shifting the element x_{n+1} to the left end of the buffer. This circulation does not happen for the specification $Buff^{(n+1)}$ since it has no parallel composition.

Theoretically, this is a striking example which illustrates that weak equivalence is not preserved by an arbitrary substitution of names.

13.7 Reduction in the λ-calculus

For our last application of weak equivalence we shall fulfil the promise of Section 11.6, and prove that our translation of the λ-calculus into the π-calculus respects the main reduction rule of the λ-calculus; that is, we prove

Theorem 11.22 $[\![(\lambda x \, M)N]\!] \approx [\![\{N\!/x\}M]\!]$.

Proof The result depends mainly on the properties of replication proved in Section 12.6; the only property we shall need of weak equivalence is that $P \approx \tau.P$. We shall assume without loss of generality that x is not free in N.

Definition 11.18 gives the translation $[\![\ ]\!]$; in this proof we shall abbreviate $[\![M]\!]\langle u \rangle$ to $[\![M]\!]u$. We easily find that

$$[\![(\lambda x \, M)N]\!]u \ \sim \ \tau. \, \text{new } x \, ([\![M]\!]u \mid !x[\![N]\!]) \, ;$$

it will therefore suffice to show that for all u, x, M and N with x not free in N

$$\text{new } x \, ([\![M]\!]u \mid !x[\![N]\!]) \ \approx \ [\![\{N\!/x\}M]\!]u$$

which we shall do by induction on the structure of M.

Case $M = x$. Then

$$
\begin{aligned}
\mathsf{new}\, x \, ([\![M]\!]u \mid {!}x[\![N]\!]) \;&=\; \mathsf{new}\, x \, (\overline{x}\langle u\rangle \mid {!}x[\![N]\!]) \\
&\sim\; \tau.\,[\![N]\!]u \mid \mathsf{new}\, x \, {!}x[\![N]\!] \qquad (x \text{ not free in } [\![N]\!]) \\
&\sim\; \tau.\,[\![N]\!]u \qquad\qquad\qquad\quad \text{as required.}
\end{aligned}
$$

Case $M = y \neq x$. Then both sides are strongly equivalent to $\overline{y}\langle u\rangle$.

Case $M = \lambda y\, M_1$. Then $[\![M]\!]u = u(yv).\,[\![M_1]\!]v$, so

$$
\begin{aligned}
\mathsf{new}\, x \, ([\![M]\!]u \mid {!}x[\![N]\!]) \;&\sim\; u(yv).\,\mathsf{new}\, x \, ([\![M_1]\!]v \mid {!}x[\![N]\!]) \\
&\approx\; u(yv).\,[\![\{^N\!/\!x\}M_1]\!]v \qquad\qquad \text{by induction} \\
&=\; [\![\lambda y\, \{^N\!/\!x\}M_1]\!]u \\
&=\; [\![\{^N\!/\!x\}M]\!]u \,.
\end{aligned}
$$

Case $M = (M_1\, M_2)$. Then $[\![M]\!]u = \mathsf{new}\, v \, ([\![M_1]\!]v \mid \mathsf{new}\, y \, (\overline{v}\langle yu\rangle \mid {!}y[\![M_2]\!]))$, so by Theorem 12.34 we can distribute the replicated resource ${!}x[\![N]\!]$ over the parallel composition, and using simple strong equivalences we get

$$
\begin{aligned}
\mathsf{new}\, x \, ([\![M]\!]u \mid {!}x[\![N]\!]) \;\sim\; &\mathsf{new}\, v \, (\mathsf{new}\, x \, ([\![M_1]\!]v \mid {!}x[\![N]\!]) \mid \\
&\mathsf{new}\, y \, (\overline{v}\langle yu\rangle \mid \mathsf{new}\, x \, ({!}y[\![M_2]\!] \mid {!}x[\![N]\!]))) \,.
\end{aligned}
$$

Now by Theorem 12.36 we have

$$
\mathsf{new}\, x \, ({!}y[\![M_2]\!] \mid {!}x[\![N]\!]) \;\sim\; {!}y(w).\,\mathsf{new}\, x \, ([\![M_2]\!]w \mid {!}x[\![N]\!]) \,,
$$

so by applying the induction hypothesis to both M_1 and M_2 we get

$$
\begin{aligned}
&\mathsf{new}\, x \, ([\![M]\!]u \mid {!}x[\![N]\!]) \\
&\quad\approx\; \mathsf{new}\, v \, ([\![\{^N\!/\!x\}M_1]\!]v \mid \mathsf{new}\, y \, (\overline{v}\langle yu\rangle \mid {!}y[\![\{^N\!/\!x\}M_2]\!])) \\
&\quad=\; [\![\{^N\!/\!x\}(M_1\, M_2)]\!]u \qquad \text{as required.}
\end{aligned}
$$

This completes the proof of the theorem. $\qquad\qquad\qquad\qquad\qquad\square$

This result entitles us to say that functional programming lives inside the π-calculus as a very special case of interactive systems. Of course, this does not diminish the importance of functional programming. The λ-calculus can also be modelled by Turing machines, which we would hardly say provide an insight into functional computation. But the encoding of λ-calculus into π-calculus is intriguingly simple; furthermore, Turing machines themselves are not hard to express in the π-calculus. This suggests that the primitives of the π-calculus may have some central significance.

14

Discussion and related work

The π-calculus has been introduced as a new and fundamental way of thinking about mobile interactive processes, and one which is amenable to rigorous treatment.

For the calculus to be a success, this introduction must take root. This does not mean that the π-calculus should become the lingua franca for designers of interactive systems; it is at too low a level for that, and in dealing with real systems one needs modes of explanation at a higher level, often using different formalisms for different kinds of application. But this very phenomenon – that there are many ways of thinking about interactive systems – implies the need for something to tie these ways together. If a basic set of ideas such as the π-calculus can supply this integrity then designers will respect it, one may dare to hope, in the way that mechanical or electrical engineers respect the differential calculus, which ties together their ways of thinking.

The strategy in the book has therefore been to take simple examples of interactive systems (scheduler, buffer, mobile phones, ...) and simple high-level concepts (data structures, objects, functions, processes, ...) and to render them in the π-calculus. In each case the rendering can be done more rigorously, but to do so would take us beyond an introductory text. We have been content to show that the 'tying together' of these various systems and concepts can be done without distortion; one then sees that they do indeed have something in common. This common element can claim to be the essence of interactive behaviour.

Beyond this conceptual unification, a good outcome for the π-calculus would be to generate new higher-level languages and analytical tools, much in the way that its predecessors CCS and CSP contributed to the design of LOTOS, a language designed to express communications protocols.

The theory in this book has been limited to various notions of *equivalent behaviour*, both of systems and of their components, based upon a primitive

153

notion of reaction or transition. We have treated structural, strong and weak equivalence; and they are congruences, i.e. in each case substituting an equivalent component yields an equivalent system.

By limiting our concern to equivalence we do not deny that there are wider concerns. A very general question is: How should we rigorously express the *specification* or required behaviour of a system, perhaps in terms of some logical formalism; and then what does it means for a system – perhaps represented by a π-calculus term – to *satisfy* such a specification? There is no reason why the system and its specification should be expressed in the same formalism. A fortiori, there is no reason to expect that the satisfaction of a specification by a system should always be expressed as the equivalence between two terms in the same formalism. But the study of behavioural equivalence, as far as it goes, has the advantage that only a single formalism is required. Furthermore, equivalence is in a certain sense fundamental; to echo the introductory chapter, until we know what constitutes equivalent behaviour we do not really understand what the term 'behaviour' means!

Origins The theory in this book is a direct continuation of my Calculus of Communicating Systems (CCS) [9, 10]. That work, together with Hoare's Communicating Sequential Processes [6] and the Process Algebra initiated by Bergstra and Klop and continued by Baeten [2] and others, constituted a new mathematical approach to non-sequential interactive computing. In [10] the sources of CCS were described in some detail, and the reader is referred to that account. Here, I would like to mention explicitly the strong contribution by David Park [13] of the concept of bisimulation which was used in that book, which is considerably better than my original treatment in [9].

None of those treatments dealt with mobility among processes. In the case of CCS the challenge to treat mobility in a fundamental way was early recognised as important and difficult. During the winter of 1979-80, when I visited Aarhus University and gave the lectures on which my first book [9] was based, I talked many times with Mogens Nielsen about how to fit such a treatment into CCS, but we failed. Some years later Nielsen together with Uffe Engberg [5] made a strong advance, showing how the notion of behavioural equivalence can be extended to handle processes which pass 'labels' to each other.

This stimulated the design of the π-calculus around 1989 [12]. Perhaps the main contribution of the π-calculus is its identification of many apparently different things – labels, channels, pointers, variables, ... – as simply one thing: *names*. This simplification gets the π-calculus off the ground, and allows it clearly to represent many computationally familiar things such as data structures, functions and imperative programming, as particular aspects of mobility among components of various kinds.

Developments Several developments of the π-calculus have take place more recently, and it would be hard to do justice to them all. I shall indicate a few which appear to me to be central.

My tutorial paper [11] introduced reaction rules (as opposed to transition rules) as a way of defining behaviour, inspired by the Chemical Abstract Machine of Berry and Boudol [3], and also introduced the sorting disciplines described in this book.

Davide Sangiorgi in his PhD Thesis [16] demonstrated that although the π-calculus only treats the mobility of *names*, this is enough to represent the mobility of *processes* themselves; in other words, processes may be passed as data in a communication. This important step showed the π-calculus to be more fundamental than was initially expected by many.

Another remarkable development was by Kohei Honda [7] who showed that an even simpler calculus, the π-calculus without summation, has almost all the expressive power of the π-calculus; this so-called *Asynchronous π-calculus* is probably the simplest version of π-calculus which comprises its most important features.

A different formal development is by Joachim Parrow and Björn Victor [14], who have devised a more powerful calculus with two attractive properties; it reduces the two kinds of name-binding (restriction new $x\,P$ and input $y(x).P$) to just one kind, and simultaneously introduces a pleasing symmetry between input and output. The asymmetry of the π-calculus in this respect was a topic of long discussion among its originators; the matter is still very much alive!

David Walker was the first to demonstrate [20] that essential ideas of object-oriented programming can be elegantly represented in the π-calculus; in Section 11.4 of this book I have taken advantage of his approach. Together, Walker and Sangiorgi have written a book [17] which develops the π-calculus theory to a more advanced level, and is a natural sequel to the present book for people who want a fuller theoretical account. For example, it contains material on proof techniques, types, encoding of higher-order calculi, a more detailed study of encoding functional calculi, and applications of the semantics of object-oriented languages.

On the practical side, the π-calculus is the basis for a new kind of programming language in which mobility of links and processes is available, taking advantage of Sangiorgi's work already cited. The main example of such a language is Pict, designed and implemented by Benjamin Pierce and David Turner [15].

Conclusion When we consider where computer science began, with the study of sequential programs running on a single machine and performing calculational tasks well known to mathematicians, we may marvel at the way the subject has developed and changed its emphasis. Thanks to communication technology, the world at large now thinks of computing as interactive, and the metaphors and theories of computer scientists are following in this direction. We must recognise that computer science is a *science of the artificial* in the sense of Herbert Simon [18]; our concepts and models follow pioneering technology, not the reverse. But they will be essential to underpin a mature engineering practice.

At the present time we cannot expect a theoretical model such as that which is provided by this book to be definitive; the new developments are too immature for that. But as we seriously address the problem of modelling mobile communicating systems we get a sense of completing a model which was previously incomplete; for we can now begin to describe what goes on *outside* a computer in the same terms as what goes on *inside* – i.e. in terms of interaction. Turning this observation inside-out, we may say that we inhabit a global computer, an informatic world which demands to be understood just as fundamentally as physicists understand the material world.

References

[1] Abadi, M. and Gordon, A., *A calculus for cryptographic protocols: the spi cal-culus*, Information and Computation, to appear.

[2] Baeten, J.C. and Weijland, W.P., **Process Algebra**, Cambridge University Press, 1990.

[3] Berry, G. and Boudol, G., *The chemical abstract machine*, in Proc. 17th Annual SIGPLAN Symposium on Principles of Programming Languages, 1990.

[4] Cardelli, L. and Gordon, A., *Mobile ambients: foundations of system specifica-tion and computation structures*, Lecture Notes in Computer Science, Vol 1378, Springer-Verlag, pp 140–155 (1998).

[5] Engberg, U. and Nielsen, M., *A calculus of communicating systems with name-passing*, Technical Report DAIMI PB-208, Computer Science Department, Uni-versity of Aarhus, Denmark, 1986.

[6] Hoare, C., **Communicating Sequential Processes**, Prentice Hall 1985.

[7] Honda, K. and Tokoro, M., *An object calculus for asynchronous communication*, in P. America (ed), Proc. ECOOP 1991, Lecture Notes in Computer Science, Vol 512, Springer-Verlag, pp133–147, 1991.

[8] Hopcroft, J.E. and Ullman, J.D., **Introduction to Automata Theory, Languages and Computation**, Addison Wesley, 1979.

[9] Milner, R., **A Calculus of Communicating Systems**, Lecture Notes in Computer Science, Vol 92, Springer-Verlag 1980.

[10] Milner, R., **Communication and Concurrency**, Prentice Hall 1989.

[11] Milner, R., *The polyadic π-calculus: a tutorial*, in **Logic and Algebra of Spec-ification**, ed. F.L. Bauer, W. Brauer and H. Schwichtenberg, Springer Verlag, 1993, pp203–246.

[12] Milner, R., Parrow, J. and Walker, D., *A calculus of mobile processes, Parts I and II*, Information and Computation, 100, 1, 1992, pp1–77.

[13] Park, D., *Concurrency and automata on infinite sequences*, in Lecture Notes in Computer Science, Vol 104, Springer-Verlag 1980.

[14] Parrow, J. and Victor, B., *The Fusion Calculus: Expressiveness and Symmetry in Mobile Processes*. Proc. 13th Annual IEEE Symposium on Logics in Computer Science, 1998.

[15]   Pierce, B. and Turner, D., *Pict: A programming language based on the Pi-calculus*, Report CSCI 476, Computer Science Department, Indiana University, 1997. To appear in **Proof, Language and Interaction: Essays in Honour of Robin Milner**, eds. Gordon Plotkin, Colin Stirling and Mads Tofte, MIT Press, 1998.

[16]   Sangiorgi, D., *Expressing Mobility in process algebras: first order and higher-order paradigms*, PhD Thesis, Computer Science Department, University of Edinburgh, 1993.

[17]   Sangiorgi, D. and Walker, D., **The π-calculus: A Theory of Mobile Processes**, Cambridge University Press, 2001.

[18]   Simon, H., **The Sciences of the Artificial**, MIT Press, third edition, 1996.

[19]   Sudkamp, T.A., **Languages and Machines**, Addison Wesley, 1988.

[20]   Walker, D., *Objects in the π-calculus*, Information and Computation, Vol 115, pp253–271, 1995.

Index

159

Printed in the United States
By Bookmasters